A TROUBLING
IN MY SOUL

The Bishop Henry McNeal Turner Studies
in North American Black Religion

Editor:

James H. Cone,
Union Theological Seminary, New York

The purpose of this series is to encourage the development of biblical, historical, theological, and pastoral works that analyze the role of the churches and other religious movements in the liberation struggles of blacks in the United States and the Third World. What is the relationship between black religion and black peoples' fight for justice in the U. S.? What is the relationship between the black struggle for justice in the U. S. and the liberation struggles of the poor in Asia, Africa, Latin America, and the Caribbean? A critical investigation of these and related questions will define the focus of this series.

This series is named after Bishop Henry McNeal Turner (1834–1915), whose life and work symbolize the black struggle for liberation in the U. S. and the Third World. Bishop Turner was a churchman, a political figure, a missionary, a pan-Africanist—a champion of black freedom and the cultural creativity of black peoples under God.

The Bishop Henry McNeal Turner Studies
in North American Black Religion
Volume VIII

A TROUBLING IN MY SOUL

Womanist Perspectives on Evil and Suffering

**Edited by
Emilie M. Townes**

ORBIS BOOKS

Maryknoll, New York 10545

The Catholic Foreign Mission Society of America (Maryknoll) recruits and trains people for overseas missionary service. Through Orbis Books, Maryknoll aims to foster the international dialogue that is essential to mission. The books published, however, reflect the opinions of their authors and are not meant to represent the official position of the society.

Biblical translations are from *The New Revised Standard Version*

Library of Congress Cataloging-in-Publication Data

A Troubling in my soul : womanist perspectives on evil and suffering /
    edited by Emilie M. Townes.
        p.   cm. — (Bishop Henry McNeal Turner series; v. 8)
    Includes index.
    ISBN 0-88344-783-5 (pbk)
    1. Suffering — Religious aspects — Christianity.   2. Theodicy.
3. Feminist theology.   4. Black theology.   I. Townes, Emilie
Maureen, 1955-   .   II. Series.
BT732.7.T76   1993
231'.8'082 — dc20
                                                        93-23875
                                                            CIP

for the womens

evil is a force outside us
suffering makes you stronger
lies
lies
lies
to my very deepest soul
there is a troubling in my soul

Contents

PART III
LOVE'S THE SPIRIT

PART IV
AS PURPLE IS TO LAVENDER

Acknowledgments

Womanist reflection and action cannot be a solo effort. There are many who form the cloud of witnesses for such a volume. Each contributor is aware of her own special folk in the cloud. Those whom I would like to thank begin with my family. My parents, Mary M. and Ross E. Townes, have done a remarkable thing for parents. They have given me both a sense of family and the courage and stubbornness to demand such from society as a whole. The Townes and McLean families are far from perfect, but they are present when the going gets rough and more than a shoulder to lean on to shout or to celebrate. We are accountable to each other. This is the lesson of family I hold dear from my own. My sister, Tricia, continues to be a source of inspiration and humor. The commitment she has to her dream and the will to follow it serve as a beacon of hope and a leaven to the bread. My aunts, Agnes Moore and Helen McLean, continue to teach me the value of humor and beginning life again and again.

I also wish to thank those who have been more than friends and supporters in the journey. They include Susan Ebersold, Katie Cannon, Emma Justes, Dody Matthais, Pat Hunter, and Frances Wood. The women in the womanist academy, who are only touched on in these pages, have been a place of grace and challenge, including Toinette Eugene, Cheryl Gilkes, Renita Weems, and Delores Williams. These are the generation who have gone before and created a way for those of my generation. Their concern and spirit of womanish comfort speak volumes and has provided a rich proving ground for generations of scholars and practitioners. Because of them, our numbers are growing in both the Black church and in the academy.

My colleagues have been a warm presence. They have pushed my growth and struggled to enter into the African-American experience out of true partnership. Their willingness to grow and be challenged to expand their horizons as I am similarly challenged has made Saint Paul School of Theology and the Kansas City area places of unexpected richness. The students, staff, and administration have each contributed from their perspective. We may not be the biggest school, but we strive for wisdom and community. Special thanks to Tex Sample, Kris Culp, and Amy Oden for their support and concern.

Finally, three people participated in the crucial stages of this project. My student assistant, Gail Madsen, was an invaluable resource. Her keen eye for consistency and grammar is remarkable. Her gifts extend beyond the editorial page to the local church. Her ministry will grace the lives of many through her ability to listen, care, think, and act out of her Christian witness. Robert Ellsberg and Susan Perry from Orbis Books were remarkable. Robert displayed patience and a staunch willingness to stand by the project as deadlines were missed. Susan revealed that the job of attending to the minutia is really an art and a ministry. With such a vast cloud of witnesses, this volume has truly been blessed.

Introduction

On Creating Ruminations from the Soul

Emilie M. Townes

This collection of essays was born in water and fire. Its final days were shadowed in the inferno and anger of the Rodney King verdict. The subsequent urban rioting and long unacknowledged unrest and frustration were conscious partners in the final editing and arrangement of this anthology. As politicians began to throw up their collective hands in frustration in an emerging awareness that the issues looming large from the reaction to the King verdict could not be solved by political spin or shifting line items on an ill-conceived budget and nebulous national agenda, the essays in this anthology point a prophetic finger at the results of neglect and callousness endemic to United States society. The ongoing question of this collection is "Where is the Black church (and its women, men, and children) as we face evil and suffering in the United States and in our world?"

The shape of the volume has emerged over time. At first, this was a solo project, but the breadth of task was too large for one person. Others were asked to join in the project. The womanist scholars and practitioners in this volume represent some of the voices of African-American women in the church. The essays are interdisciplinary and ecumenical. The common theme each author addresses is the nature of evil and suffering from a womanist perspective as she confronts the reality and the hope of the African-American community.

The four parts of the book are based on the definitions of womanist found in Alice Walker's *In Search of Our Mothers' Gardens*.[1] African-American women in the church and in theological education have begun to explore Walker's definitions in light of the gospel message of salvation and hope. Perhaps the most common understanding of womanist is that she is a woman committed to an integrated analysis of race, gender, and class. This arises from a deep concern to address the shortcomings of traditional

1

feminist and Black theological modes of discourse. The former has a long legacy of ignoring race and class issues. The latter has disregarded gender and class. Both modes of discourse have begun to address these internal flaws. Yet womanist reflection maintains its critical perspective of feminist and African-American traditional ways of analytical reflection.

This critical perspective extends to Eurocentric discourse as well. Much of what womanist thought seeks to debunk is the notion of universals and absolutes. Womanist thought is intentionally and unapologetically biased. Its bias is for a diverse and faithful community of witnesses. These witnesses are an active force for love and justice in the midst of oppression and fallenness. With such a bias, all forms of theological discourse are open for reconsideration and critique. This includes womanist discourse as well.

Yet the anchor for womanist thought is the African-American church and its people. The history of the Black church is not only religious, it is social. The social conditions and worldviews of its people have had an intricate connection. Womanist thought reflects some of this intimacy. Examples of this can be found in the deeply spiritual and moral aspects of such writers as James Baldwin, Toni Morrison, Alice Walker, and August Wilson. The gospel renderings of Cissy Houston and Thomas Dorsey are grist for the mill. West African religions, vodun, and folktales are mediums. Life in the church—from preacher's admonitions to choir crescendos to board meetings and power struggles—all are resources and guardians of communal memory and accountability. Academic theological discourse is also a part of womanist reflection and thought. Such are the touchstones for womanist reflection.

With such a rich proving-ground, the essays in this book are, of necessity, theoretical and practical. The impulse of womanist thought is to challenge, as it remains a part of (and issues from) the African-American religious community as well as traditional academic discourse. It is both descriptive and prescriptive in light of the real life and death struggle that Black women wage, individually and communally, in seeking to shape a just social order.

The opening essay of the anthology is by Clarice J. Martin. She provides a helpful introduction to the question of theodicy by exploring Maria Stewart's reflections on evil and suffering to answer the pointed question, "If God exists, why is there evil?" Martin concentrates her analysis in three areas: (1) the sociopolitical, (2) the spiritual autobiography as mediator for the tensions of an evil world and a gracious God, and (3) the central place the Bible holds in addressing divine causation and human freedom. Jarena Lee and Julia A. J. Foote join Stewart as the primary resources for assessing Black women's theological reflections on the experiences of suffering and evil in the drama of human existence.

Frances E. Wood argues that United States society tolerates, indeed, designates, certain populations as permissible victims. Our level of tolerance of such designations is heightened in the absence of serious challenge by community leaders. Historical and contemporary Christian attitudes and practices, within the context of the larger community, have offered no substantive opposition to this social norm. Christianity reinforces beliefs elevating the suffering and victimization of Black females to the status of martyrdom for the cause (of others) and a level of pseudomoral superiority designated to assure that we do not view ourselves as entitled to nurturance and care or deserving of pleasure and joy in this life.

Wood examines the proposition that there is some evil inherent in every institution. She discusses those elements within religious institutions that idealize suffering and perpetuate the oppression of Black women. She concentrates on attitudes and behaviors that support misogyny, reinforce internalized racism, maintain gender-role stereotypes, prohibit women's expressions of sexuality, promote body-spirit dualism, and reflect a Christology that apotheosizes human suffering. She ends with an alternative vision and praxis for the community of African-American followers of Christ.

In her essay, Jamie T. Phelps reveals how the Spirit has been checkmated by the social sins of racism and sexism. Such a search, for Phelps, does not concentrate on the question of God and evil, for the goodness of God and God's will for a just society are assumed as intrinsic to the Christian message and witness. An African-American Roman Catholic perspective informs this essay as Phelps explicates the historic disenfranchisement of African-American women and men in the church of Rome.

Phelps' essay begins with a historical construction of classism, racism, and sexism. It then provides a critique of the historical and contemporary teachings of social evil. The final section of the essay suggests recommendations for the future mission of the church as it seeks to be a truly faithful and prophetic witness to justice and a just society. Phelps argues that this is acutely necessary as the Roman Catholic church endeavors to reach out to the African-American community in the United States and to women on a global scale.

Marcia Y. Riggs examines the nineteenth-century Black club women's understanding of moral evil and their response to the way in which such was perpetrated in society. Using traditional ethical understandings of moral evil as a point of departure, Riggs brings the Black club women's thought into dialogical critique with those understandings. Her essay explicates the Black club women's understanding of the nature of evil and suffering as institutionalized moral evil, their social analysis of such, and the activities that club women undertook to alleviate the impact of such evil upon the African-American community in the United States. In her final section, Riggs discusses the implications of the Black club women's socioethical paradigm which synthesizes moral suasion and social activism for Black liberation ethics.

The essay by Emilie M. Townes is both descriptive and prescriptive. Descriptively, the African-American experience is the ground for reflection. More particularly, the lives of African-American women provide the lenses for focus. The traditionally "good" moral characteristics of personal loss, denial, and sacrifice provide the interpretive framework for elucidating Black women's lives.

The prescriptive component of Townes' essay constructs a womanist ethic as a praxis for the elimination of suffering. The social justice rhetoric and activity of Ida B. Wells-Barnett guides this discussion. Wells-Barnett provides a praxis for an articulate and effective challenge to an acquiescence to evil. She does not sanction suffering as ennobling in the lives of African Americans. Through her rhetoric and actions, a reinterpretation of suffering emerges. This is crucial to a renewed understanding of the impact of evil and the options for change and transformation.

The socioethical claim Townes makes in her essay is that womanist ethical reflection rejects suffering as God's will and understands suffering as outrage. Her use of Wells-Barnett's rhetoric and social witness provides a historical base from which to question the moral valuing of loss, denial, and sacrifice. For Townes, womanist ethics advocates a renewed emphasis on authority, liberation, and reconciliation that will move and guide the contemporary African-American community and its people of faith.

Rosita deAnn Mathews relates her experiences and involvement as a chaplain and director of pastoral services in a veterans administration hospital. Her perspectives include that of being a woman, an African American, and a clergyperson working within a nonparish setting. Issues arising from this exploration include framing a theological construct that deals with systems, systems theory, diagnosing a system and its culture, and the psychological effects of working within a system—particularly as an African-American female. For Mathews, understanding systems theory and psychological foundations is an integral part of working in a corporate setting and addressing problems of evil.

Mathews addresses the theological-womanist contributions that speak to corporate survival regarding isolation, tokenism, discrimination, and power. She speaks to the role of a chaplain-clergyperson within a system: the tension of existing as priest, prophet, and employee. Finally, she explores how parish clergywomen can shape their ministry to address the needs of their parishioners who work in these settings and who may be hospitalized as patients.

M. Shawn Copeland makes an historical and theological investigation of and reflection on selected narratives of the lives and experiences of enslaved and/or emancipated women of African descent during the nineteenth century in the United States. She examines the ways in which enslaved and/or emancipated Black women experienced, conceived, judged, and grappled with instances of suffering and evil in their lives. Historical and sociocultural analysis function to contextualize these women's lives and experiences, thus grounding her theological interpretation in the concrete.

For Copeland, religious consciousness is *the* crucial mediation of African-American personal and communal, spiritual and political transformation. Her aim is to get at the content of the experience which that religious consciousness objectifies and mediates. First, she identifies the content and expressions of experiences of evil and suffering in the lives of enslaved and emancipated Black women. Next she explores the distinction between evil and suffering in the lives of these Black women. Finally, Copeland explores the ways in which religious consciousness empowers, heals, and transforms these women and their lives, and informs and revolutionizes their political practice.

Copeland seeks to insinuate into Christian theology Black women's religious, sociocultural, and political experiences and traditions. She identifies neglected historical resources for critical theological reflection and shapes the emerging womanist perspective in theology by accentuating Black women's sociopolitical practices.

Delores S. Williams explores the ways in which the development of Black Christian theological thought and sin and suffering have been discussed and defined with regard to Black people's experience with white racism. On the one hand, some of this Black theological thought corresponds with Paul Tillich's understanding of sin as alienation from God, neighbor, and/ or self. White racism is cited as the cause of much of this alienation. On the other hand, some Black theological thought defines sin in a social sense and claims that failure to join the liberation struggle of the oppressed of the earth constitutes sin in a Christian context.

Williams' essay reviews both trajectories of Black theological thought on sin. She claims that by focusing upon African-American women's historic experience of suffering, we not only arrive at a new understanding of sin, we also uncover a structure of domination that historically has been active in Black women's lives but has been invisible in theological scholarship by Black males. This structure of domination (and suffering it has caused Black American women) is responsible for this new understanding of sin relevant for all Christians.

Cheryl A. Kirk-Duggan draws on her background as a musician and theologian. For her, cultural works or artifacts document a society's existence and that society's use of power. African-American spirituals are artifacts that symbolize the political and religious Afrocentric experience in the United States. African Americans used spirituals to respond to the events of seventeenth- through nineteenth-century slavery. The civil rights campaigns of the late twentieth century adopted many of the same traditional spirituals for spiritual and psychological assistance against anti-Black racism.

Kirk-Duggan contends that African-American spirituals delineate an Afrocentric concept of theodicy, a Christian response to the problem of the actuality of evil. The resurgence of racism directed against African-Americans in the 1990s functions as a catalyst for contemplating the exegetical meaning of contemporary African-American spirituals first encountered in North American seventeenth- through nineteenth-century slavery-based culture. These spirituals apprise us of previous responses to the evil based on *the color line* and the slavery-based economy. These spirituals lead to an informed hermeneutic comprised of four parts. The first is sociohistorical. Kirk-Duggan explores how these insights describe how the supporting mythology has led to rituals that practice institutional evil, especially racism, as a faith experience and disclose those tendencies that produce institutional evil. The second is narrative-dialectical. This emphasis helps Kirk-Duggan define the Afrocentric experience as a DuBoisian "veil" or double consciousness to break the coded communication. The third part of the hermeneutic, the rhetorical-musical critical, examines the text and music of these spirituals as a complete unit, to discern the literary and musical structural patterns and devices. These patterns and devices reveal the dynamics of these musical performances as living, integrated, oral discourse. The final part of her hermeneutic, the philosophical-theological, is a matrix Kirk-Duggan uses to encompass theodicy and to review options for contemporary response.

This technique enables Kirk-Duggan to analyze spirituals that were prominent through both historical periods. These particular spirituals reflect on the past and foreshadow the future. Her multifaceted methodology introduces these spirituals as entities worthy of in-depth philosophical and theological insight and reveals how these spirituals confront and exorcise evil by juxtaposing faith and humor.

Karen Baker-Fletcher explores the life and witness of Dr. Anna Julia Cooper. Cooper was an active participant in the Black women's club movement of the late nineteenth and early twentieth century. She used her skills as a teacher and lecturer to argue for the education of Black women and the social uplift of African-American children, men, and women. Baker-Fletcher scrutinizes Cooper's *A Voice From the South* (1892) as a radical collection of lectures and speeches. From this, Baker-Fletcher discusses the impact and importance of voice in womanist experience. Voice is key to any movement toward freedom and equality.

Patricia L. Hunter approaches beauty and health from another perspective. For her, the Christian faith teaches that God created women and men. The Christian faith also teaches that all God created is good. Women are wonderfully complex passionate-powerful creations of God that yearn to be active in the world. Hunter argues that women and men are aware of the passion-power of women. Further, it would seem that if believing that all God created is good, that women are created by God and in the image of God, and a significant aspect of womanliness is passion-power, then it would stand to reason that a woman's passion-power is also good. However, for Hunter, misogyny controls women's passion, discounts women's power, and labels both as evil. Too many women believe that passion-power is something to be feared, denied, and controlled because of its inherent evil nature. Therefore, women as creations of God are evil.

Hunter sees the impact of misogyny and the apparent confusion and the ambivalence regarding women's relationship with the Creator affecting all aspects of women's lives. Women's understanding of their spiritual relationship with God directly affects their image of themselves as sexual beings in the world and determines whether they see their passion-power as something to be embraced and encouraged or something to be feared. For Hunter, women's ambivalence toward their goodness or sinfulness in the sight of God affects how they love, work, and relate to other women. Confusion with their spirituality keeps women wondering whether they are fine just the way God created them or if their purpose in life is to make physical improvements where God left off.

Hunter explores the connection between the cosmetic industry as a multibillion dollar industry (and how the cosmetic industry feeds on women believing they are not good enough) and the effects of racism on women's understanding of themselves being good creations of God. Living in a racist society influences women's images of other women and what women consider acceptable and unacceptable treatment from men. Hunter sees that women of color have often denied their passion-power to help men of color feel better about themselves. She is convinced that once women view their spiritual relationship with God as positive and believe that they are a part of God's "good" creation, women can acknowledge their sexuality as a gift of God's grace, instead of something to be feared, mistrusted, and seen as evil.

Notions of service and servanthood are intrinsic to Christianity. Jacquelyn Grant turns her attention to the concept of servanthood as it relates to women's life and service in the church. Servanthood is far from a neutral or immediately ennobling term. When cast in light of human indignity, notions of servanthood quickly degenerate to victimization and exploitation. Rather than servanthood, argues Grant, African-American women in the United States experience servitude.

After providing recent interpretations of feminist redemptions of service by Letty Russell and Rosemary Radford Ruether, Grant provides a historical overview of Black women's domestic service. This history is one of economic and sexual exploitation. Service and servitude are one, with little hope of empowerment or liberation. This, for Grant, is a theological dilemma. Operating from a womanist theological stance, Grant challenges obsequious theological formulations that promote dehumanization and unjust suffering.

Grant turns to W. E. B. DuBois' understanding of double consciousness for understanding the healthy aspects of African-American dichotomous existence. The "twoness" of double consciousness has helped Black folk understand that if he or she were "uncle" or "aunty" in a dominated social order, they were "deacon" and "sister" in God's liberating plan. It is out of this double consciousness that Grant suggests the triple consciousness of Black women's existence. This triple consciousness enables African-

American women to follow a liberating Jesus into genuine Christian discipleship.

Katie Geneva Cannon's essay considers the African-American folk sermon as the most vital factor in African-American culture although these sermons have been passed over, basically unnoticed. The substantial omission of African-American sermons from both theological and literary discourse flows quite naturally from scholars using analytical frameworks that take the European-American religious experience as the norm. For Cannon, the African-American folk sermon is the earliest form of the spoken religious arts. It is the fundamental religious lore embodying people's understanding of good and evil.

Cannon concentrates on Zora Neale Hurston's sermon, "The Wounds of Jesus," a pivotal text in African-American letters. Hurston captures the distinctive style of Black oratory so as to give evidence of previously spoken-only understanding of certain religious truths. Hurston's sermonic eloquence can be judged equal, if not superior, to the very best masters of the oratory arts in any age. The overt religious dimensions in Hurston's canon help redress the preoccupation of traditional scholarship that has concentrated on European-American religious and academic sources. In other words, by fictionalizing this genre, Hurston uncovers aspects of African-American religious culture that have circulated orally from one generation to the next. By extension, this novelist opens up the dimensions of the sacred in everyday life as it relates to risk-and-security, weakness-and-strength, life-and-death.

By naming sermons as genre and preaching as process, Cannon seeks a mode of critical inquiry that allows her to examine the theological language in these texts, to identify the basic religious concerns related to evil and suffering that arise in the plots, and to elucidate the theoethical justification of goodness in the face of manifold evil interwoven in Hurston's folk sermons.

For Cheryl Townsend Gilkes, racial oppression and cultural humiliation are powerful forces that undercut the self-esteem of African-American women and men. For Gilkes, a womanist perspective that takes seriously Alice Walker's observation that one "loves food" and "loves roundness" and "loves herself" stands in stark contrast to the dominant cultural dictum that one can be neither too rich nor too thin. In a world of political and economic inequity, one can be too rich and first-world anorexia and third-world starvation mean one can be too thin.

Gilkes focuses on cultural humiliation as a major component of racial oppression. She seeks to uncover the sociohistorical and embodied experiences of Black women as paradox and conflict. Gilkes discusses the ways in which white culture has exploited and selected certain aspects of the African-American appearance through beauty pageants and the contradictory way in which Black culture has responded to the cultural humiliation imposed on the community concerning beauty and women's social roles.

From this, Gilkes juxtaposes African-American women's experiences with societal hegemony.

She argues for the "revolutionary nature of the womanist idea." This idea and ideal provide resources for African-American women's healthy resistance to cultural and racial oppression. For Gilkes, these resources become strategies for the liberation of African-American women and men.

Womanist reflection is far from monolithic in voice and tone. The contributors to this anthology have a unique perspective on the nature of evil and suffering in the lives of African-American women and the African-American community as a whole. They begin with their particular experience as a rigorous sounding board and offer piercing analysis as they construct an alternative vision. These visions have an underlying theme of justice and equality. However, the method and the strategy to achieve such ends vary in a womanist stance. Rather than appeal to a common methodology, which begets a common ideology, womanist reflection encourages creativity rather than conformity in proposing solutions to evil and suffering.

There is a troubling in the souls of the contributors. Yet there is a witness to the power of hope. Such hope emerges in the midst of the struggle. The hope given testament to in this collection is far from naive. It is crafty, calculated, joyful, and faith-filled. This is a hope that demands an active witness. Such a hope can only be sustained by the Spirit.

NOTE

1. Alice Walker, *In Search of Our Mothers' Gardens: Womanist Prose* (New York: Harcourt Brace Jovanovich, 1983).

PART I

RESPONSIBLE,
IN CHARGE

1

Biblical Theodicy and Black Women's Spiritual Autobiography

"The Miry Bog, the Desolate Pit,
a New Song in My Mouth"

Clarice J. Martin

I waited patiently for the Lord;
  he inclined to me and heard my cry.
He drew me up from the desolate pit,
  out of the miry bog,
and set my feet upon a rock,
  making my steps secure.
He put a new song in my mouth,
  a song of praise to our God.
                    Psalm 40:1–3[1]

The psalmist's trenchant description of his deliverance from the depths and travails of human suffering, anguish, and evil represents an appropriate starting place to begin a discussion of African-American women's reflections on suffering and evil. That Maria W. Stewart, America's first African-American political writer[2] and a woman of profound religious faith, quoted Psalm 40:1-3 in her autobiography, *Productions of Mrs. Maria W. Stewart* (1835),[3] is not surprising, for she, like the psalmist, "wrestled with the perennial conundrum of a supposedly just and merciful God's ostensible willingness to tolerate the continued, undeserved suffering of the innocent."[4]

The desire for deliverance from the "miry bogs" and the "desolate pits" of human existence raises the larger question of the inevasible problem of evil in the universe. As the question has been formulated, "*Si deus est, unde malum?"* or, "If God exists, why is there evil?"[5] This decidedly pointed and direct question focuses on "the problem of evil," often referred to by the term *theodicy.* The term *theodicy,* coined by the eighteenth-century German philosopher Gottfried Wilhelm Leibniz, is based on the conjunction of the Greek words *"theos"* (God) and *"dikē"* (justice). The term *theodicy* thus represents the attempt to affirm divine justice despite the suffering in the world.[6]

Men and women in the Judeo-Christian tradition in particular have sought to mediate the tensions between theological affirmations of the goodness and omnipotence of God (who, according to Gen. 1:31, observed that everything that had been made was "very good"[7]) and the ubiquity of evil and suffering in the world. Certainly, the nature of the "kind" of God and the "character" of God one believes in comes to the forefront of theological and moral reflection, discourse, and debate when individuals broach the subject of theodicy, or suffering and evil in the human condition. As men and women through the centuries have queried, "if God is omnipotent, if God can prevent evil, how could a good God permit so many evils in the world?"[8] Perhaps God lacks goodness, or power, or both.[9] Further, if God is willing and able to prevent evil, "whence then is evil?"[10]

Experiences of privation, oppression, deliberate suppression of the flowering of human independence and wholeness, misery, and unwarranted suffering and violence have always attended human existence. If joy, happiness, and contentment brighten the horizons of our moral landscape, death, disease, and natural calamities remind us of the limits of human control over the affairs of our lives.[11]

Religious responses to suffering function in at least three ways. First, they attempt to provide a context into which the existence of evil is integrated into the larger picture of reality.[12] Second, recognizing that suffering may not be avoidable, but in fact may be a phenomenologically and primarily existential experience that one "lives through," attempts at "intellectual" and "spiritual" explanation are nevertheless attempted to place the experience in perspective. As Clifford Geertz observes, "The problem of suffering is, paradoxically, not how to avoid suffering, but how to make physical pain, personal loss, worldly defeat, or the helpless contemplation of others' agony something bearable, supportable, something, as we say, sufferable."[13] Third, as Peter Berger observes in his book, *The Sacred Canopy,* while theodicies are not employed to provide people with a false sense of happiness, nor to simply affirm some type of personal redemption, theodicy-making does function to maintain religious meaning in spite of suffering and evil.[14]

The psalmist's exultant affirmation of a God "mighty to save," who provides comfort and deliverance in the face of travail and anguish, recurs with magniloquent clarity in the spiritual autobiography of Maria W. Stewart. Stewart's autobiography is an instructive *Abbildung* for assessing the ways in which African-American women of faith have appropriated biblical texts in their lives within the context of their own personal and corporate experiences of suffering and evil in the world. How have African-American women reconciled their own experiences of racial and gender oppression in particular with belief in the all-powerful Judeo-Christian God?

The essay will examine the subject of Maria Stewart's reflections on suffering and evil within the context of early nineteenth-century American life with an analysis of three topics. First, what was the sociopolitical and religious context in which Stewart gave voice to her musings? The subject will be examined broadly under the rubric: "Black Autobiography and the Context of Theodic Reflection."

Second, why was the literary medium of spiritual autobiography an appropriate genre for Maria Stewart's attempts to mediate the tensions of evil in a world created by a gracious God? Discussion of some of the characteristic features and concerns of nineteenth-century African-American women's autobiography is presented in the section: "Nineteenth-Century African-American Women's Spiritual Autobiography: The Genre of Theodic Reflection."

Third, how did biblical texts function philosophically and practically in Stewart's attempt to address issues of "divine causation" (suffering and evil occur because it is God's will) and "human freedom" (suffering and evil occur because human beings choose to sin)? What is (or are) the hermeneutics operative in her interpretation and appropriation of biblical texts in general, such that she refused acquiescence to the traditionally delineated roles of African Americans as ontologically inferior and intellectually deficient, and such that she refused conformity to the "place" of women as socially and religiously dependent and subordinate to men? How did Stewart use the Bible to nurture a politics of cojoined socioreligious discourse and action that actuated a liberation praxis illustrating the power of the sentiment *fiat justitia, ruat caelum* ("let justice be done, though the heavens fall") in the face of inequity, suffering, and evil? The section " 'The Miry Bog, the Desolate Pit, a New Song': Maria Stewart's Perspectives on Theodicy Issues" will explore these concerns.

Black Autobiography and the Context of Theodic Reflection

If, as Vicchio observes, religious responses to suffering include in their ideological and conceptual formulations an attempt to identify the *context* into which the existence of evil is integrated into the larger picture of reality,[15] it is immediately apparent that one can safely postulate early nineteenth-century American life as the *Sitz im Leben* of Stewart's pensive and hortatory musings. A thorough treatment of the subjects of African-American women in the nineteenth century and, in particular, the tradition of African-American women's autobiography in the nineteenth century, is beyond the scope of this essay; however, the following observations regarding some of the characteristic features and functions of Black autobiography provide useful prolegomena for assessing Stewart's personal narratives both ideologically and socially.

> Autobiography in America is not only a genre with significant origins and distinguished classics, it is also an industry, a sometimes hand-made, sometimes machinemade common commodity, like "grubby" clothes and three-piece suits, old family mansions and pickup trucks with campers. And like clothes, cars, and houses, it is a necessity, or almost a necessity, that we have to have—for work and for entertainment—in order to say who we are and where we've been.[16]

Sayre's observation underscores the "varieties of form" and "diversities of writer" who have penned autobiographies. From the masterfully classic autobiographies of Saint Augustine (*Confessions*)[17] and John Bunyan (*The Pilgrim's Progress*),[18] to the intimately personal and passionate-personal letters of the seventeenth-century writer Madame de Sévigné,[19] to the rhetorically sustained and declarative autobiography of Malcolm X (*The Autobiography of Malcolm X*),[20] to the graphically detailed and symbolically engaging autobiography of Maya Angelou (*I Know Why the Caged Bird Sings*),[21] all forms of autobiography generally provide some clues and insights into the *auto* and the *bios* of their creators.

Knowledge of some features of the "context" of both female and male autobiographers' lives is requisite for negotiating the landscape of their narratives. The term *context* literally means "to weave together, to twine, to connect."[22] The interweaving of the wide range of experiences, expectations, smaller and larger social-structured networks and forces (including family and kin, for example) all contribute to and influence the shaping and parameters of a life.[23] While the constructs of such factors as gender, race, and class are not necessarily rigidly determinant of the identity of the writer, they are nonetheless intricately meaningful elements that contribute to the whole complex of dynamic processes and influences that gives meaning to the context of human life.

In his excellent compendium of selected ethnic autobiographies, *The Ethnic I. A Sourcebook for Ethnic-American Autobiography*, James Craig Holte observes that in the creation of an autobiography, the writer transforms the complex and creative interaction of self and society into a literary form: "Whether this imposition of form on experience takes place during the actual activity or is an act of literary imposition that occurs during the construction of a narrative may be unanswerable, but there is evidence that many writers use the autobiography as a means of imposing order on experiences that are disruptive and confusing."[24]

It would not be unreasonable to think that Maria Stewart's memoirs imposed order on what was more typically a "chaotic" life for African Americans in the nineteenth century. The death-dealing realities of chattel slavery, second-class citizenship, and unbridled discrimination and segregation, formed a part of the transactions between "self and society." African Americans everywhere, whether on the very fringe of survival or free, were immersed in the struggle to move beyond mere existence and survival.[25]

African-American autobiographical writing in the nineteenth century represented more than a socially detached and reflective attempt to create a "self-portrait." The writer could be an uninhibitable prophetic "disturber of the peace,"[26] whose expressions about her or his experience of reality (both internal and external to themselves) could be conveyed with sermonic, didactic, spiritual, or mystically-nuanced fluency.

There are at least four elements of African-American autobiography that generally tend to recur as constants in the literature. First, there is an expressed desire to live as one chooses,[27] to affirm fully and positively one's self-worth through unrestrained possibilities for self-actualization.

A second characteristic feature of African-American autobiography is "the tacit or explicit criticism of external national conditions that . . . work to ensure that one's freedom of choice is delimited or nonexistent."[28] There is, then, a refusal to engage in abstract pretensions about both the origin and the reality of racial oppression and suffering, about those factors that contribute regularly and almost uninterruptedly to personal and communal chaos in the life.

African-American autobiographies are also, in a third and related point, a "mirror of white deeds."[29] If autobiography links both history and literature,[30] objective fact and subjective awareness, then it serves to remove fully the mask that seeks to camouflage the ugly reality of the continuing legacy of slavery and the ubiquitous and pervasive expressions of racism. Stephen Butterfield describes the way in which African-American autobiography authenticates historical consciousness and experience and its potentially transformative dimension:

Black autobiographies fill in many of the blanks of America's self-knowledge. They help us to see what has been left out of the picture of our national life by white writers and critics, how our critical judgment has been limited, indeed, crippled, by a blind spot toward Afro-American culture. . . . as so many black autobiographies demonstrate, one is never content to remain a thing. The humanity won by the slave and his descendants belongs to humanity everywhere. The door of the white prison is opened, not closed, by his story. If the very worst effects of oppression have been unable to wipe out intelligence, compassion, honor, faith, hope, and the courage to resist in the mass of its black victims, then these qualities are preserved for all, including the children of the ruling culture. The slave's victory is the victory of the best in ourselves.[31]

A fourth characteristic feature of African-American autobiographies is their transcendence of the "self," or a preoccupation with individuation, or "Renaissance individualism," toward a more integrated communal consciousness. The "self" of African-American autobiography is no mere "lonely sojourner" on the road of life, no isolate with a private career, but "a soldier in a long, historic march toward Canaan ... a member of an oppressed social group, with ties and responsibilities to the other members. ... The self belongs to the people, and the people find a voice in the self."[32]

One may conclude, then, that particularly for the African-American female or male autobiography, reflections on the "context" in which suffering and evil are experienced—though communicated and portrayed through one voice (the writer's)—tend to integrate and interweave both individual and communal grapplings with the chaos they seek to negotiate.

Nineteenth-Century African-American Women's Spiritual Autobiography: The Genre of Theodic Reflection

If Ann Allen Shockley is correct in her chronicle of African-American women writers from the eighteenth century to the early twentieth century, African-American women's autobiographies began to burgeon between 1830 and 1840. Phyllis Wheatley and Lucy Terry, among the earliest "stolen females" and muses of the African diaspora, had established themselves as the first African-American female poets. Ann Plato, writing sixty-eight years after Phyllis Wheatley published her first volume of verse, *Poems and Various Subjects, Religious and Moral* (1773), wrote the second book authored by an African-American writer.[33] Published in 1841, Plato's *Essays; Including Biographies and Miscellaneous Pieces in Prose and Poetry* was one of many exposés that illumined the personal thoughts and lives of African-American people in general, and African-American women in particular.[34]

If Black women's very narrations of their autobiographies constituted a political act—resolute self-affirmation and self-reclamation of the significance of the "Afra-American self"[35] in general—their spiritual autobiographies comprised illuminating self-disclosures of their relations to the divine, the otherworldly, and the spiritual, in particular.

Definitions and varieties of spiritual autobiographies have varied widely over time. According to Daniel B. Shea, when applied to seventeenth- and eighteenth-century American life, "spiritual" connotes concern primarily with the question of grace (including whether the individual has been accepted into the divine life, as demonstrated, in retrospect, by discernible psychological and moral changes commensurate with conversion). But the Quaker and Puritan autobiographers tended to focus less on the conversion process and more on either the nature of the "witnessing life" or the examination of "any experiences and events that might bear on their spiritual conditions," respectively.[36]

Mary G. Mason, on the other hand, argues that the expressions and modes of interior disclosure vary according to gender. Augustine's structure of conversion in the *Confessions*, which presents the self as involved in a battle of opposing forces — spirit against flesh — with a climactic victory for spirit that completes the drama of the self, "does not accord with the deepest realities of women's experience and so is inappropriate as a model for women's life-writing."[37]

According to Mason, a characteristic feature of women's autobiographical writing — including women's spiritual autobiographies — is the intimate and almost determinant symbiotic relationship between "the Other" and "self-identity."

> Both Julian [of Norwich] and Margery Kempe, writing in the mystical tradition of personal dialogue with a divine being who is Creator, Father, and Lover, discover and reveal themselves in discovering and revealing the Other. . . . Julian establishes an identification with the suffering Christ on the cross that is absolute; yet, while such a total identification might seem to suggest a loss of self, the fact is that Julian is in no way obliterated as a person, for her account is shot through with evidence of a vivid, unique, and even radical consciousness.[38]

Margery Kempe's autobiography, *The Book of Margery Kempe* (ca. 1432), "a schort tretys and a comfortabyl for synful wrecchys" that narrates her life's devotion to "ower souereyn Sauyowr Cryst Ihesu,"[39] displays (unlike Julian of Norwich's "single-visioned" *Revelations*) her twofold sense of vocation in her spiritual pilgrimage: the wife-mother and pilgrim-mystic roles. This retention of a dual focus in Kempe's life "represents a rather more common pattern of women's perceptions of themselves as maintaining equally demanding identities, worldly and otherworldly, both of which, however, are ultimately determined by their relation to the divine."[40]

Mason's observation about women's presentation and evolution of self-identity in relation to the divine is germane to the spiritual autobiographies of nineteenth-century African-American women. Black women's reflections on the spiritual life of individuals and communities, their records of conversions, religious pilgrimages, of confrontations with both family members and the predominantly male "gatekeepers" of the ordained ranks, reveal no tendency to self-annihilation or "absorption" by the deity, but an ever-emergent, reempowered self-identity in relation to the deity, the community, and the wider society.

Nineteenth-century African-American spiritual autobiographies were penned largely by Northern, freeborn women, who, whether as slaves, former slaves, or freeborn, responded to a "call" to a mission that commanded their total allegiance and loyalty.[41] The religious Black women may have sought sanction for their usually itinerant ministries within traditional ecclesiastical hierarchies, but given that repudiation of their preaching and evangelistic efforts was more often the "norm" than the exception, they were prepared to face daunting and unforeseen personal and social hindrances to respond to the Highest Authority. Nineteenth-century Black women demonstrated the freedom that they achieved through faith as they described both the search for Christian perfection and the development of their gifts of leadership and service, and as they heralded the importance of religious duty and instruction in the quest for sanctification and wholeness.

The African-American women gospel-bearers who refused to permit the Black male clerical establishment's insistence on male dominance and female subordination to overrule the higher calling of God in their lives were many, representing a wide range of denominational affiliations: Jarena Lee, an unordained but licensed minister of the African Methodist Episcopal Church;[42] Zilpha Elaw, a minister of the Methodist Episcopal faith;[43] Rebecca Cox Jackson, who established a Black Shaker sisterhood in Philadelphia;[44] a Quaker named Elizabeth (with no last name), born into slavery in 1766.[45]

One of the chief results of the conversion experience on many of the writers of spiritual autobiographies was what William Andrews describes as "a very real sense of freedom from a prior self and a growing awareness of unrealized, unexploited powers within."[46] For many African-American women, this "realignment of the self" fostered the boldness and inner conviction of spirit to result in "independence, self-reliance, strength, autonomy,"[47] and the verve to challenge male authority. It was this kind of "self-realignment" that led Julia Foote to admonish her sisters in ministry to persevere in their proclamation of the gospel:

> Sisters, shall not you and I unite with the heavenly host in the grand chorus? If so, you will not let what man may say or do keep you from doing the will of the Lord or using the gifts that you have for the good of others. How much easier to bear the reproach of men than to live at a distance from God.[48]

The African-American women missionaries, preachers, exhorters, and visionaries thus asserted the literary self to narrate the stories of the spiritually "transformed, transforming self." The awareness of their true place and calling in the presence of Almighty God in an imperfect world prompted the use of a narrative rhetoric marked as much by awe of a gracious Sovereign as by reflective analyses of unjust power relationships in church and society.[49]

Even if it is true that African-American women sought to "realign the self" in their spiritual autobiographies, neither should one conclude that African-American women sought only to "create and recreate the self-in-experience in literature,"[50] but rather, claiming equal access to the love, forgiveness, and care of the Judeo-Christian God, they established firmly their rightful claims to full humanity in both church and society: "they wanted their words to change the hearts of the men and the women whom they reached."[51] That is, conversion, salvation, and security about the efficaciousness of God's saving grace was not the *terminus ad quem*, but became a lens through which they evaluated and reinterpreted their experiences of a particular *racial* community *as women* within that community.

Black spiritual autobiographies functioned — for both women and men — as a medium through which they could document the power of spiritual healing to effect some relief from the powerfully oppressive winds of racial denigration. They also provided a vehicle through which their authors could gain literary power and authority in the language of the dominant culture.[52] Further, the genre provided an opportunity to elaborate freely on the Book of Books, "the white text in a black voice, and through a black perspective."[53]

For African-American women, the spiritual autobiographies were an appropriate forum to challenge the boundaries set by a dominant white society that promulgated "supremacy" based on race, and it was an appropriate forum to challenge the boundaries set by a majority of African-American men who promulgated "authoritative male hegemony" in the religious sphere based on gender. The courageous African-American female autographs claimed that their struggle to be free was as urgent for them as citizens of the United States as it was for them as citizens of the Heavenly Kingdom. They claimed that their sense of call and commitment to God's work as missionaries, evangelists, and preachers was consistent with the notion of the "democracy of saved souls," where women and men alike were on "equal standing"[54] before the God who gives gifts in accordance with the divine will alone, irrespective of gender distinctions.

"The Miry Bog, the Desolate Pit, a New Song": Maria Stewart's Perspectives on Suffering and Evil

If the inhospitable and ruthlessly anti-African-American sentiment and sociopolitical policies of pre-Civil War America comprised the *context* for Maria Stewart's life, and autobiography the *literary medium* through which she purposefully and emphatically "gave voice" to her profound religious faith and passionate social activism, *biblical traditions* provided for Stewart a vital and life-empowering witness for both theological reflection about and oppositional engagement against racial suffering and evil.

Black Suffering and the Praxis of Oppositional Engagement

Maria Stewart's reflections on the problems of suffering and evil as they relate to racism in particular suggest that she sought more than a "sufferable" existence with reference to this perfidious evil.[55] Moreover, the "maintenance of religious meaning"[56] in spite of suffering and evil required for Stewart more than "pensive navel-gazing" on the theoretical and philosophical complexities of an authentic Christian response to the problem of suffering. Stewart's religious vision and her sociopolitical agenda were intrinsically bound, defined one by the other.[57] A praxis of active, oppositional engagement against racial suffering and evil was a fundamental aspect of her theodic ideology. "Resistance to oppression was, for Stewart, the highest form of obedience to God."[58] Stewart states her convictions about devotion to God and social activism with unapologetic candor, noting that it was her conversion experience that intensified her desire to ameliorate the "wretched and degraded" situation of African Americans:

> From the moment I experienced the change, I felt a strong desire, with the help and assistance of God, to devote the remainder of my days to piety and virtue, and now possess that spirit of independence, that, were I called upon, I would willingly sacrifice my life for the cause of God and my brethren.[59]

But what is the nature of this suffering, the amelioration and annihilation of which Stewart would gladly sacrifice her life?

In his helpful discussion of "Theodicy and Racism,"[60] William R. Jones outlines three essential features of Black or ethnic suffering. First, it is "maldistributed." That is, Black suffering is not spread more or less randomly over the total human race, but instead, a "double portion of suffering is experienced by or concentrated in a particular ethnic group."[61]

A second characteristic feature of Black suffering is its "enormity." That is, it designates not only a statistically widespread impact upon the total number of Blacks, but "enormity" also refers to the "range of intensity" of the experience: "Enormity also designates suffering unto death or that oppression which reduces life expectancy and frustrates self-realization."[62]

A third characteristic feature of Black suffering is that it is "noncatastrophic." That is, ethnic suffering does not "strike quickly" and then leave, or its effects dissipate after a short or terrible siege: "Rather, it strikes not only the father but the son and the grandson; it is, in fine, transgenerational."[63] Similarly, the insidious effects of the durative quality of noncatastrophic Black suffering strikes the mother, the daughter, and the granddaughter in transgenerational fashion.

That Maria Stewart witnessed and experienced the threefold aspects of African-American suffering as "maldistributed," marked by "enormity" and persistently "noncatastrophic," emerges in her descriptions of Black suffering in her lifetime. Though born a freeborn New Englander in 1803 and reared in Hartford, Connecticut (she was orphaned at age five and "bound out" to a minister's family),[64] her personal knowledge and experience of the odious character of racism and of Southern slavery emerges quite clearly in her autobiography:

> I have heard much respecting the horrors of slavery; but may Heaven forbid that the generality of my color throughout these United States

should experience any more of its horrors than to be a servant of servants, or hewers of wood and drawers of water![65]

Stewart dolefully laments the cavalier lack of commitment of white women and men to the struggle of African-American peoples to secure rights of full citizenship and opportunity. Death may, in some circumstances, she argues, appear to be a more attractive alternative to an existence where the opportunity to develop full personhood is denied:

> I have asked several individuals of my sex, who transact business for themselves, if, providing our girls were to give them the most satisfactory references, they would not be willing to grant them an equal opportunity with others? Their reply has been—for their own part, they had no objection; but as it was not the custom, were they to take them into their employ, they would be in danger of losing the public patronage.
>
> And such is the powerful force of prejudice. Let our girls possess what amiable qualities of soul they may; let their characters be fair and spotless as innocence itself; let their natural taste and ingenuity be what they may; it is impossible for scarce an individual of them to rise above the condition of servant.
>
> Few white persons of either sex, who are calculated for anything else, are willing to spend their lives and bury their talents in performing mean, servile labor. And such is the horrible idea that I entertain respecting a life of servitude, that if I conceived of there being no possibility of my rising above the condition of a servant, I would gladly hail death as a welcome messenger. O, horrible idea, indeed! to possess noble souls aspiring after high and honorable acquirements, yet confined by the chains of ignorance and poverty to lives of continual drudgery and toil. Neither do I know of any who have enriched themselves by spending their lives as house-domestics, washing windows, shaking carpets, brushing boots, or tending upon gentlemen's tables. I can but die for expressing my sentiments; and I am as willing to die by the sword as the pestilence; for I am a true born American; your blood flows in my veins, and your spirit fires my breast.[66]

Stewart's reflections on the tension of how to reconcile her experience of racial oppression with belief in the all-powerful Judeo-Christian God focus less on attempts to "absolve the deity of responsibility for injustice," or to "protect the deity's honor," pronouncing a "not guilty" verdict over God for that which destroys the affairs of human beings, and the world;[67] rather, Stewart assumes both ontologically and epistemologically that God is near to and acts on behalf of the powerless and the disenfranchised in the interests of divine justice.[68]

Assuming, as have African Americans before and after her, that racial oppression was detrimental to the highest good of both African Americans and the wider society, Stewart affirmed and promulgated the actions of a God who fights against the oppressive evils of life. As many of the Spirituals that emerged from the Black church in slavery averred, "Christianity has to do with fighting with God against the evils of this life."[69] The God who liberated Israel from the oppression of slavery (Exod. 1:1–15:27) was believed to be no less affronted about Black slavery. The biblical witness of a God who is involved in history, who acts within history to advance social, economic, and political justice for the poor and unwanted in society has always been a fundamental and bedrock tenet of African-American religious faith.[70] Biblical traditions that highlight this theme recur in Black religion.

> It is, indeed, the *biblical witness* that says that God is a God of liberation, who calls to himself the oppressed and abused in the nation and assures them that their righteousness will vindicate their suffering. It is the Bible that tells us that God became man in Jesus Christ so that his kingdom would make freedom a reality for all men. This is the meaning of the resurrection of Christ. Man no longer has to be a slave to anybody, but must rebel against all principalities and powers which make his existence subhuman (italics added).[71]

The Bible witnesses to a God who not only liberated disparate groups who were perceived to be "nobodies," existing on the fringes of ancient Near Eastern society, it also witnesses to God as one who maintains and works out forcefully and creatively freedom and the formation of community for the alien and the alienated.[72] The "formation of community" was central to the challenge that the newly liberated Israel faced in its covenantal relationship with the God Yahweh who was responsible for its liberation.

Liberation from suffering, evil, and oppression was thus perceived to represent only the beginning of a journey wherein one acts *with God* to exemplify the realities of freedom and justice and community formation within the sociopolitical and religious institutions of a society. It is the combination of "the mighty acts of God" (as seen in the Exodus event and in the life, death, and resurrection of Jesus Christ) and "human response" that reverses the suffering and evil of oppression that thwarts the purposes of God in the "purposeful ordering of society as a sign of God's intention for creation."[73] "It is not simply by divine fiat, but by conflict, struggle, and overt human choice that men are liberated and community is formed . . . the freedom sought and effected is both political and spiritual, the fellowship created is both social and religious."[74]

Black Suffering: Hermeneutical Strategies in Oppositional Rhetoric

Maria Stewart accepted readily the notion that liberation from racial suffering and evil required a human response of participation with God in securing and encoding the realities of justice within the lives of African-American peoples. As statements from her spiritual autobiography have shown, she adhered to a "praxis of oppositional engagement" (in which the sufferer actively confronts and resists the causes and effects of human suffering and evil) as an appropriate and imperative response to the expressions of individual and institutional racism.

The subject of how Maria Stewart appropriated biblical traditions within the narrative of her spiritual autobiography is germane, given the pervasive use of biblical texts throughout *Productions of Mrs. Maria W. Stewart*. A close analysis of the rhetoric and argument of the autobiography reveals at once that she was an avid student of both the Old and New Testaments. Biblical texts drawn from the Old Testament, in particular, are woven throughout the argument of her political essays and lectures, although copious quotations of Matthew, various of the Epistles, and Revelation are included as well.[75]

As one assesses Stewart's use of biblical traditions in such a way as to advance her praxis of oppositional engagement against racial suffering and evil, it is essential to evaluate her hermeneutical strategies with a view to how the rhetoric of her arguments could or would shape human actions. Preliminary comments on the science of hermeneutics (interpretation) and particularly the "effects" of hermeneutical strategies are appropriate at this point.

Roger Lunden, Anthony C. Thistleton, and Clarence Walhout[76] have observed correctly that "hermeneutics" is not simply a cognitive process wherein one seeks to determine the "correct meaning" of a passage or text. Neither are questions of penultimate truth and universality solely determinative of meaning. Also of essential importance in the interpretive task are such matters as the nature of the interpreter's goals, the effects of a given interpretation on a community of people who have an interest in the text being interpreted, and questions of cultural value, social relevance, and ethics. "What is at stake in hermeneutics is not only the *truth* of one's interpretation, but also the effects interpretation and interpretive strategies have on the ways in which human beings shape their goals and their actions. These effects may be indirect . . . but the difference they make is to be seen in the final analysis in their role, small or large, in the shaping of human actions."[77]

Maria Stewart's reflections on the pernicious effects of racial suffering and evil include appeals to conscience as well as to a vital praxis. They contain a critique of the abuse of power and herald a vision to the creation of a society in which men and women value true piety as much as human rights. In short, Stewart advanced adherence to Christian faith and promoted unremitting involvement against those forces that sought to overwhelm and nullify the purposes of God for the human community.

One hermeneutical strategy employed by Maria Stewart in her oppositional stance against racial suffering and evil is an *eclectic use of disparate sources*, including, especially, biblical traditions, to marshall evidence against all claims that racial suffering and evil is philosophically and morally defensible.

Given that Stewart closely interwove the concerns of both religion and social justice in her analysis, it is not surprising to see her invoke both the Bible and the Constitution of the United States to reinforce the universal birthright to justice and freedom. The use of the two documents together intensifies Stewart's persuasive argument against the racial dominance of one group over another:

> This is the land of freedom. The press is at liberty. Every man has a right to express his opinion. Many think, because your skins are tinged with a sable hue, that you are an inferior race of beings; but God does not consider you as such. He hath formed and fashioned you in his own glorious image, and hath bestowed upon you reason and strong powers of intellect. He hath made you to have dominion over the beasts of the field, the fowls of the air, and the fish of the sea. He hath crowned you with glory and honor; hath made you but a little lower than the angels; and, according to the Constitution of these United States, he hath made all men free and equal. Then why should one worm say to another, "Keep you down there, while I sit up yonder; for I am better than thou?" It is not the color of the skin that makes the man, but it is the principles formed within the soul.[78]

If, as Stephen B. Reid observes, the task of Black biblical hermeneutics "involves the interpretation of Black culture and the biblical text," with both Black culture and the biblical text functioning as "partners" (neither identity nor interpretation takes priority),[79] then the Bible and the Constitution—both primary and authoritative cultural artifacts in the history of African-American social and communal life[80]—can be viewed correctly by Stewart as complimentary (and not "competing") resources in her rhetorical argument.

A second hermeneutical strategy that Stewart uses in her diatribe against racial suffering and evil is the use of selected biblical traditions to make *polemical pragmatic comparisons* between prominent biblical personages who induced brutal suffering on a particular group within biblical narratives, and polemical pragmatic comparisons with those who tolerated and inflicted racial suffering and evil against African Americans.

The phrase "pragmatic comparison" is used to identify a comparative language class ("comparative language" refers to similes and metaphors and other literary strategies for making comparisons)[81] in which the activity or result of one thing is compared with another.[82] Psalm 5:9 describes a situation wherein "the throats of the wicked gape like an open grave, and with the same implication for their victims." Another example of a pragmatic comparison is found in Mark 4:30, where the kingdom is described as working like yeast, "but so also does the bad example of Pharisees and of Herod" (Mark 8:15).[83]

Within the context of Maria Stewart's protests against racial suffering and evil, the sometimes intensely intrepid tone of her discourse makes the phrase "polemical pragmatic comparison" quite apropos. One example of a polemical pragmatic comparison likens those who perpetuate racial suffering and evil to Pharaoh, who perpetrates unjust suffering and evil against Israel. Stewart had been informed of an attempt by the Colonization Society to relocate African Americans to Liberia. Her response is forthright as she questions the motives of the Society's collection of funds to this end:

I am informed that the agent of the Colonization Society has recently formed an association of young men, for the purpose of influencing those of us to go to Liberia who may feel disposed. . . . if the colonizationists are real friends to Africa, let them expend the money which they collect, in erecting a college to educate her injured sons in this land of gospel light and liberty; for it would be most thankfully received on our part, and convince us of the truth of their professions, and save time, expense and anxiety. Let them place before us noble objects, worthy of pursuit, and see if we prove ourselves to be those unambitious negroes they term us. But, ah! methinks their hearts are so frozen towards us, they had rather their money should be sunk in the ocean than to administer it to our relief; and I fear, if they dared, like Pharaoh, king of Egypt, they would order every male child among us to be drowned. But the most high God is still as able to subdue the lofty pride of these white Americans, as He was the heart of that ancient rebel.[84]

Stewart uses a second polemical pragmatic comparison (albeit involving a more symbolic figure) in her comparison of America with "the great city of Babylon," whose criminous excesses are described in Revelation 14:8; 17:1–18:24:

It appears to me that America has become like the great city of Babylon, for she has boasted in her heart — I sit a queen, and am no widow, and shall see no sorrow? She is indeed a seller of slaves and the souls of men; she has made the Africans drunk with the wine of her fornication; she has put them completely beneath her feet, and she means to keep them there; her right hand supports the reins of government, and her left hand the wheel of power, and she is determined not to let go her grasp. But many powerful sons and daughters of Africa will shortly arise, who will put down vice and immorality among us, and declare by Him that sitteth upon the throne, that they will have their rights; and if refused, I am afraid they will spread horror and devastation around. I believe that the oppression of injured Africa has come up before the Majesty of Heaven; and when our cries shall have reached the ears of the Most High, it will be a tremendous day for the people of this land; for strong is the arm of the Lord God Almighty.[85]

The comparison of America's easy tolerance of racial injustice with Babylon's[86] abominations, immorality, and idolatry intensifies the severity of the indictment of America's spiritual vacuity and moral deterioration in the area of race relations. The effect of the polemical pragmatic comparisons of America with both Pharaoh and Babylon suggests that the God who chastens and judges Pharaoh and Babylon would be justified in leveling similar judicial judgments and calamitous penalties on obstinate and unrepentant America.

Maria Stewart employs a third hermeneutical strategy in her oppositional stance toward racial suffering and evil that may be called a *hermeneutics of reiterative remembrance.* The focus of the strategy is conspicuously more personal, involving a declarative rehearsal, a "reiteration" of the ways in which God has delivered, rescued, transformed, and reempowered the self or the community in the face of suffering or calamity.

The quotation of biblical texts or testimony that narrates the mighty acts of God and God's power to deliver and sustain in the midst of suffering and evil was a familiar leitmotif in both the Hebrew Bible and the New Testament. The Psalms in particular often represented testimony that substantiated and reiterated the trustworthiness of Yahweh, who has served as protector and refuge (e.g., Ps. 16; 23; 30; 39; 91; 121). In the New Testament, Luke portrays the bold, itinerant believers and missionaries of the earliest church as gathering to share in a triumphant profession of God's protection following the release of Peter and John before the religious authorities in Jerusalem (Acts 4:5–30). The reiteration of the conviction that God helps those beset by antagonists is thus a practice firmly rooted within the Judeo-Christian tradition.[87]

As noted above,[88] autobiography is a means of imposing order on experiences that are disruptive and confusing. African-American autobiographies typically include expressed desires for full and uninhibited self-actualization, a critique of external national conditions, and an interweaving of individual and communal consciousness. It is the African-American "spiritual" autobiography that contains some of the most poignantly stirring recitations and reiterations of the conviction that God sustains life as it exists in a whirlwind of chaos. God rescues, delivers, and succors the sufferer and besieged sojourner on the road of life.

Two of the most rhetorically powerful and enduring spiritual autobiographies that include within the narrative development the reiteration of examples of God's faithfulness are those of Harriet Tubman and Sojourner Truth. Both Harriet Tubman, who rescued over two hundred women, men, and children from slavery, and Sojourner Truth, abolitionist and advocate for women's rights and civil rights, were stellar representations of nine-teenth-century religious and political reformers.

While neither Tubman nor Truth acquired the gift of literacy, both women had others transform their oral stories into written words. The women's autobiographies, *Harriet Tubman, The Moses of Her People*, and *Narrative of Sojourner Truth*, illustrate the vitality of written spiritual auto-biography in the personal "as told to" narrative.[89]

The spiritual autobiographies of Tubman and Truth reveal what Joanne M. Braxton calls "radical" uses of traditional forms of spirituality that led them to question fearlessly what they perceived to be illegitimate authority, to "wage war" against "an intemperate, sexist, and slaveholding society."[90] Their spiritual autobiographies thus became a testament of witness to what God had done and would do within the context of the drama of their own experiences of suffering and upheaval:

> They believed that God was on their side, and that they acted on divine authority. . . . They believed in the power of prayer and the presence and accessibility of God; nothing they asked for would be denied. Both experienced dreams and visions of a prophetic nature and were so guided in their daily experiences; both relied on inner voices, which they presumed to be of divine origin. God was their immediate protector.[91]

Sojourner Truth's autobiography provides an electrifying account of her assumption that the God who had helped her in times past would help her again. Truth recounts the story of her attempts to recover her five-year-old son, sold by Truth's mistress to a wealthy planter in Alabama. Sojourner Truth boldly confronted her mistress and demanded the return of her young son:

> I tell you. I stretched up, I felt as tall as the world.
> "Missus," says I, "I'll have my son back again!"
> She laughed.
> "You will, you nigger? How you goin' to do it? You ha'nt got no money."
> "No Missus but God has—an' you'll see he'll help me!"[92]

Sojourner Truth did eventually regain her son, returned to her with his back "all covered with scars and lumps" from floggings that he had received.

Sojourner Truth's convictions of a God who "helps" within the context of racial suffering and evil were shared by Harriet Tubman, who brought her brothers, aged parents, and many others to freedom in the North (mak-ing at least twenty trips back into the slave states[93]). Tubman was resolute in her conviction that God had and would help her on the treacherous journeys into Canada:

I was free; but dere was no one to welcome me to de land of freedom, I was a stranger in a strange land, and my home after all was down in de old cabin quarter, wid de ole folks and my brudders and sisters. But to dis solemn resolution I came; I was free and dey should be free also; I would make a home for dem in de North, and de Lord helping me, I would bring dem all dere.[94]

Tubman's determination to secure freedom for both herself and others is a marked illustration of the kind of interweaving of individual and communal consciousness characteristic of those who have suffered racial suffering and evil. Tubman's asseveration, "de Lord helping me," was doubtless as much a prayer as a confident profession of a reality that she believed to have been verified each time she crossed into Canada delivering another woman, man, or child into Freedom's arms.

The stories of Harriet Tubman and Sojourner Truth's claim on a "God who helps" the sufferer, empowering her or him to assume an oppositional and life-affirming praxis against death-dealing forces reflect a similar theme echoed in Maria Stewart's autobiographical reflections. In particular, Stewart utilizes a "hermeneutics of reiterative remembrance" to proclaim God's faithfulness in delivering her "from all my distresses" in her quotation of Psalm 40:2–3a:

Come, all ye that have breath, and I will tell you what great things the Lord hath done for my soul: how he hath delivered my feet from the miry clay and the horrible pit, and hath put a new song in my mouth, even praise unto our God.[95]

Maria Stewart who, like her sisters Harriet Tubman and Sojourner Truth, had waged war and rebellion against the suffering and oppression of a segregated and slaveholding society, reiterated in the midst of the struggle that God was a faithful Deliverer and Sustainer in battle. The hermeneutics of reiterative remembrance functioned to *reclaim* and *proclaim* emphatically and unequivocally to a self under siege that even in the midst of the struggle against racial suffering and evil, when the very soul of one's personhood is threatened with depredation or extinction,[96] God is the "Lover of the soul"[97] who will not let go, and moreover, who will restore to life: "God hath put a new song in my mouth." God has done it before, God will do it again!

Stewart's quotation of Psalm 40:2–3a is located in "Meditation XIII" of the *Productions of Mrs. Maria W. Stewart*, within the literary context of an extended discourse on God's care of the "widow, the fatherless, the poor and the helpless." Clearly, Stewart's reiteration of God's faithfulness and care within this context is inclusive of, but not limited to, the distresses occasioned by racial suffering. The sweep of the challenges faced in the whole of her life are brought into sharp relief here as she recalls both the loss of her parents and her husband (Stewart was orphaned at the age of five; she married in 1826 and was widowed three years later).

The pictorial message of Psalm 40:2–3a is graphic, with an abundance of anthropomorphic imagery used in reference to God. God moves to activity on behalf of the sufferer, and in relationship with the sufferer to "deliver the feet from the miry clay and the horrible pit" (the Hebrew text adds: "and set my feet on a rock, making my steps secure").[98]

The "miry clay" and "the horrible pit" are likely references to deep cisterns, often used as prisons in the ancient Near East. The Hebrew Bible mentions "desolate" or "horrible pits" as places of imprisonment (Exod. 12:29; Isa. 24:22; Zech. 9:11; Lam. 3:53). Joseph was thrown into a cistern (Gen. 37:20–29; 40:15), as was Jeremiah: "So they took Jeremiah and cast him into the cistern of Malchiah, the king's son, which was in the court of the guard, letting Jeremiah down by ropes. And there was no water in the cistern, but only mire, and Jeremiah sank in the mire" (Jer. 38:6).

Cisterns represent a sphere or place from which one must "be" delivered. They have no lateral access, but drop precipitously from above, making it impossible for someone to extricate himself or herself from it. Additionally, rain water that flows into the cistern remains there, due to a lime plaster covering around the base of the bottom.[99] It was often the case that as a mixture of dust, bits of earth, and water found their way into the cistern, a "mire" would be created into which one could sink, hence the phrase "miry bog" or "miry clay." The imprisoned person would often slip and struggle to be extricated from the mud and slime, unable to stand, "until exhaustion or suffocation ended his misery."[100]

The figure of the "miry bog" and the "horrible pit" describes a situation of complete helplessness. Just as Jeremiah had to be lifted out of the miry bog of the cistern (Jer. 38:6-13),[101] so Stewart needed to find help for deliverance from her own threats of death and hell from within, and especially from outside, herself. If G. A. F. Knight is correct, the "desolate pit" was a phrase used to describe the lowest level of Sheol, the abode of the dead: "To reach there, God would have had to go down into those depths" before someone could be drawn up from the mud.[102] Stewart exults in God's "going down into the depths" for her and raising her up to a place of stability and safety.

A "new song" follows the rescue, and even the new song is a gift from God, a celebration of "our" God's saving deeds. As Stewart, Tubman, and Truth would all concur, one "cannot flounder in the mud," and once rescued, "be silent on the rock."[103] Their spiritual autobiographies are not surprisingly punctuated as much with cameos of "some battles lost," as with songs of deliverance and praise to the God who has helped them to achieve "some battles won," rescuing and delivering them, and ratifying their efforts to secure freedom and justice for "those with a sable hue." A hermeneutics of reiterative remembrance would thus have served to reignite the flames of perseverance when the soul's reserves were low; it would have parodied the demons of racial suffering and evil who feigned that they would have the last word. Maria Stewart's words and life show, above all, that in Christ, taking a stand against the racial suffering and evil which was so inescapably widespread in nineteenth-century America (and remains so in the twentieth century) represents a victory over "praxis paralysis" and affirms the integrity of an active partnership with God in the securance of truly human life and personhood for African-American humanity.

NOTES

1. Bruce M. Metzger and Roland E. Murphy, eds., *The New Oxford Annotated Bible with the Apocryphal / Deuterocanonical Books*, New Revised Standard Version (New York: Oxford University Press, 1991), 707. All citations of the Bible in this essay are taken from the *New Oxford Annotated Bible*, New Revised Standard Version.

2. Marilyn Richardson, *Maria W. Stewart, America's First Black Woman Political Writer: Essays and Speeches* (Bloomington and Indianapolis: Indiana University Press, 1987).

3. Maria W. Stewart, *Productions of Mrs. Maria W. Stewart*. Presented to the First African Baptist Church and Society of the City of Boston (Boston: Friends of Freedom and Virtue, 1835). Reproduced in *Spiritual Narratives*. The Schomburg Library of Nineteenth-Century Black Women Writers, Henry Louis Gates, Jr., General Editor (New York: Oxford University Press, 1988), 3–98. All quotations of Stewart's autobiography will be taken from this primary source as reproduced in the Schomburg edition.

4. Richardson, *Maria W. Stewart*, 15. For Stewart's quotation of Psalm 40:1–3, see *Productions*, Meditation XIII, 48.

5. Barry L. Whitney, *What Are They Saying About God and Evil?* (New York: Paulist Press, 1989), 3.

6. Ibid., 2, 94.

7. Genesis 1:31.

8. Nelson Pike, ed. *God and Evil* (Englewood Cliffs, NJ: Prentice Hall, 1964), 86–87.

9. C. S. Lewis, *The Problem of Pain* (London: Collins, 1940), 14.

10. David Hume, *Dialogues Concerning Natural Religion*, ed., Norman Kemp Smith (New York: Bobbs-Merrill, 1947), 198.

11. Stephen J. Vicchio, *The Voice from the Whirlwind: The Problem of Evil and the Modern World* (Westminster, MD: Christian Classics, 1989), vii, 5.

12. Ibid., 6.

13. Clifford Geertz, *The Interpretation of Culture* (New York: Basic Books, 1973), 171.

14. Peter Berger, *The Sacred Canopy* (New York: Anchor Books, 1969), 53–54, 60.

15. Vicchio, *The Voice from the Whirlwind*, 6.

16. Robert F. Sayre, "Autobiography and the Making of America." *Autobiography: Essays Theoretical and Critical*. James Olney, ed. (Princeton: Princeton University Press, 1980), 147–148.

17. Saint Augustine, *Confessions*, trans. William Watts, rev. by W. H. D. Rouse, 2 vols. (Loeb Classical Library, 1977).

18. John Bunyan, *The Pilgrim's Progress*. James Blanton Wharey, ed. 2d ed., rev. Roger Sharrock (Oxford: Clarendon Press, 1960).

19. Madame de Sévigné, *Correspondance*, ed. Roger Duchene (Paris: Gallimard, 1974–78).

20. Malcolm X, with Alex Haley, *The Autobiography of Malcolm X* (New York: Grove Press, 1965). See also, *Malcolm X Speaks*, ed. George Breitman (New York: Grove Press, 1965).

21. Maya Angelou, *I Know Why the Caged Bird Sings* (New York: Bantam Books, 1971).

22. Joy Wester Barbre and Members of the Personal Narratives Group, "Conditions Not of Her Own Making." *Interpreting Women's Lives: Feminist Theory and Personal Narratives*, ed. The Personal Narratives Group (Bloomington and Indianapolis: Indiana University Press, 1989), 19.

23. Ibid., 19–20.

24. James Craig Holte, *The Ethnic I. A Sourcebook for Ethnic-American Autobiography* (New York: Greenwood House, 1988), 3.

25. Bert James Loewenberg and Ruth Bogin, eds., *Black Women in Nineteenth-Century American Life: Their Words, Their Thoughts, Their Feelings* (University Park and London: Pennsylvania State University Press, 1976), 5, 6.

26. Fred L. Standley, "James Baldwin: The Artist as Incorrigible Disturber of the Peace." *Southern Humanities Review* 4 (1970), 18–30.

27. Roger Rosenblatt, "Black Autobiography: Life as the Death Weapon." James Olney, ed., *Autobiography: Essays Theoretical and Critical* (Princeton: Princeton University Press, 1980), 170.

28. Ibid.

29. Stephen Butterfield, *Black Autobiography in America* (Amherst: University of Massachusetts Press, 1974), 3.

30. Ibid., 1.

31. Ibid., 4.

32. Ibid., 3.

33. Ann Allen Shockley, *Afro-American Women Writers, 1746-1933: An Anthology and Critical Guide* (Boston: G. K. Hall, 1988), 4.

34. Ann Plato, *Essays; Including Biographies and Miscellaneous Pieces in Prose and Poetry*. The Schomburg Library of Nineteenth-Century Black Women Writers. Henry Louis Gates, Jr., General Editor (New York: Oxford University Press, 1988).

35. I am indebted to Jeanne M. Braxton for the phrase "Afra-American self." See, Braxton, *Black Women Writing Autobiography: A Tradition within a Tradition* (Philadelphia: Temple University Press, 1989), 139.

36. Daniel B. Shea, Jr., *Spiritual Autobiography in Early America* (Princeton: Princeton University Press, 1968), xi.

37. Mary G. Mason, "The Other Voice: Autobiographies of Women Writers." *Autobiography: Essays Theoretical and Critical*. James Olney, ed. (Princeton: Princeton University Press, 1980), 210.

38. Ibid.

39. Ibid., 209. See also, *The Book of Margery Kempe*, Sanford Brown Meech, ed. (London: Oxford University Press, 1940). *Julian of Norwich*, trans. Edmund Colledge and James Walsh (New York: Paulist, 1978).

40. Mason, "The Other Voice," 211.

41. Nellie Y. McKay, "Nineteenth-Century Black Women's Spiritual Autobi-

ographies. Religious Faith and Self-Empowerment." *Interpreting Women's Lives Feminist Theory and Personal Narratives*, ed. The Personal Narratives Group (Bloomington and Indianapolis: Indiana University Press, 1989), 142.

42. Jarena Lee, *Religious Experiences and Journal of Jarena Lee, Giving an Account of Her Call To Preach the Gospel* (1849) in William L. Andrews, ed., *Sisters of Spirit* (Bloomington: University of Indiana Press, 1986).

43. Zilpha Elaw, *Memoirs of the Life, Religious Experience, Ministerial Travels and Labours of Mrs. Zilpha Elaw, an American Female of Color; Together with Some Account of the Great Religious Revivals in America* (1846) in Andrews, *Sisters of Spirit*.

44. Rebecca Cox Jackson, *Gifts of Power: The Writings of Rebecca Jackson, Black Visionary, Shaker Eldress* (n. d., but Jackson's writings span the period from 1830–64). See Ann Shockley, *Afro-American Women Writers, 1746–1933: An Anthology and Critical Guide* (Boston: G. K. Hall, 1988), 6. Cf. Rebecca Cox Jackson, *Gifts of Power: The Writings of Rebecca Cox Jackson, Black Visionary, Shaker Eldress*. Edited and with an Introduction by Jean McMahon Humez (Amherst: University of Massachusetts Press, 1970).

45. *Elizabeth: Coloured Minister of the Gospel, Born in Slavery* (Philadelphia, 1889), 2–12. This tract was published by the Philadelphia Quakers and was based on an interview with Elizabeth recorded when she was ninety-seven years old.

46. William L. Andrews, ed., *Sisters of the Spirit: Three Black Women's Autobiographies of the Nineteenth Century* (Bloomington: Indiana University Press, 1986), 12.

47. Cheryl Townsend Gilkes, " 'Together in Harness': Women's Traditions in the Sanctified Church." *Signs: Journal of Women in Culture and Society* 10, no. 4 (Summer 1985): 678–99.

48. Julia A. J. Foote, *A Brand Plucked from the Fire: An Autobiographical Sketch (1866) in Spiritual Narratives*. With an Introduction by Sue E. Houchins. The Schomburg Library of Nineteenth-Century Black Women Writers, Henry Louis Gates, Jr., General Editor (New York and Oxford: Oxford University Press, 1988), 112–113.

49. But some spiritual autobiographies were concerned largely with "spiritual matters," such as the writer's dreams, visions, or her analysis of the call and inspiration for her special mission. For a discussion of this tendency in the spiritual autobiography of Rebecca Cox Jackson, see Braxton, "Fugitive Slaves and Sanctified Ladies: Narratives of Vision and Power," in *Black Women Writing Autobiography: A Tradition within a Tradition* (Philadelphia: Temple University Press, 1989), 61–62.

50. McKay, "Nineteenth-Century Black Women's Spiritual Autobiographies," 140.

51. Ibid.

52. Ibid., 152.

53. William L. Andrews, *To Tell a Free Story: The First Century of Afro-American Autobiography, 1760–1865* (Urbana: University of Illinois Press, 1986), 54.

54. Andrews, *Sisters of the Spirit*, 19.

55. See Clifford Geertz's observation in the opening section of this essay above, that one aspect of the problem of suffering is "how to make physical pain, personal loss, worldly defeat, or the helpless contemplation of other's agony something bearable, supportable, something, as we say, sufferable" (cf. n. 13).

56. Peter Berger has argued that "theodicy-making functions, in part, to maintain religious meaning in spite of suffering and evil." See the reference to his thesis in the opening section of this paper, and n. 14 above.

57. Richardson, *Maria W. Stewart*, 9.

58. Ibid.

59. Stewart, *Productions of Mrs. Maria W. Stewart*, 4. (See n. 3 above for the full bibliographic information of *Productions*.)

60. William R. Jones, "Theodicy: The Controlling Category for Black Theology." *The Journal of Religious Thought* 30 (1973): 28–38.

61. Ibid., 34.

62. Ibid.

63. Ibid., 34–35.

64. Loewenberg and Bogin, *Black Women in Nineteenth-Century American Life*, 183.

65. Stewart, *Productions of Mrs. Maria W. Stewart*, 51–52.

66. Ibid., 52–53.

67. James L. Crenshaw, ed., *Theodicy in the Old Testament* (Philadelphia: Fortress Press, 1983), 1.

68. Ibid. Sages in Israelite thought (especially in Wisdom literature) often linked the concepts of creation and justice, suggesting a belief that the God who created the world possessed sufficient power to ensure both order and equity.

69. James H. Cone, *Black Theology and Black Power* (New York: Seabury, 1969), 94. Cone cites as telling examples of this conviction the following Negro Spirituals: "Oh, Freedom," "I'm A-Going to Do All I Can for My Lord," and "I Want to Live So God Can Use Me." The songs bear witness to the conviction that one fights "with God" against the evils of life.

70. James H. Cone, *A Black Theology of Liberation*. The C. Eric Lincoln Series in Black Religion (Philadelphia and New York: Lippincott, 1970; Maryknoll: NY, 1990), 19.

71. Cone, *A Black Theology of Liberation*, 66–67.

72. Robert A. Bennett, "Black Experience and the Bible," *Theology Today* 27 (1971), 422.

73. Ibid., 423.

74. Ibid.

75. Richardson, *Maria W. Stewart*, 9, 15.

76. Roger Lunden, Anthony C. Thistleton, and Clarence Walhout, *The Responsibility of Hermeneutics* (Grand Rapids: Eerdmans, 1985).

77. Ibid., x, xi.

78. Stewart, *Productions of Mrs. Maria W. Stewart*, 4, 5.

79. Stephen Breek Reid, *Experience and Tradition: A Primer in Black Biblical Hermeneutics* (Nashville: Abingdon Press, 1990), 16.

80. The observation about the importance of the Constitution is made even in light of the fact that the Constitution did sanction human slavery based on race and color, with a decree that those held in bondage were each counted as three-fifths of a person. For a brief summary of this history, see Judge George W. Crockett, Jr., "Racism in the Law." *The Voice of Black America*. Vol. 2. Philip S. Foner, ed. (New York: Capricorn, 1975), 518–525.

81. G. B. Caird, *The Language and Imagery of the Bible* (Philadelphia: Westminster Press, 1980), 144–145.

82. Ibid., 147.

83. Ibid.

84. Stewart, *Productions of Mrs. Maria W. Stewart*, 68–69.

85. Ibid., 71.

86. "Babylon" is a cryptic name for Rome, or the Roman Empire. Cf. Sib. Or. 5:143, 159; 1 Pet. 5:13; Eusebius, *Ecclesiastical History* 4.23.11.

87. For a helpful exploration of the characteristics and function of antagonists in the Psalms, see Steven J. L. Croft, "The Identity of the Individual in the Psalms," *Journal for the Study of the Old Testament.* Supplement Series 44 (Sheffield, England: University of Sheffield, 1987).

88. See the section of the essay entitled, "Black Autobiography and the Context of Theodicean Reflection."

89. Braxton, *Black Women Writing Autobiography*, 72–73. The full bibliographic data for Tubman and Truth's autobiographies are as follows: Sarah H. Bradford, *Harriet Tubman, The Moses of Her People* (n.p.: For the Author, 1886); Sojourner Truth, *Narrative of Sojourner Truth: A Bondswoman of Olden Time, Emancipated by the New York Legislature in the Early Part of the Present Century: With a History of Her Labors and Correspondence as Drawn from Her "Book of Life."* Olive Gilbert, ed. (Battle Creek, MI.: For the Author, 1878).

90. Braxton, *Black Women Writing Autobiography*, 73.

91. Ibid., 73–74.

92. Sojourner Truth, *Narrative of Sojourner Truth*, 163.

93. Loewenberg and Bogin, *Black Women in Nineteenth-Century American Life*, 219.

94. Tubman, *Harriet Tubman*, 31–32.

95. Stewart, *Productions of Mrs. Maria W. Stewart*, 48.

96. Some of the slave narratives describe the unutterable evils of the institution of slavery with the rhetorical figure of "inexpressibility," the assertion of a subject's ineffability in such a way as, paradoxically, to say something about it. Henry Bibb says of his own experience of slavery: "[N]o tongue, no pen, has or can express the horrors of American slavery. Consequently, I despair in finding language to express adequately the deep feeling of my soul, as I contemplate the past history of my life." The institution's violation of the slave's soul, with the frequent impossibility of describing adequately that transgression, is one of its horrors. See on this point: G. Thomas Couser, *Altered Egos: Authority in American Autobiography* (New York and Oxford: Oxford University Press, 1989), 133; Henry Bibb, *Narrative of the Life and Adventures of Henry Bibb, An American Slave, Written by Himself (1849)*. Reprint, *Puttin' On Ole Massa*, Gilbert Osofsky, ed. (New York: Harper & Row, 1969), 51–171.

97. The phrase "Lover of the soul" is taken from Charles Wesley's (1707–1788) classic hymn of refuge, "Jesus, Lover of My Soul," long a favorite in the African-American religious experience.

98. Psalm 40:2.

99. Othmar Keel, *The Symbolism of the Biblical World: Ancient Near Eastern Iconography and the Book of Psalms* (New York: Seabury, 1978), 70–71.

100. E. M. Blaiklock, *Commentary on the Psalms.* Vol. 1 (Philadelphia and New York: J. B. Lippincott, 1977), 101.

101. The African Ebed-Melech, the Ethiopian eunuch who was in King Zedekiah's household, initiated the efforts to have Jeremiah rescued from the cistern. It took three additional men to "draw him up with ropes" and lift him out of the cistern.

102. G. A. F. Knight, *Psalms.* Vol. 1 (Philadelphia: Westminster Press, 1982), 193.

103. Blaiklock, *Commentary on the Psalms*, 101.

2

"Take My Yoke upon You"

The Role of the Church in the Oppression
of African-American Women

Frances E. Wood

Introduction

Human struggle with the existence of evil and suffering is recounted
throughout recorded history. These struggles can be found in sources as
diverse as the book of Job; meditations of mystic Howard Thurman; essays
of Holocaust witness Elie Wiesel; and discussions of theodicy by womanist
ethicist Katie Geneva Cannon.

Jesus' invitation to "take my yoke upon you, and learn of me,"[1] in all its
paradoxical import, frequently has been distorted in theological and philosophical discourse, as well as ministerial instruction. Philosophers and
theologians have offered ontological rationalizations and theological expli-
cations in their attempts to explain the unexplainable and decipher the
perplexing phenomenon of human suffering, particularly suffering that
results from intentional harm at the hands of another human being, com-
monly understood as moral evil.

Among those calling themselves Christian, there are some widely
accepted notions concerning suffering, its purposes and meaning. Many, if
not all, are based on explanations offered by church fathers whose interpretations have gone unquestioned for centuries. They include suffering as
punishment for sin; suffering for the building of character; suffering as
evidence of specialness in the sight of God; suffering (particularly for
females) as a consequence of Eve's disobedience. When these explanations
are applied to the situation of Black females in this country, they function
to maintain a lethal sociological and ecclesiastical status quo. Neither the
secular nor religious communities pay much attention to the implications

for lives of African-American women who have internalized the explanations of church fathers.

Philosophers as well as some behavioral scientists argue that what sets human beings apart from other mammals is the capacity to reason. Coupled with this capacity is the ability to reflect on our life circumstances and environment, and to effect changes in them. I understand our differences from other animals also lie in our capacity to love and call forth love in one another. Sadly, there is yet another ability exhibited only by human beings. That is the ability to oppress one another. No other life form on the planet engages in intentional acts of oppression or wanton destruction. These are actions over which we have choice, and in which we engage with forethought. In our attempts to justify certain behaviors we place them on an arbitrary scale of lesser and greater harm; often engaging in horizontal oppression, or constructing hierarchies of oppression. By so doing, we seek to exonerate ourselves from the roles we play in perpetuating evil and suffering. Although evil and suffering take myriad forms, my purpose is not to dissect the existence of evil or suffering in the abstract. This essay addresses the particular shapes and forms that manifest themselves in the oppression of African-American women within the Christian community.

The social status quo, despite various modern liberation movements, continues to be one in which females are treated as inferior to males. Moreover, the dominance and submission mode of gender relations within the Black Christian community, as well as the dominant culture, meets criteria for moral evil: sustaining and reinforcing attitudes, beliefs, policies, and practices that deny certain individuals or groups the status of full humanity, create negative concepts of "otherness," and justify patterns of discrimination against the oppressed group. One may argue that Black men are exempt from the role of oppressor in this definition of evil. However, it is important to bear in mind that despite the tenuousness of gender privilege afforded them, the exercise of that privilege by Black men contributes to the oppression of Black women. In this regard, James Cone asks a critical question: "What kind of society do we (Black men) wish to create? Do we want a genuinely new society or just the right to replace white men with black men?"[2]

With this question in mind I will discuss (1) the reality of women who bear the yoke of violence rooted in sexism, which is part of women's fee for membership within the church; (2) the role of the church community in either adding to the burden or denouncing and removing the yoke; and (3) offer some requisites for change in the African-American community claiming membership in the body of Christ. The context for my discussion is the social situation of women in the United States, with particular attention to the treatment of gender as it is constructed in the dominant culture, and reflected in the attitudes and behaviors of the African-American Christian community.

The Yoke of Oppression

The experiences of women of the African diaspora residing in the United States have begun to be examined sporadically in the teaching of history, sociology, literature, law, theology, and other disciplines. Increasingly, these accounts reflect women as subjects, rather than objects. Black women are depicted as moral agents, rather than immoral beings reacting to the agency of others. African-American women's stories are being shared in ways previously unheard of. Ironically, although the core of African-American Christian tradition has as its foundation, "telling the story" of God's liberating and saving grace in the person of Jesus Christ, there persists an awful silence in telling the *whole* story. This silence can be likened to that afflicting the adults in the children's story, *The Emperor's New Clothes.* Within the African-American church community the silence about the realities of women's experience and how it differs from men's experience has taken the proportions of a version of the "big lie," and is a deadly yoke. This yoke consists of silencing, ignoring, degrading, and dismissing women's experience, especially those experiences that reveal the nature and extent of oppression perpetrated against them within the community. Idealization and romanticization of Black women's suffering is as insidious a habit in the African-American community as it has been historically in the dominant society. Elevating women's suffering to a form of martyrdom for the cause (of others) virtually guarantees that it will remain unexamined. Herein lies a peculiar dilemma for the community. On the one hand, women's suffering is apotheosized. By so doing, we subscribe to the suffering-servant motif in Christology. On the other hand, if the proximate cause of the suffering is the men within the community, the response of the community is active or passive denial. Black women who risk telling their story in this context are shamed, denounced, and treated as pariahs rather than prophets. The yoke of silencing, degrading, ignoring or dismissing women weighs down the Black Christian community in a conspiracy against its own total liberation. In the name of racial solidarity, this yoke is a burden borne by all the members, although disproportionately by those who are female.

As is true in any paradigm of oppression, whenever the alleged inferior group seeks, as womanists have, to define itself on its own terms or, in any other way, shift the status quo, a backlash ensues. Whatever forms it takes, backlash is intended to keep a group "in their place." In the dominant culture this is evidenced in the discussion of issues such as fetal protection or the mommy track, as euphemisms for discriminating against women in employment. In the Black community it takes forms such as the myth of the Black woman being in academic conspiracy with white males, or discussions of Black men's definitions of "real" women. It is worth noting that one of the prerogatives exercised in paradigms of oppression is the dominant group defining the target group. One of the vicissitudes of "real" women (as opposed to those constructed by male fantasy), regardless of ethnicity or race, is that we are treated as "permissible victims."[3] Leadership in the Christian community has failed to demonstrate any seriously considered opposition to this treatment. The legendary strong Black woman has become the personification of the permissible victim. She is the sister whose solo on Sunday morning moves the congregation in a special way, despite her having been assaulted at home on Saturday night. In a younger version, she is the young teen who is an exemplary student and is being forced to keep secret the horrors of being molested. The woman is kept silent with a strong dose of Saint Paul; and the teenager, learning her lessons in being silenced, listens to a sermon on obedient children.[4] Females are regarded as legitimate targets of abuse. Little boys equate being physically vanquished by their male peers with being "like a girl." Grown men continue to view the battering or rape of a woman as simply a hazard of being female, as opposed to a consequence of the behavior of men who choose to victimize women. The assaults that women and girls experience in their homes are seen as normative. More to the point, the abuse is perceived as what women and girls should expect as the result of being female.

With few exceptions (primarily when the victim of violence perpetrated by a *stranger* is *his* daughter, wife, mother, sister), assaults of women go unmentioned in the writing, civic commentary or sermons of male religious leaders. Assaults that occur within the family receive virtually no mention or condemnation at all. Abusive behavior, which we call taboo, is not the real taboo; speaking the truth about the abuse is. In the paterfamilias model of family, proprietary considerations supercede considerations of justice. When African-American male ministers list issues of justice confronting society, the abuse perpetrated against females by family members and friends is conspicuous by its absence.

To add insult to injury, when a battered woman approaches her pastor for assistance, she is frequently advised either to become a better wife; bear her cross in faith; or pray for her husband. The abusive behavior goes unchallenged; the suffering is "explained"; the one who knows best has spoken. Those taking seriously the prophet's injunction to "seek kindness, love justice, and walk humbly with your God"[5] must be willing to sort through and challenge popular myths, stereotypes and illusions that reinforce victimization; to peel away the tough outer layers of the fruit so that the tender truths at the core are revealed. The pastor as interpreter of meaning for the sister in trouble will be held accountable someday for his interpretations.

Men of color have an obligation to extract from their eyes the lens of sexism through which they view the world, no less than white men have an obligation to remove the lens of racism through which they view the world. In responding to situations of oppression one must take care always to ask:

Whom does this circumstance serve or disserve? Who benefits from things as they are? In discussing "good news" Bernice Johnson Reagon states:

> It's good news when you reject things as they are; when you lay down the world as it is, and you take on the responsibility of shaping your own way. . . . It's hard times when you decide to pick up *your own cross*. You gonna catch hell if you don't do it the way they say do it. [italics added][6]

This statement is as true in the African-American Christian community as it is in secular institutions and organizations. I understand it to apply particularly to women who struggle to claim their *own* identity and shape their *own* way within the community. Doing it "the way they say do it" has required silence about women's experiences of sexual and domestic violence as well as other forms of oppression manifested by the hydra-headed monster called misogyny.

The Institutional Church: An Added Weight on the Yoke

Founded, constituted, and led by African Americans, the Black church emerged from a people in bondage, who understood the good news as a liberating message. The church has been comforter, leader, moral agent, intercessor, locus of status, and definer of all that is good and right for people who fear the Lord. In many communities, it remains the moral center of public activity. When issues of justice arise, the voice of religious leadership from the Black community is often the most audible and adamant. Because of this voice, we mistakenly have come to believe that matters of justice affecting *all* Black people are at the top of the agendas of Black church leaders. Sadly, this is not the case. Absent from the Black church is any substantive discussion of gender justice as it pertains to women. When one uses the criteria of denying others' full humanity, viewing "otherness" in a negative light, and perpetuating patterns of discrimination as the measure of social evil, one can conclude that the treatment of women in Black churches all too often fits those criteria. There continue to be churches that thwart women's calls to pastor and preach. The excuse that "our church is not ready for a woman, yet" continues to have validity across denominational lines. Jokes from the pulpit that demean women consistently elicit laughter and go unchallenged. Some church organizations prefer slow deterioration under poor male leadership over *any* female leadership.

Within the church, as in all social arrangements, there are those who are treated as pillars who support the group, and scapegoats who are blamed when the structure is crumbling. Both these designations are applied schizophrenically to Black women. Simultaneously placing women on pedestals and denouncing them as the root cause of the demise of the

Black community results in an insidious double bind for Black women and men, as well. Labeling women according to the madonna/whore syndrome is not the sole province of white denominations. Indeed, these characterizations of women are found from storefront to cathedral; from the most isolated rural settings to the most populated cities. The madonna most frequently is noted on Mother's Day when the woman in the congregation who has borne the greatest number of children (with benefit of wedlock) is singled out for recognition. The whore is identified primarily in relation to the number of men in the congregation who either actually or allegedly have had sex with her. A woman's place in this seemingly polarized arrangement is subject to shifting arbitrarily as she engages in behavior deemed worthy of praise or blame. We must examine our collusion with these characterizations of women, and what these role assignments reveal about what we *truly* think of women, as opposed to what we say we believe about women. Regardless of the language we use, the dynamics related to pillar and scapegoat syndrome are alive and well. They are but one set of behaviors which reveal our collective bias against women. A concomitant situation of women in the church is the dubious distinction of being identified as the "backbone" of the church. In discussing the backbone phenomenon Jacquelyn Grant offers this analysis:

> The telling portion of the word "backbone" is "back." It has become apparent to me that most of the ministers who use this term are referring to location rather than function. What they really mean is that women are in the "background" and should be kept there.[7]

With many congregations having a 70 percent female membership, we must reflect on the extent to which internalized misogyny erodes the spiritual welfare of the church, and denounce misogynistic practice as antithetical to Christian liberation, and an insidious form of spiritual death. This malaise is not peculiar to Black churches, but it is a form of suffering in the community about which Black folk speak little, if at all. In those rare instances where serious questions are raised against misogynistic assumptions, presumptions, and practices (such as women being capable of preparing but not distributing communion), the questioner, if female, is denounced as a manhater or, if male, as a dominated wimp. The label of manhater or wimp implies that one has engaged in a treasonous act, and broken the contemporary eleventh commandment: thou shalt not criticize male behavior. All challenge or criticism that could remotely hold Black men accountable for their behavior vis-à-vis women is interpreted as maligning African-American manhood. By treating men as fragile egos who cannot bear the truth, women both infantalize men and forfeit an opportunity to call forth the *best* in men. Men frequently equate challenges to gender privilege with being unloved by women. The irony of the situation in the church and wider society is there is no other group that loves and supports Black men as do Black women; and Black men *know* that Black women love them. These two major premises form the foundation for both the support African-American women provide men and the legitimate challenges against injustice that results from the exercise of gender privilege. With these as major premises, how do we incorporate an understanding within the community that deals with the enormously painful and complex reality of the oppressed as oppressor? What is the word of liberation and hope spoken to the battered wife of the head of the deacon board? Where is the accountability required when the head of the trustee board repeatedly sexually harasses "our women"? What are we to make of the double standard for teenage sexual behavior that allows boys to sow their oats, yet expects girls to keep their panties up and their dresses down? How are we teaching our children the meaning of justice when the term "our youth" means our *boys*? What are we to make of the practice in some churches of shunning pregnant teenage girls, and elevating their male counterparts to leadership roles? How do we account for the disgraceful refusal of congregations to consider an ordained woman for pastoral leadership? Before we dismiss these questions as not applicable in our own situations, we must take a moment to think about practices in our own congregations. What are the signposts we need to guide us along the perilous path toward liberation and justice for us all? How will our future communal life honor our forebears' living and dying for equality?

Bearing the Yoke of Jesus

Before we can take on the yoke of Jesus in the work of gender justice, we must name the burdens and claim the memories under which we struggle and labor. This naming is an essential first step if the church is to be able to "remember, repent, and do the works."[8] Remembering is often difficult to do when one is in the midst of crisis. The axiom of America getting a cold and the Black community getting pneumonia is painfully evident throughout the country. However, as William R. Jones would remind us, if the illness is incorrectly diagnosed, the wrong remedies will be applied.[9]

The first memory that must be claimed is that we were never meant to survive as human beings.[10] Second, we must demythologize the notion that African-American women and men working side by side in the cotton rows somehow automatically has translated into gender equality. Whereas partnership as a model for shared work between Black women and men is an ideal, we must understand that "before there is partnering and sharing with someone, there is the becoming of oneself."[11] The becoming of oneself does not supplant partnership. It is, however, a prerequisite for authentic partnership. The third memory we must acknowledge and name is that misogyny against Black women did not begin with their enslavement in the United States. Neither did the habit of mimicking the worst assumptions and values of the oppressor only begin after the Civil War. Just as Black feminists and womanists are not suffering from some disease caught from white women, but rather are women engaged in wrestling with both the awful truths and awesome power of our lives, neither are Black men who exercise male privilege suffering from some disease they caught from white men. How have we come to the place where a group so attuned to the adverse effects of racism, as are Black churchmen, is inured to their own sexism? Given the depth of this anesthetized state, we are long overdue in asking African-American Christian men the question:

> What [man] here is so enamored of [his] own oppression that [he] cannot see [his] heelprint upon [a] woman's face? What terms of oppression have become precious and necessary to [him] as a ticket into the fold of the righteous, away from the cold winds of self scrutiny?[12]

Denial of the oppression of women within the African-American Christian community constitutes a mockery of authentic claims for justice in the face of the variety of "isms" confronting us. The metaphor of getting one's own house in order is apt here. We cannot simultaneously denounce injustice on the part of white society and perpetuate injustice within our own communities. In the last decade of this exceedingly violent century we can no longer tolerate an analysis of the issues of conflict between Black women and men as simply the result of women being "too well educated."[13]

We must acknowledge that "things as they are" are not serving the community well, and that clinging to prerogatives rooted in the oppression of women mitigate against the full personhood of us all. Further, we must be mindful that things as they *are* do not constitute what they necessarily *will be* in the future. In spite of contention within the community, the Black church continues to have

> tremendous potential for fostering constructive, instructive, and reconciling discussion on issues of mutuality, sexuality and spirituality for women and men. It is obvious that the foundational theory and the theology are all in place to accomplish this dialogue, yet the praxis is still limited or lacking if we are at all honest in our reflection upon our lived experience. The recovery of a *meaningful* value system enriching the relationships between black women and men still remains underdeveloped, or at best only moderately achieved.[14] [italics added]

The conditions of misogyny in our churches are neither a "man thing" nor a "woman thing." Rather they are conditions that impede the work of justice and undermine the capacity to "do the works" of justice required of us. Any call to justice in this last decade of the twentieth century, in order to be authentically Christian, must incorporate *metanoia*, a transformation at the deepest levels of one's self. In addressing the issue of feminist activism and maleness, one writer counsels, "One must change the core of one's being. The core of one's being must love justice more than manhood."[15] I would add that what conventionally have been used as attributes of true manhood, that is, social and economic dominance, sexual prowess, and theological supremacy, are bankrupt and need to be put to rest. The prophets of ancient Israel frequently mention the rueful destiny that will befall a stiff-necked people. A destiny of destruction need not be the inheritance of African-American Christian men and women.

Several years ago, when asked about the declining numbers of priests and the increasing role of women and lay men in ministerial leadership, a Roman Catholic archbishop replied: "I believe the Holy Spirit has spoken to us, but we refuse to accept what is being said."[16] Another way of putting the bishop's response is that maybe God is trying to tell us something. Living together in the Spirit in the Christian community is not limited to shouting, sermonizing, and lifting every voice to sing. Being in the Spirit also demands that we risk examining assumptions and presumptions about roles and relationships in the community. Jesus' strongest denunciations in the Gospels are reserved for the "hypocrites, snakes and viper's brood," those in leadership roles who dominated and exacted heavy burdens of the Jewish people. The situation among the male leadership in too many congregations and denominational structures can best be described as sexist apartheid, wherein the minority clings to a structure of domination over the majority. Until or unless this fundamental structural reality is acknowledged, and its implications for women examined, calls for justice outside the church will ring as hollow as the calls for international human rights on the part of U.S. politicians. Christian manhood does not consist of the capacity to rule. Christian womanhood does not consist of a critical, silent collusion with the yoke of sexism.

The yoke that we are called to bear, what is *required* of us, is seeking justice, loving kindness, and walking humbly with our God. It is in this seeking and loving that we will find the signposts to assist us in remembering, repenting, and returning. We must remember that all the Blacks are not men. We must repent from the idolatrous worship of maleness. We must return to an ethic of mutuality.

Seeking justice demands that we not only look outward, but also that we look inward. Looking inward demands that we no longer exploit the concept of racial solidarity to mask bigotry. Looking inward demands that pastoral search committees pay more than lip service to female candidates for the ministry. Looking inward demands an end to pedestaling and scapegoating women. Looking inward demands that men forego a solidarity that places sharing the hormone testosterone as its highest value. Looking inward demands that women begin to realize that we do not serve the best interests of women, children, *or* men when we refuse to hold men accountable for oppressive behavior. In our lifetime there are those who have died being true to the belief that resistance to evil is part of the Christian heritage. The evils we resist today are no less real than those our predecessors fought: oppression, nostalgic revisionism, lying. The context, however, has shifted: the oppression we fight is that of women; the nostalgic revisionism we resist is the fiction that "once we were one"; the lying to which we will not accede is female subjugation as a requisite of racial solidarity.

As long as men continue to define themselves by using the masters' tools of dominance and subordination, whether by commission or omission, as their measure of manhood, there will be no justice in the church. Until there is a new understanding and regard for the full personhood of all women with their gifts and talents in the church, we will not bear the yoke of Jesus. Instead, we will continue to bear the yoke of preserving patriarchal privilege.

Must women bear the yoke alone, and all the men go free?

NOTES

1. Matthew 11:29.

2. James H. Cone, *My Soul Looks Back* (Maryknoll, NY: Orbis Books, 1986), 123.

3. The term "permissible victim" refers to those groups or individuals who can be harmed with little or no negative consequence befalling the perpetrator. The least permissible victim in U.S. society is a white, wealthy, heterosexual male.

4. Ephesians 5:22–23; 6:1–3.

5. Micah 6:8.

6. Sweet Honey in the Rock, "Good News," 7th Anniversary Concert, 7 November 1980. Songtalk Publishing Co., 1980.

7. Jacquelyn Grant, "Black Women and the Church," in *All the Women Are White, All the Blacks Are Men, But Some of Us Are Brave*, Gloria T. Hull, Patricia Bell Scott, and Barbara Smith, eds., (Old Westbury, NY: Feminist Press, 1982), 141.

8. Revelation 2:2–5.

9. Author of *Is God a White Racist? A Preamble to Black Theology* (Garden City, NY: Anchor Books, 1973) addressing the National Council of Churches of Christ (NCCC) Commission on Family Ministry and Human Sexuality (CFMHS) on the issue of racism, Sarasota, Florida, November, 1990.

10. Audre Lorde, "The Transformation of Silence into Language and Action," in *Sister Outsider: Essays and Speeches* (Trumansburg, NY: The Crossing Press, 1984), 42.

11. Jeanne Noble, *Beautiful Are the Souls of My Black Sisters* (New York: Prentice-Hall, 1978), 343.

12. Lorde, 132.

13. The Reverend Wallace Charles Smith addressing the National Council of Churches of Christ, CFMHS, at a consultation on the Black Church and the Family, November, 1989.

14. Toinette M. Eugene, "While Love Is Unfashionable," in *Women's Consciousness, Women's Conscience*, Barbara Hilkert Andolsen, Christine E. Gudorf and Mary

D. Pellauer, eds. (San Francisco: Harper & Row, 1985), 133.

15. John Stoltenberg, *Refusing To Be a Man* (Portland, OR: Breitenbush Books, 1989), 185.

16. Former Seattle Archbishop Raymond G. Hunthausen addressing members of the Chancery staff, 1984.

3

Joy Came in the Morning
Risking Death for Resurrection

Confronting the Evil of Social Sin
and Socially Sinful Structures

Jamie T. Phelps, O.P.

Introduction

The classic theological question of evil centers around the problem of reconciling the historical presence of evil and the belief that God is the all-good, all-powerful Creator of the universe. How could an all-good God be the source of evil? How could an all-good God permit evil? Why doesn't an all-powerful God prevent or eliminate evil? Such questions have occupied theologians for centuries. These are not the questions that concern the current discussion. Interesting and as intellectually stimulating as these questions may be, this author would like to pose the question of evil in a less speculative and more historically concrete fashion. Looking at the world, one notices two major types of evil, traditionally identified as natural evil and moral evil: evil resulting from natural catastrophes such as hurricanes, earthquakes (natural evil) and evil resulting from human exercise of free will and choice (moral evil). I will restrict my concerns to moral evil. Further, I will focus not so much on individual private acts of evil, but on socially constructed evil. Socially constructed evil involves patterns of relationships that are directed toward the denial of the human dignity and value of some human beings for the benefit of other human beings. This dehumanization and marginalization contradicts the reality that all human beings are made in the image and likeness of God and are called by God to eternal communion with the whole human community and the Triune God. Such dehumanization is the source of existential and physical suffering including death. Those who consciously participate in the construction and perpetuation of socially sinful institutions, which mediate existential and physical suffering and death, are participating in what is designated morally as social sin.

At the end of the twentieth century worldwide patterns of dehumanization and marginalization are evident. From the perspective of the oppressed, it seems as though human beings are valued or devalued in our society not on the basis of their identity as children of God or individual merit and goodness, but on the basis of characteristics that are inherited socially or biologically, that is, their national identity, race, gender, class. Persons born in the nations located in the Northern Hemisphere are generally more valued than those born in nations located in the Southern Hemisphere. Whites are more valued than Blacks and other people of color. Men are more valued than women. The rich are more valued than the poor. One's access to food, clothing, shelter, education, employment, and housing is conditioned by one's nationality, race, gender, and class.

These patterns of inequality are not compatible with the Christian belief in the equality of all human beings from the perspective of God's universal love for all the works of the Creator's hands. These patterns are not compatible with Christ's redemptive act, which inaugurated the coming of the Kingdom of God. These patterns are not compatible with the church's understanding of its universal mission and the universal call to salvation. Christian discipleship demands that we be willing to confront death in our struggle to transform these sinful patterns, which are embodied in sinful social structures of our church and society.

In the following pages, I will describe the historical development of class, race, and sexual discrimination of African Americans within the social and ecclesial institutions or structures of the United States; second, review the development of the social justice teachings of the Roman Catholic magisterium relative to race, class, and gender discrimination; third, define and develop the concept of social sin as it has emerged in these teachings; and finally, describe and discuss the contemporary situation of African Americans within the Catholic church. This final section will include a review of the fruits of the Black Catholic movement and Catholic collaboration and dynamics that are currently active in transforming these ecclesial institutions to bring them into conformity with the church's understanding of mission of preparing for the kingdom of God.

Historical Development of Race, Class, and Gender Discrimination toward African Americans within the United States

To be Black in white America is to suffer. Blacks may suffer existentially, questioning their value and worth within the society, and/or they may suffer physically from hunger, homelessness, unemployment, ill-health, drug abuse, and so forth. While much of this suffering is self-inflicted, most of it is rooted in the historical patterns of inequality that have characterized the sojourn of African Americans within the United States.

The United States was established to guarantee freedom and human dignity for those men and women fleeing poverty and religious and political oppression existing in various European countries. The paradox of their freedom-seeking was that in the process of their escape to freedom, the freedom and human dignity of Native Americans, Africans, and others were denied.

For many of the African ancestors of today's African Americans, this denial of freedom took the form of chattel slavery. Slavery was not the natural condition of the newly arrived Africans; rather slavery was a socially constructed system that guaranteed a permanent labor force. The institution of the slavery system gave structure to the process of denying the human dignity of Africans and devaluing them as subhumans who were morally and intellectually inferior.

Although Africans first arrived in North America as temporary indentured servants, the "equality of status" that they shared with white indentured servants deteriorated as the need for a permanent labor force grew. By the 1640s, a clear racial caste pattern was emerging as indentured servitude yielded to lifelong slavery. By the eighteenth century, enslaved Blacks were defined as chattel.[1] By the end of the nineteenth century, segregation as a legal system, overtly legislating social, political, and economic separation and covertly supporting white supremacy, was established. Economic, social, and political dynamics converged to transform a de facto segregated society into an explicitly segregated one. The process of dehumanization was gradual, from indentured servants to slavery to Black Codes to Jim Crow laws to finally the 1896 *Plessy vs. Ferguson* decision of the Supreme Court. This latter ruling of "separate but equal" neutralized the Fourteenth and Fifteenth Amendments of the Constitution and the civil-rights legislation of that era. The legal system of segregation had been formalized. This act was the triumphant victory of white supremacists and the white male power elite was the greatest beneficiary.[2]

The racism that permeated the agrarian institutions of the Old and New South intensified in the late nineteenth century. As the class stratification based on the economic dynamics of production and change became more dramatic, the power dynamics of race relations became more acrimonious. The superior-inferior evaluation of race distinctions is neither natural or inevitable, yet race relations are socially constructed on such assumptions. Racism is based on the fictive of "white supremacy." It has been socially constructed and maintained by power dynamics that have been so intricately woven within the fabric of the fundamental institutions of our nation that it is almost inseparable from those institutions as they currently exist.[3]

European Americans developed theories of racial superiority, legalized segregation by political maneuvering, and established economic patterns of employment, which divided the work force sexually and racially. Enslaved

African Americans were treated as chattel and within slavery there were some gender distinctions. In many instances, labor was assigned according to gender. Males did only so-called men's work such as carpentry, stonemasonry, milling, shoemaking, and chopping wood. Black female slaves were used as breeders and concubines by slave owners. However, when profit motive prevailed, such gender divisions of labor were overlooked, and men and women were used according to their individual strengths. Field workers were male and female. Enslaved Black women and Black men had no rights over their bodies, products produced by their labor, or the maintainence of family bonds.

Free African Americans never enjoyed the social, economic or political privileges of their white counterparts. As freed African Americans entered the labor market, their upward mobility was limited. Economically, the majority of African Americans moved from slavery, to sharecropping, to low-paying jobs as domestics and farmers. Free Black women worked as seamstresses, dressmakers, laundresses, and hairdressers, both before and after Emancipation. A small Black enterpreneurship emerged among Black men and women during the early twentieth century.[4]

The social structure of legal segregation lasted for almost sixty years. It was not successfully challenged until 1954 when the *Brown vs. the Board of Education* Supreme Court decison outlawed segregated schools. The Civil Rights Act of 1964 augmented this strike against segregation and supported racial equality by legislating against discrimination and segregation in voting, education and the use of public facilities.[5]

"Separate but equal" was never equal. Legal segregation in reality supported unequal access and inferior opportunities not only in education, but also in the areas of employment, housing, and politics. Such restriction led to a cycle of poverty for many African Americans. Poverty increased a Black person's potential for hunger, miseducation, unemployment, homelessness, and lack of proper health care. Some twenty-five years after the Civil Rights Act of 1964, the National Research Council's 1989 report on Blacks and American society documents the continuance of the structures of inequality. Residential segregation, racial discrimination, and "exclusion from social networks essential for full access to economic and education opportunities" are commonplace.[6]

The disproportionate victimization of African Americans through economic poverty had been documented earlier in a report by Ammot and Matthaei:

In 1988, nearly one-third of all Blacks lived in poverty. The share of Blacks who were very poor — living on less than half of poverty-line income — increased by 69 percent between 1978 and 1987 . . . a Black person's chances of being persistently poor in the late 1980s are eight times higher than those of a white person.[7]

The report continues to state that the poverty trends are concentrated among female heads of household living in the inner city with children caught in "the long-term cycle of poverty, segregated into inferior housing, schools and jobs." One-third of Black women are in low-paid, low-status jobs. Both Black men and women suffer from high unemployment (twice that of their white counterparts) and low earnings (Black women earn 60 percent and Black men earn 73 percent of white men's medium income).[8]

Common Destiny predicts that approximately one-third of the Black population will continue in poverty. Drugs and teenage pregnancy, poor education, unemployment "will maintain their grip on large numbers of the poor and near-poor blacks." Residential segregation will continue and de facto inequality in society and class divisions among Blacks still pose a formidable problem to the nation.[9]

Racism, sexism, and classism have been oppressive factors in the life of African Americans since the beginning of our nation. As reported above, the prevailing social, economic, and political dynamics of our nation have been socially constructed to primarily benefit a white male power elite comprised of businessmen and politicians. Such a construction, however, was and is maintained by careful orchestration and maintenance of hostility and division between the races and diverse ethnic groups, rich and poor, male and female.[10]

The common denominator of these and other "isms" is the systemized oppression of one group (race, class, gender, nation or age group) by another. These "isms" are such an integral factor of the established patterns of relationships within the social structures of church and society that the benefactors of the status quo and some of its victims view the patterns as natural or inevitable.

The dynamics of racism, sexism, and classism continue to intermesh, making it more difficult for African Americans within the society and church to exercise their legal and moral rights as children of God and citizens of the United States. As a result, many Blacks experience existential death and physical suffering.

The Role of Christian Churches with Emphasis on the Roman Catholic Church within the United States

Historically most Christian churches initially participated in and legitimized slavery in the New World. As the historian Lester B. Scherer noted, in the colonial and provincial churches of the seventeenth and early eighteenth century, being a Christian did not prevent one from participating in any aspect of the slave trade or slavery. Protestant ministers read slave codes from their pulpits, and debated the feasibility of instructing slaves and admitting them to the sacraments.[11]

Christians intent upon prosperity of every American province adopted attitudes that blinded them to the immorality of the slave trade and slavery.

By 1772, Christian theory opposing slaveholding had developed, but then Black people were systematically treated with contempt and white "children from the first dawn of reason [were taught] to consider people with black skin on a footing with domestic animals, form'd [sic] to serve and obey."[12]

Roman Catholics and Slavery

Roman Catholics did not distinguish themselves as an exception. Catholics owned slaves and participated in the slave trade. Although church directives mandated a more humane treatment of slaves, many Catholics concurred with the prevalent racial attitudes of the times. The Roman Catholic church's stance against slavery and racism evolved gradually. Although the natural law supported a belief in the common unity or familyhood of the human race, this common unity was understood exclusively as a spiritual kinship. Likewise, the prevalent Catholic understanding of the social order subscribed to an understanding of social relationships that were hierarchial in nature. Therefore, class distinctions were considered a natural consequence of natural differences in ability and skills.[13] As Roman Catholicism in the United States confronted racism manifested through the system of slavery, it failed to understand the moral implications of the system. Slavery did not appear to Francis Patrick Kenrick, the leading American moral theologian of that time, to "abolish the natural equality of men."[14] Blinded by the times, Catholic bishops remained officially neutral on the question of slavery and found themselves personally lined up on both sides of the abolitionist question and the Civil War. Officially they expressed a preference for "gradual emancipation."[15]

Even though Pope Gregory XVI had condemned the slave trade in 1839 and Leo XII had condemned slavery in 1888 and 1890, it was not until 1965 that slavery was articulated as totally "incompatible with God's design" because it was "a violation of the integrity of the human person . . . and an offense against human dignity." In this same article of *Gaudium et Spes* "forms of social or cultural discrimination in basic personal rights on the grounds of sex, race, color, social conditions, language and religion" were identified as practices to be "curbed and eradicated as incompatible with God's design.[16]

Select Roman Catholic Teachings on the Poor, the Racially Oppressed, and Women

Ecclesial institutions as social structures must submit to the same self-critical evaluation in the matter of discrimination as they demand of other social systems and institutions. The Roman Catholic church has explicitly acknowledged that as a visible institution it is "at once holy and always in need of purification" and therefore must constantly follow "the path of penance and renewal."[17] The progress of the church's official intellectual conversion is manifested in some of the documents written and promulgated by the pope and bishops beginning with the Second Vatican Council.

Vatican II defined the nature of the church as a universal sacrament of salvation which is essentially missionary. This mission includes the preaching of the gospel to all, especially those who are poor or afflicted.

> The joy and hope, the grief and anguish of the men [and women] of our time, especially of those who are poor or afflicted in any way, are the joy and hope, the grief and anguish of the followers of Christ as well. Nothing genuinely human fails to find an echo in their hearts. For theirs is a community composed of men [and women] who, united in Christ and guided by the Holy Spirit, press onwards towards the kingdom of the Father and are bearers of a message of salvation intended for all men [and women].[18]

The United States Catholic bishops, responsive to concerns of its membership and the teachings of the Council and subsequent synod documents on social justice, notably the 1977 proclamation *Justice in the World*, have issued pastorals on racism and sexism and the economy. They evidence their understanding of the church's complicity with the social sins of racism and sexism and classism, and have called on its members to conversion, renewal, and transformation of its attitudes and practices toward people of color, women, and the poor within the Catholic church and the society.

In their pastoral letter on racism, *Brothers and Sisters to Us*, the bishops acknowledge that "Racism is an evil which endures in our society and Church." It goes on to state that:

> Racism is a sin: a sin that divides the human family, blots out the image of God among specific members of that family, and violates the fundamental dignity of those called to be children of the same Father [and Mother]. Racism is a sin that says some human beings are inherently superior [white supremacy] and others essentially inferior because of race. It is that sin that makes racial characteristics the determining factor for the exercise of human rights and mocks the words of Jesus: Treat others the way you would have them treat you. ... Racism ... is a denial of the truth of the dignity of each human being revealed in the mystery of the Incarnation.
> ... Racism is not merely one sin among many; it is a radical evil that divides the human family and denies the new creation of a redeemed world. To struggle against it demands an equally radical transformation in our minds and hearts as well as *in the structures of our society*.[19][*emphasis added*]

In a similar manner, the 1988 first draft of the pastoral letter, *Partners in the Mystery of Redemption: a Pastoral Response to Women's Concerns for*

Church and Society, the United States Catholic bishops describe the negative effects of the sin of sexism on women and human relationships:

The sin of sexism depersonalizes women. It makes them objects to be possessed and used. . . .
Women and men by virtue of their baptism, are reborn in Christ and are therefore intended for equal partnership in celebration of their mutuality and uniqueness before God. Sadly this human longing for union with God and communion with one another and, by extension, with cosmic creation has been severely distorted by the universal influence of sin, which simultaneously alienates human beings and shatters the solidarity of the human community.[20]

The pastoral declares sexism a social and moral evil:

When anyone believes that men are inherently superior to women or women are inherently superior to men, then he or she is guilty of sexism. Sexism is a moral and social evil.[21]

Finally, in the pastoral entitled *Economic Justice for All*, the bishops addressed their concern for the poor. They acknowledged that the rate of poverty among female-headed "minority" families is over 50 percent and although most poor people are white, poverty is disproportionately high among Blacks and those who have been victims of racial prejudice and discrimination. The pastoral continues by suggesting that the norms for decision making would be meeting the "basic needs of the poor" and increasing the participation of all in the economic life of the nation. Such participation will enable the development of greater social solidarity and will require "fundamental changes in the social and economic life" of the nation.[22]

Earlier the bishops challenged themselves and other members of the church:

Though in the Gospels and in the New Testament as a whole the offer of salvation is extended to all peoples, Jesus takes the side of the most in need, physically and spiritually. The example of Jesus poses a number of challenges to the contemporary Church. It imposes a prophetic mandate to speak to those who have no one to speak for them, to be a defender of the defenseless, who in biblical terms are the poor. It also demands a compassionate vision that enables the Church to see things from the side of the poor and powerless and assess lifestyle, policies, and *social institutions* in terms of their impact on the poor. It summons the church also to be an instrument in assisting people to experience the liberating power of God in their own lives so that they may respond to the Gospel in freedom and dignity. Finally, and most radically, it calls for an emptying of self, both individually and corporately, that allows the Church to experience the power of God in the midst of poverty and powerlessness.[23]

Social Sin

The church's teaching magisterium has offically acknowledged and condemned racism, sexism, and classism *within the church and society* and has called for structural change inaugurated by personal conversion. Blacks and whites, males and females, rich persons and poor persons are called to transform those barriers that prevent them from working together for the social and spiritual transformation of the church and society. Yet Blacks, women, and poor people continue to daily experience oppression within the society and the church. Black middle-class women and men in church and society experience double oppression. Black poor women and men experience triple oppression. Racism, sexism, and classism are alive and well in most Christian churches. Why?

First, many are unaware or insensitive to the experience Black Catholics have within the church. Second, those who benefit from the current arrangements see no reason for change. Third, both those who benefit from the status quo, and those who are victimized by it, fear change.

Isolation of Black Catholics in segregated institutions or marginalized within "integrated" institutions can lead to insensitivity to the experience of Black men, women, and youth. Their intellectual, spiritual, and cultural gifts remain invisible. Their creative talents remain unused. Their particular needs and concerns are not addressed.

Those who benefit from the current structural arrangements and patterns of relationships are often insensitive to the negative impact of racism, sexism, and classism upon the quality of their own and other persons' lives. Many who share in institutional power and are aware of the church's teaching on racism, sexism, and the economy seem to think that these teachings should have no implications for the internal structures of the church. Yet racism, sexism, and classism have had profound impact on how and with what authority one participates in the ministry and decision making of the church.

Most human beings are resistant to change. Personal change is difficult. Structural change is formidable. Change is perceived to involve too much personal or institutional risk. One fears loss of order, security, power, or control. Many consider it "impolite" to raise the issues of racism, sexism, or classism directly or publicly. Such issues generate feelings of guilt, anger or helplessness.

Failure to study and personally integrate the social justice teachings of the church, and the unconscious and conscious inaction on the part of those who possess institutional power and those who are victims of the current structural arrangements, has blocked change and perpetuated the socially sinful status quo. Social injustice, social sins and the perpetuation of socially unjust structures are made possible by the unspoken cooperation of the oppressor and the oppressed. The moral theologian Hormis Mynatty defines social sin as

> the conscious and willful participation of a group or a society in co-operating with sinful social structures and thus maintaining and perpetuating them and failing to do anything to change them when it is possible.[24]

The contemporary patterns of social segregation and exclusion of Black men and women from participation in ministries and decision making within the church are grounded on historical patterns. As church historians Cyprian Davis and Stephen J. Ochs reveal in their works on Black Catholics, the Roman Catholic church in the United States related to African Americans in the same patterns of domination, segregation, and racism as the social insitutions within our nation.[25]

Even today, African-American Catholics are generally segregated within all Black parishes or marginalized in predominantly white parishes. These segregated parishes exist in all the regions of the country. In the rural South it is still not unusual for towns to have two separate Catholic churches, one all white, the other all Black. In the North, racially segregated living patterns have produced racially segregated parishes. In some instances, the Catholic parish is predominantly white even though the church is located in a predominantly Black community.

While some predominantly Black parishes have an African-American priest, deacon, brother, sister, or lay minister on their pastoral staff, most pastors and other offical ministers of these Catholic parishes are white. Lack of cross-racial experience and knowledge and respect of the history, culture, and experience of African Americans can make one consider her- or himself culturally and racially superior, and prohibit the appropriate inculturation of the gospel, religious rituals, and organizational structures.

The current and past structures and processes within the church have systematically tended to exclude all but a relatively few Black Catholic men and women from seminaries, religious congregations, and the official ministries, offices of administration, and ministerial activities of the church.

The perpetuation of these socially sinful systems, however, has required the complicity of many, and the conscious decision and action of a few. As Mynatty suggests, the evil embodied in socially sinful structures is manifested by the "drastic evil consequences" of dehumanization and destruction of life even without the "immediate involvement and agency of all people."[26]

Church institutions still manifest patterns of racism, sexism, and classism, which are destructive to African-American Catholics and others. Catholics from every race, ethnic group, and social and ecclesial category (laymen and laywomen, deacons, priests, sisters, brothers, and bishops) must cooperate with God's empowering grace and assume postures of moral fortitude to act to transform these sinful church institutions and organizations. The attitudes, social structures, and patterns of relationship that prohibit African Americans from responsible participation in prayer life, ministry, and decision making must be altered.

Parish Ministry

Within some local parishes, Black Catholics are still arbitrarily oppressed by persons in authority. Such pastors, pastoral associates, pastoral teams, and small groups of lay parishioners prevent the establishment of quality, spirit-filled liturgies, prayer and study groups. Some block the participation of lay people in the evangelizing and social justice ministry of their local churches. Adult Catholics are treated like children and are manipulated to serve the interest of the pastor or small power groups. Such ecclesial paternalism and maternalism embodies racist attitudes. It assumes that the ordinary Black Catholic is neither skillful, intelligent, moral, or spiritual enough to be an active adult participative member of the Christian community. These same parishes fail to establish study groups and training sessions to impart knowledge, develop skills, and promote spiritual growth of their membership.

Some Black Catholic parishes in contrast are culturally sensitive, vibrant centers of prayer, study, and community action. With quality leadership, these parishes are successful in maintaining and developing their membership. These parish communities are spirit-filled. Taking discipleship seriously, these members make a spiritual and social impact upon the neighborhood. They work collectively to confront the social problems of drug addiction, AIDS, child abuse, homelessness, lack of availability of quality education, gangs, suicide, unemployment, teenage pregnancy, low self-esteem, and family disintegration, which is epidemic within some economically poor Black communities.

Black lives are lost daily, not only by the physical violence of crime and drugs, but also by the social violences of devaluation, dehumanization, and marginalization caused by social alienation or marginalization. A church that describes itself as having a universal mission, as a sacrament of salvation, which continues the ministry and mission of Jesus Christ, must engage in prayer, study, fasting, and action in the midst of Black communities that are poor and afflicted.

Many Black Catholics today have already witnessed the closing of schools and churches within their community without their participation in the decision making. Some of these parishes were places of domination and dehumanization rather than communities of Christian love and discipleship. These were justifiably closed. However, a wholesale closing of schools and churches solely for economical reasons seems to evidence a lack of priority for the concerns of the poor as expressed in the economic pastoral letter. The continuance of parishes within the inner cities of our dioceses must be a high priority. Such parishes, however, must be characterized by a vibrant mission-consciousness evidenced by their involvement in mission outreach, responsiveness to the life needs of the community, and rootedness in the spiritual and sacramental ministry of the parish.

One of the positive effects of the "closing crises" could be the emergence of a more aware and responsible Black Catholic laity who will insist on participation in the decision making and mission of the local parish. To collaborate with the ordained ministers and religious men and women, committed Black Catholic men and women who express some sense of call to church ministry should be recruited and supported in obtaining the necessary training and credentials to be parish administrators and ministers.

Where church integration is a new phenomenon, pastoral staffs and church leaders must become active in welcoming the newcomers to the neighborhood, rather than becoming the organizing site for resistance to racial and ethnic transitions. Never again should a person feel rejected or limited in their participation in the sacraments and community life of a local church because of their race, class, or gender.

In municipal and rural areas where social integration has occurred, Catholic parishes and other Christian churches and religious institutions must develop structures to provide for the inclusion of class, racial, cultural, and gender diversity in the planning and the exercise of ministry within the church. Structuring such diversity in planning and ministerial groups makes it possible for pastoral staffs to become sensitive to issues that are confronting these distinct groups of members. Sensitivity to these issues makes it possible for parish liturgies, homilies, instruction classes, community action, and ministerial priorities to be responsive to issues and experiences of spiritual growth and development in the context of the real life of its members.

The social sins of racism, sexism, and classism have for too long allowed the stifling of the spiritual and ministerial development of Black Catholics and others who feel called to active discipleship. A skilled and prayerful spirit-filled leadership, committed to preach and realize the mission of Jesus Christ of establishing right relationships within the human community, and between that community and God, can attune many members of the church to the power of God within them. Thus awakened to the presence of God within, they will be able to be responsive to the needs of the poor and afflicted in the community. An oppressive, spiritually dead, egocentric leadership can be an obstacle to church members responding to God's call to each Christian to participate in the preparation of the coming of God's kingdom, which will enable them to be responsive to the needs of the poor and oppressed within our communities and nation. An oppressive, spiritually dead, egocentric leadership can prove a stumbling block to persons called by God to participate in the building up of the kingdom within their neighborhood, city, nation, and the world community.

Black Catholic Self-Help, Self-Determination and Catholic Collaboration

The spirit-led development of the contemporary Black Catholic movement has made some impact on the U.S. Catholic church at large. The founding of the National Black Clergy Caucus, the National Black Sisters Conference, the National Office of Black Catholics, and the National Black Seminarians Association during the last twenty-five years provided supportive structures and ministerial vision for Black Catholic priests, sisters, brothers, deacons, seminarians, and women in religious formation. The establishment of the Institute for Black Catholic Studies at Xavier University, almost ten years ago, has provided a degree and certificate program to provide an Afrocentric perspective of the Catholic tradition and Black Catholic thought and culture for those ministering in the Black Catholic community.

The appointment of thirteen Black Catholic bishops, the issuance of pastoral letters on racism and evangelization (*What We Have Seen and Heard*), the establishment of offices for Black Catholic Ministry and the employment of African-American Catholic consultants in diocesan offices, the establishment of the National Association of Black Catholic Administrators, and the publication of the Black Catholic hymnal, *Lead Me, Guide Me*, are also fruits of twenty-five years of individual and collective action on the part of Black Catholics who were struggling to combat the effects of institutional racism within the church. Those Black Catholics who have been active participants in the movement are well aware of the active presence of the Spirit empowering them to continue in the face of suspicion and negative responses by Blacks and non-Blacks. Black Catholics touched by this movement continue to be hopeful and enthusiastic about their ministry and mission, despite the the bleak social and ecclesial environment which surrounds them.

More Black Catholic bishops, deacons, laity, priests, sisters, and brothers have become involved in the ministries among African Americans during the twenty-five years since Vatican II. Such an increase is a testimony to the action of the Holy Spirit and the responsiveness of Blacks and whites who have not placed themselves as barriers to this action of the Spirit, but who have been active supporters and nurturers of those enlivened by God's grace. Despite the presence of personal and structural obstacles, and personal and structual sinfulness, grace has abounded. Black Catholics currently number approximately two million. This pattern of growth has been stimulated by conversion and immigration of Catholics from Africa and the Caribbean. If it is to continue, the barriers to Black male and female participation in church life and ordained, vowed, and lay missions must be removed.

The convening of the Sixth National Black Catholic Congress in 1987 was the collective fruit of these Black Catholic bishops and National Black Catholic organizations and the Knights and Ladies of St. Peter Claver. As in the first five congresses, the sixth congress invited Blacks and whites to participate in developing a pastoral plan for the future of evangelization within the Black community. The fruits of this congress cannot be measured but the congress itself has become a vehicle for addressing the pastoral needs of the Black community.[27] The congress has sponsored interim conferences and annual pastoral workshops. The Seventh National Black Catholic Congress, convened in July, 1992, passed public policy statements addressing medicaid, universal health care, welfare reform, africentric education and job training as these impact the African-American community. Among its pastoral statements support was given to continued development of programs to support family development and evangelization and the provision of quality africentric Catholic schools in the African-American community.

Many U.S. bishops have been responsive to and supportive of the convening of the National Black Congresses and the establishment of the Secretariat for Black Catholics as part of the United States Catholic Congress. Some archdioceses and dioceses are struggling to restructure themselves in a manner that will allow Blacks, Hispanics, Native Americans, and Asians to be more involved in directing the diocesan mission and ministry within these cultural communities. Leadership conferences of men and women religious have gathered to discuss the presence of racism within their congregations. Some have taken constructive action to identify, nurture, and sustain vocations from the African-American community and have established new ministries within the African-American community. Some schools of theology and seminaries are struggling to overcome social sinfulness in their structures by making concerted efforts at recruitment and curriculum changes that are more culturally, racially and globally sensitive.

The struggle to overcome the social sins of racism, sexism, and classism and their dehumanizing effects require the collaborative participation of the representatives from all races and ethnic groups, males and females, rich and poor. Collaborative styles of planning, decision making, and action are not easy for those trained in and accustomed to authoritarian models of leadership. Members of pastoral staffs and congregations must struggle to overcome their personal and cultural-racial patterns of domination or submission and feelings of innate superiority and inferiority. Collaboration is time-consuming and painful for those fearful of change. Yet it is in this struggle of intellectual and moral conversion expressed in concrete action that one begins to partially see and experience the hope, joy, and love of living in the patterns of right relationships, characteristic of God's kingdom. It is in the struggle that we come together in prayer and eucharist to remember that Jesus was crucified because his life style and preaching signaled a change in the social, political, and religious institutions of his day. Yet death was not triumphant. Joy came in the morning as the resurrected Jesus revealed his presence as the risen Christ.

NOTES

1. Paula Giddings, *When and Where I Enter: The Impact of Black Women on Race and Sex in America* (New York: Bantam Books, 1988), 33–39.

2. John W. Cell, *The Highest Stage of White Supremacy: The Origins of Segregation in South Africa and the American South* (New York: Cambridge University Press, 1982), 86. This is an excellent critical analysis and debate among historians about the complex development of segregation in two segments of our world community.

3. Ibid., 117, 119.

4. Teresa L. Amott and Julie A. Matthaei, *Race, Gender, and Work: A Multicultural Economic History of Women in the United States* (Boston: South End Press, 1991), 146–168.

5. John Hope Franklin and Alfred A. Moss, Jr., *From Slavery to Freedom*, 6th ed. (New York: Knopf, 1988), 367, 449.

6. Gerald David Jaynes and Robin M. Williams, Jr., eds., *A Common Destiny: Blacks and American Society* (Washington, DC: National Academy Press, 1989), 9. A critique of this report and an African-American perspective on the issues of family, education, social, political, and economic issues including health care is available from the William Monroe Trotter Institute, University of Massachusetts, Harbor Campus, Boston, MA, in the publication series entitled "Assessment of the Status of African-Americans."

7. Amott and Matthaei, 190.

8. Ibid., 189–190.

9. Jaynes and Williams, 26.

10. Cell, 115, 117. See quotations from Fredrick Douglass and W. Dubose.

11. Lester B. Scherer, *Slavery and the Churches in Early America: 1619–1819* (Grand Rapids: Eerdmans, 1975), 63, 91.

12. Ibid., 128.

13. Pope Leo XIII, *Rerum Novarum* in *The Papal Encyclicals*, Vol. 2. Claudia Carlen, IHM, ed. (Salem, NH: McGrath Publishing Co., 1981), 241–261. In 1891, five years before *Plessy vs. Ferguson*, Leo XIII spoke directly to the labor concerns arising in the newly industrialized nation. Catholic immigrants were striving to unionize for just working conditions and wages. *Rerum Novarum* primarily spoke out against socialism, but warned also about the negative consequences of extreme capitalism or individualism. The encyclical supported private property, the rights of workers to organize and the need of the state to intervene to protect the rights of people. (See Jay P. Dolan, *The American Catholic Experience* [New York: Doubleday, 1985], 334.) American immigrants and bishops paid little attention to the encyclical except for its implicit support of unions. Preoccupied with the concerns of the immigrant populations, which were their ethnic group of origin, few if any American bishops concerned themselves with the implications of this encyclical for labor rights of African Americans. The encyclical itself failed to sufficiently analyze the origins of class distinctions but assumed that they were the natural consequence of inequity in wealth and property ownership based on Christian morality, hard work and differences in capacity, skill, health, strength (*Rerum Novarum*, #17, 245).

Two distinct classes were evident, the powerful who held wealth and manipulated power and trade "for its own benefits and purposes" and the "needy and powerless" multitudes who needed to be encouraged to work hard to acquire property and therefore access to wealth and power (*Rerum Novarum*, #47, 253).

14. Joseph D. Brokhage, *Francis Patrick Kenrick's Opinion on Slavery* (Washington, DC: Catholic University Press, 1955), 54–55.

15. Jamie T. Phelps, "The Mission Ecclesiology of John R. Slattery: A Study of An African American Mission of the Catholic Church in the Nineteenth Century," Ph.D. diss., The Catholic University of America (Ann Arbor: University Microfilms International, 1989), 108. For a more extensive review of U.S. Catholics and slavery see pages 67–109 of the dissertation and Jamie T. Phelps, "Caught Between Thunder and Lightning: An Historical and Theological Analysis of the American Bishops and Slavery" in *Many Rains Ago* (Washington, DC: United States Bishops' Conference, 1990).

16. *Gaudium et Spes* in *Documents of Vatican II*, Vol. 1, Austin Flannery, ed. (Northport, NY: Costello Publishing Co., 1981), #27, 928. See also Leo XII, *In Plurimas* and *Catholicae Ecclesiae* in *The Papal Encyclicals*, Vol. 2, Claudia Carlen, IHM, ed. (Salem, NH: McGrath Publishing Co., 1981), 159–167, 233–235.

17. *Lumen Gentium* in *Documents of Vatican II*, Vol. 1, Austin Flannery, ed., (Northport, NY: Costello Publishing Co., 1981), #8, 358.

18. *Gaudium et Spes*, #1. The English translations of the documents of Vatican II and church documents from Rome still often use the term *men* "generically" to refer to men and women. While this was characteristic of the 1960s, given the feminist critique of sexist language in the United States, this stylistic convention should have been altered in translation and writing of documents of the 1980s and 1990s. This is not always the case.

19. U.S. Catholic Bishops, *Brothers and Sisters to Us: U.S. Bishops Pastoral on Racism in Our Day* (Washington, DC: United States Catholic Conference, 1979), 3, 10.

20. U.S. Catholic Bishops, "Partners in the Mystery of Redemption: A Pastoral to Women's Concerns for Church and Society" in *Origins* 17, no. 45 (April 21, 1988): 758–788. Article #28, 35.

21. Ibid., Article #39. Because of strong opposition from Euro-American Catholic women's organizations and strong division within the episcopal body centered on the pastoral's negative stance on women's ordination, the women's pastoral was tabled and commended to committe for further study. As a consequence the U.S. Bishops Conference never officially passed or promulgated the proposed pastoral on women.

22. U.S. Catholic Bishops, *Economic Justice for All: Pastoral Letter on Catholic Social Teaching and the U.S. Economy* (Washington, DC: National Conference of Catholic Bishops, 1986), 45–48. Article #87, 93.

23. *Economic Justice*, #52, 28–29.

24. Hormis Mynatty, "The Concept of Social Sin," *Louvain Studies* 16 (1991): 17.

25. Cyprian Davis, *The History of Black Catholics* (New York: Crossroad Publishing Co., 1990) and Stephen J. Ochs, *Desegregating the Altar* (Baton Rouge: Louisiana State Press, 1990).

26. Mynatty, 12.

27. See the papers presented at the Sixth National Black Catholic Congress of

1987 in *The U.S. Catholic Historian*, 7, nos. 2 and 3 (Spring-Summer 1988): 299–356. The National Black Catholic Pastoral Plan has been published under the title *Here I Am, Send Me* (Washington, DC: National Conference of Catholic Bishops, 1989).

PART II

IT WOULDN'T BE THE FIRST TIME

4

"A Clarion Call To Awake! Arise! Act!"

The Response of the Black Women's Club Movement to Institutionalized Moral Evil

Marcia Y. Riggs

One of the tasks of a womanist ethicist is to retrieve Black women's history as a source for ethical reflection. This essay is an example of such historical retrieval, focusing upon the thought and work of the Black women's club movement during the late nineteenth and early twentieth centuries. The aim of this essay is to describe the Black club women's understanding of the nature of and remedy for injustice in society as a critical point of departure for thinking about the ethics of Black liberation for African Americans today. The essay has three parts: (1) a discussion of some sociohistoric and socioeconomic features of Black women's lives during the late nineteenth and early twentieth centuries as the basis for the emergence of a Black women's club movement; (2) a description of the thought that undergirded the work of the club movement; and (3) an interpretation of the significance of this historical retrieval for Black liberation ethical reflection.

Sociohistoric and Socioeconomic Features of Black Women's Lives

During the late nineteenth and early twentieth centuries, the "cult of true womanhood or cult of domesticity" described and prescribed the role of women and the nature of femininity in society. Women were to be wives and mothers who possessed the attributes of domesticity, submissiveness, piety, and purity. In effect, the "cult of true womanhood" was a classist and racist ideology of womanhood.

The parameters of the ideological discourse of true womanhood were bound by a shared social understanding that external physical appearance reflected internal qualities of character and therefore provided an easily discernible indicator of the function of a female of the human species: men associated "the idea of female softness and delicacy with a correspondent delicacy of constitution" . . . It is worth considering that a delicate constitution was an indicator of class as well as racial position; woman as ornament was a social sign of achieved wealth, while physical strength was necessary for the survival of women in the cotton fields, in the factories, or on the frontier.[1]

On the one hand, upper-class white women of leisure were best able to maintain some semblance of this ideal of womanhood, and white middle-class women sought to align their behavior with the "cult" as a vehicle for social mobility.[2] On the other hand, working-class and all Black women were considered transgressors of the "cult." Also, working-class women and all Black women were considered to be freely available for sexual use by upper-class white males.

Moreover, all Black women were bound together and oppressed as a distinct sociohistorical group by this ideology of the "cult of true womanhood," on the one hand, and the racial ideology of the Black child-savage,[3] on the other hand. The social myth of the "bad black woman" resulted from an intertwining of these gender and racial ideologies, and all Black women (poor, working class, professional) found that their nature and role was defined by society largely in terms of that myth. Thus, while it is true that Black women and men experienced a common oppression deriving from life in a racist society, Black women experienced racism in a qualitatively different manner because of the additional constraints of gender oppression upon their lives.

Also, by the late nineteenth century and into the early twentieth century, urbanization of the Black population increased, and Black women were a significant number of the migrants into southern and northern cities. In fact, "the predominance of the female element [was] perhaps the most striking phenomenon of the urban Negro population."[4] The following reasons for and consequences of Black women's migration are crucial socioeconomic earmarks that distinguish Black women's experience at this time.

First, single mothers with children and widows were particularly prominent among migrants to cities in the South because of the difficulty of maintaining an economically viable agrarian livelihood for the support of a family. This in turn led to high percentages of female-headed families and women in the paid labor force; 50 to 70 percent of all adult Black females were gainfully employed at least part-time in large southern cities at the turn of the century. Three times as many Black as white women listed an occupation during the period from 1870–1880. Two-thirds of single Black women and one-third of single white women, 31 percent of married Black women and 4 percent of married white women reported jobs.[5] While white southern women who migrated into southern towns and cities worked in textile and tobacco factories, the majority of Black women were employed in white households or other low-paying service jobs as nurses, cooks, washerwomen, chambermaids, and seamstresses.[6]

Even in a place such as Washington, D.C., "with its large supply of clerical positions and better paying domestic service jobs,"

> only a small portion of the black female paid work force in the nation's capital (and elsewhere) held clerical positions. In 1890, according to published occupational census data, all black female clerical workers in the District of Columbia comprised less than one percent of the total black female paid work force. Even the wartime demand for labor resulted in only 2.8 percent (814) of the local black female working population becoming clerical workers in 1920, compared to 68.8 percent (41,376) of the Washington native-born white female work force. Foreign-born white women occupied a smaller percentage of clerical jobs (24.7 percent) than native-born white women, but that was still higher than the rate for black women.[7]

Second, the prospect of better wages in industrial cities of the North made these cities attractive to southern Black women who as farm laborers or urban domestics were paid $.75 a day and $1.50 to $3.00 a week, respectively. At least the northern cities held out the possibility of earning as much as $3.00 or $4.00 a day in factories and $2.50 a day for domestic work.[8] However, because of the higher cost of living in the North, the difference in wages was negligible, and Black women frequently found that their standard of living was actually lowered. Young illiterate Black girls were often lured northward by labor agents who had them sign contracts that required repayment of the cost of the trip as well as a placement fee. Many times these agents promised the girls domestic service when they were actually recruiting them for brothels.[9] Black female migrants were thus vulnerable economically as well as personally.

Since the Black female migrants primarily swelled the class of unskilled laborers, their presence contributed to antagonism between migrants and Black residents of the cities. Because of the fact that Black women worked in large numbers outside of the home and given the types of work they performed, Black womanhood was devalued. Black female migration aggravated class tensions within the Black community and fed white society's general negative assessment of Black people with respect to white middle-class standards for womanhood, family life, and economic progress.

In brief, these sociohistoric and socioeconomic features constitute some contours of Black women's experience within the late nineteenth and early twentieth centuries. Black women found that their gender leveled out their experiences across class lines, and consequently, a race-gender-class consciousness emerged among Black women, which reflected this fact. It is the negative interaction of gender with race and class within the lives of Black women (regardless of whether they were poor, working class or professional) that shaped Black women's public responses to injustice – to institutionalized moral evil – in society. The Black women's club movement was one of those public responses.

Thought of the Black Women's Club Movement

The context in which a national Black women's club movement emerged was earmarked by the growth of women's organizations in the nineteenth century generally.

The development of the Woman's Christian Temperance Unions and the success of the Grange among rural women during the last quarter of the nineteenth century heralded an era in which American women joined together to form a multitude of clubs, leagues, societies, and associations. Between 1890 and 1920, this "associating" tendency reached fulfillment as millions of women organized into thousands of separate groups.[10]

Although the types of groups within the club movement were diverse (literary societies, social clubs, professional clubs, prayer circles, Dorcas societies), most interpreters of the late nineteenth-century women's club movement characterize it principally as nonsectarian and autonomous (not an auxiliary of male organizations) and suggest that this critically distinguishes the movement from precedent groups in the earlier part of the century.[11] This characterization applies to the Black women's club movement.[12]

Black women organized the National Association of Colored Women (NACW) by merging the National Federation of Afro-American Women and the League of Colored Women in 1896. It became a *socioreligious* movement against the interaction of race, gender, and class oppression in the lives of Black women while working for the advancement of all Blacks. On the one hand, the Black women's club movement was a *social* movement in the following senses:

Social movements provide weapons for the powerless. They create milieus for people or groups with few formal institutional ties and for ideas that are not part of the institutional consensus. Social movements tend to question both accepted relations of power and the ideological underpinnings of those relations. Therefore, it is not surprising that innovative ideas often take shape within social movement organizations as they develop programs, agendas, and justifications for the world they want to create. But because the ultimate success of an insurgent program is dependent on its mobilization of broad support, such organizations must find avenues to introduce their agendas into wider discourse. Because institutional routes are usually blocked, social movement groups find allies among other insurgent groups. . . .

Because its posture of reform usually isolates a social movement from established social, political, or economic institutions, the development of support networks has the potential to create an audience for ideas that previously had little or no voice in public dialogue.[13]

In other words, the Black women's club movement created a milieu wherein Black women were empowered to challenge the ideological underpinnings of race-gender-class oppression perpetrated against them in society. Black club women developed programs and justifications for a society which they wanted to create, a reformed society for the sake of justice.

As a social movement NACW was both a sponsor of national programs and "the first cohesive national network of black women." It was a social reform organization whose very structure constituted support networks.

The structure of the organization facilitated communication: local clubs at the base, then state federations, regional federations, and at the top the national body. Information and influence flowed freely from bottom to top as well as in the reverse direction.[14]

Furthermore, the club movement derived from Black women's existence as a distinct sociohistorical group. Although the national Black women's club movement, between 1892 and 1894, developed during the time of and even parallel to the white women's club movement, the two movements had distinguishing purposes deriving from the radically different sociohistoric and socioeconomic bases of the two groups of women's lives. For example, although the two movements were led primarily by middle-class women, Black women understood that their class status was attained in spite of, and maintained under conditions of, racist caste-class oppression. They were led most often to attack systemic issues of injustice rather than issues pertinent to maintaining their own middle-class status.

Addie W. Hunton, a national organizer of the Black women's club movement, characterizes the distinctiveness of the Black women's club movement thus:

The colored woman's club is an eleemosynary organization. There may be a social feature and some attention may be given to self-culture, but these are secondary. The main purposes are to relieve suffering, to reclaim the erring, and to advance the cause of education.

Neither have colored club women seen fit to ape their fairer sisters' work to any perceptible degree. The conditions are essentially different and our women have recognized this fact. For want of means and time, it is difficult for any one of our clubs to foster a large number of enterprises. It has been the aim of each club, however, to find the thing most needed in its special community and to devote a volume of loving service to the overcoming of that need. The motto for work has grown to be "Quality rather than quantity."[15]

This discussion does not ignore the fact that racism was a critical factor inhibiting Black women's participation in the white women's club movement. However, this discussion emphasizes that Black women, as a distinct sociohistorical group because of the negative interaction of race, gender, and class in Black women's lives, organized a separate Black women's club movement as more than a defensive reaction to racist exclusion; it was an act of self-determination in order to address the particular concerns of Black women and Black people.

On the other hand, the Black women's club movement was a *religious* movement with respect to its continuing ties to the church and in terms of the socioreligious ethical sensibilities nurtured within Black women by the church. Both local member clubs (some were, in fact, women's church groups) and their leadership maintained ties with and in the church. In effect, this was a movement for racial uplift, which "... with its federation of women's clubs was the specialized political arm of black church women."[16] Emily H. Williams noted the continuing presence of churchwomen and their club work in her report during the ninth biennial convention of the NACW in 1914:

Many clubs are actively engaged in church work and so noticeable was the number of ministers' and bishops' wives present, that a conference of these women was held after one of the sessions. The president called attention to the importance of this phase of the work of the Association, saying: "When you get the Negro minister's wife, you get the Negro minister; when you get the Negro minister you get the Negro people."[17]

Moreover, as Fannie Barrier Williams, a club woman and journalist of the period, wrote in 1900:

The training which first enabled colored women to organize and successfully carry on club work was originally obtained in church work. ... The churches have been sustained, enlarged and beautified principally through the organized efforts of their women members. The meaning of unity of effort for the common good, the development of social sympathies grew into women's consciousness through the privileges of church work.[18]

Although it is significant that the movement retained ties with the church, the socioreligious ethical sensibilities ("unity of effort for the common good," "the development of social sympathies") that Williams described Black women as developing through church work, are particularly relevant to this discussion.

Therefore, when the National Association of Colored Women was organized in 1896, it represented a socioreligious reform movement led by Black women. The interrelated aims of this movement were: (1) "uplifting" the Black community, and (2) struggling for justice in the larger society. In the words of Carrie W. Clifford, president of the Ohio Federation of Colored Women's Clubs:

> It is in the club that we will gain inspiration to *do* and to *dare*. The clubs of art, literature and music; philanthropy, temperance and social science; the business leagues and home improvement societies shall all be *levers* which will serve to lift us to high and higher planes of living. The spirit of club life shall be a clarion-call to Afro-American people to awake! arise! act![19]

The thought of club women that undergirded this spirit of club life reveals a race-gender-class consciousness, which scrutinized the complexity of Black oppression. On the one hand, the women were aware of an external dimension of Black oppression, and this produced an evaluation of the relation between economics and justice in society. On the other hand, club women also recognized an internal dimension, and this led them to call for self-help and economic self-determination on the part of Black people. For example, when the club women implemented programs, such as a special study of the history of "the Race" in the United States or founded a sanitorium and training school for nurses, they were responding to the needs of Black people (the need for self-knowledge, the need for adequate health services, and the need for professional training) rather than reacting defensively to race-gender-class oppression. Club women knew that racial advancement had to rest upon a dynamic interplay between critical self-understanding of and socioeconomic response to the realities of the race's condition in society.

Black club women knew that Black people had to analyze the context in which Blacks found themselves. Yet, they also insisted that Black people not allow that context to define their responses, that Black people be self-critical and self-assured, rejecting racist, sexist, and classist norms for Black life and promoting community as functional unity for the common good instead of individualism. Mary Church Terrell, the first president of NACW, wrote about this in an article in 1900:

> As individuals, colored women have always been ambitious for their race. From the day when shackles first fell from their fettered limbs

till now, they have often single-handedly and alone, struggled against the most desperate and discouraging odds, in order to secure for their loved ones and themselves that culture of head and heart for which they hungered and thirsted so long in vain. But it dawned upon them finally, that individuals working alone, or scattered here and there in small companies, might be ever so honest in purpose, so indefatigable in labor, so conscientious about methods, and so wise in projecting plans, they would accomplish little, compared with possible achievement of many individuals, all banded together throughout the entire land, with heads and hearts fixed on the same high purpose and hands joined in united strength. As a result of a general realization of this fact, the National Association of Colored Women was born.[20]

Also, the motto of the NACW, "Lifting as We Climb," reflected the club women's sense of the interconnectedness and interrelatedness of Black people as a group. As historian Linda Perkins notes, there was an intertwining of a sense of racial obligation and duty with one of racial uplift and elevation.

Moreover, the socioreligious ethical sense from which the "clarion call" from club women issued was one of socioreligious responsibility. The club women believed that the world was ordered by God's justice and that justice for Black people was a command of God. Their ethical sense of socioreligious responsibility thus included an understanding that injustice(s) perpetrated against Black people in society were forms of institutionalized moral evil, evil that represented transgression against God's justice. Sometimes the language that the club women used characterized their work as "a battle for the rights of humanity against the demons of prejudice and injustice."[21] However, they clearly recognized the concrete manifestations of these demons in a society when they established programs to address such evils as the convict lease system, Jim Crow car laws, and lynchings. Club women, in thought and action, affirmed this: "Seeking no favors because of our color or patronage because of our needs, we knock at the bar of justice and ask for an equal chance.[22]

Significance for Black Liberation Ethical Reflection

Why turn to the thought and work of the Black women's club movement as a source for Black liberation ethical reflection? What do reformers have to say to liberationists?

First, the struggle of African Americans for Black liberation today is against a complex form of Black oppression that must be understood as race-gender-class oppression. This struggle is seriously hindered by a socioethical dilemma of competitive individualism vs. intragroup social responsibility. African Americans seem to be entrapped by a false Black consciousness, lacking an awareness or understanding of what the relationship between individual autonomy and communal autonomy should be for Black persons and Black people as a community. Accordingly, as social stratification among African Americans intensifies, upper- and middle-class individuals may be willing to emotionally and intellectually advocate the plight of the lower classes but lack the will to act on behalf of, or actually participate with, lower classes of Black people to effect mutual liberation. There is "sympathy without empathy." In fact, many upper- and middle-class persons entrapped by competitive class consciousness do not believe that they are in need of liberation. This belief leads to problems of isolation on the part of the upper and middle classes from the lower classes and alienation on the part of the lower classes from the upper and middle classes. Isolation and alienation create disunity where *functional* unity is essential for liberative struggle. The Black club women stressed a principle of collective solidarity and intragroup social responsibility ("Lifting as We Climb"), which is critical for African Americans to reappropriate if purposeful liberative struggle is to occur.

Second, the retrieval of the Black club women's sense of socioreligious ethical responsibility offers another important way to strengthen the substantive and practical implications of Black theology and the emergent Black womanist religious thought. Importantly, at the crux of the club women's sense of socioreligious ethical responsibility is a mediating posture whereby a sense of racial obligation and duty is ever interacting with a belief in the justice of God. Club women were certain that they had an obligation to institute and demand socioeconomic programs to uplift "the Race" because justice for Black people was interpreted as a command of God. We can also learn from the club women that because God's justice is the context in which struggle for liberation occurs, we must be self-critical, applying the norm of God's justice to our life within the African-American community. Careful attention to the thought and work of the club movement can yield significant insights for Black liberation scholars about how to mediate between religious, ethical, and social contextual meaning for Black liberation.

In brief, a Black liberationist moral vision must call for collective advancement for African Americans as part of a common goal to transform the socioeconomic and sociopolitical structure of United States society. African Americans must respond out of faith in God's justice because we know that it is through and within our sociohistoric community that we are judged, redeemed, and saved by God's justice, thus being called as moral agents to respond to institutionalized moral evil because the universal context of God's justice so commands us. A Black liberation ethic premised upon the moral vision of God's justice and the socioreligious ethical sense of intragroup social responsibility (like the club women's sense of socioreligious responsibility) may truly be the way to once again sound "a clarion call to awake! arise! act!"

NOTES

1. Hazel V. Carby, *Reconstructing Womanhood* (New York: Oxford University Press, 1987), 25.

2. Paula Giddings, *When and Where I Enter: The Impact of Black Women on Race and Sex in America* (New York: Morrow, 1984), 47. Cf. Catherine Clinton, *The Other Civil War: American Women in the Nineteenth Century* (New York: Hill and Wang, 1984), 34. Clinton notes that even upper-class and middle-class white women were not completely exempt from domestic labor and those who were, had substituted other women's labor for their own.

3. George M. Fredrickson, *The Black Image in the White Mind* (Middletown, CT: Wesleyan University Press, 1987), 198–225; 258–262. The ideology of the Black child/savage race undergirded "Negrophobia" and allegations of the rise of crime and increased sexual immorality on the part of Blacks.

4. Kelly Miller, "Surplus Negro Women," *Radicals and Conservatives* (New York: Schocken Books, 1968), 183.

5. Jacqueline Jones, *Labor of Love, Labor of Sorrow* (New York: Vintage Books, 1986), 73, 113, 74.

6. Dolores Janiweski, "Sisters Under Their Skins: Southern Working Women, 1880–1950," in *Sex, Race, and the Role of Women in the South*, Joanne V. Hawks and Sheila L. Skemp, eds. (Jackson: University of Mississippi Press, 1983), 20.

7. Sharon Harley, "Black Women in a Southern City: Washington, D.C., 1890–1920," in *Sex, Race, and the Role of Women in the South*, 62. Harley also thinks that race is the overriding determinative factor in clerical employment because of the fact that there was only about a 7 percent difference in the literacy rate of Black and native-born white women but a more than 90 percent difference between the number of Black and white women occupying clerical positions in 1920.

8. Florette Henri, *Black Migration: Movement North, 1900–1920* (New York: Anchor Press, 1975), 54.

9. Ibid., 61–62.

10. Judith Papachristou, "Associationism and Reform: 1890–1920," in *Women Together* (New York: Knopf, 1976), 113.

11. Ibid.; Eleanor Flexner, *Century of Struggle* (Cambridge: Harvard University Press, 1975), 182–183.

12. See Gidding, *When and Where I Enter*, chap. 6; Cynthia Neverdon-Morton, *Afro-American Women of the South and the Advancement of the Race, 1895–1925* (Knoxville: University of Tennessee Press, 1989), chap. 10.

13. Naomi Rosenthal et al., "Social Movements and Network Analysis: A Case Study of Nineteenth-Century Women's Reform in New York State," *American Journal of Sociology* 90, no. 5 (1985): 1013–1023.

14. Neverdon-Morton, *Afro-American Women of the South*, 193.

15. Addie W. Hunton, "The National Association of Colored Women: Its Real Significance," *The Colored American Magazine* 14 (1908), 419.

16. Cheryl Townsend Gilkes, "The Role of Women in the Sanctified Church," *The Journal of Religious Thought* 43 (Spring-Summer 1986), 35.

17. Emily H. Williams, "The National Association of Colored Women," *Southern Workman* 43 (September 1914), 481.

18. Fannie Barrier Williams, "The Club Movement Among Colored Women of America," in *A New Negro for a New Century* (New York: Arno Press, 1969), 383.

19. Charles Alexander, "The Ohio Federation at Dayton," *Alexander's Magazine* 1, no. 4 (15 August, 1905), 15.

20. Mary Church Terrell, "The Duty of the National Association of Colored Women to the Race," *A.M.E. Church Review* 16, no. 3 (January 1900), 340.

21. From the presidential address of Mrs. Carrie W. Clifford, president of the Ohio Federation of Colored Women's Clubs, in Charles Alexander, "The Ohio Federation at Dayton," *Alexander's Magazine* 1, no. 4 (15 August, 1905), 13.

22. Mary Church Terrell, "What role is the educated Negro woman to play in the uplifting of her race?" in *Twentieth Century Negro Literature: A Cyclopedia of Thought on the Vital Topic Relating to the American Negro*, D. W. Culp, ed. (Naperville, IL: J. L. Nichols and Co., 1902; Reprint New York: Arno Press and the New York Times, 1969), 177.

5

Living in the New Jerusalem

The Rhetoric and Movement of Liberation in the House of Evil

Emilie M. Townes

Womanist ethics begins with the traditional role and place assigned to Black women. An African-American woman contends with race, sex, class, and other sources of fragmentation. The challenge of a womanist social ethic is to create and articulate a positive moral standard, which critiques the arrogance and deadly elitism of dominance and is so bold as to name it as systemic evil. Womanist ethical reflection focuses on moral standards that are relevant to (but not circumscribed by) the African-American community. This ethical reflection also contains a universal dimension and critique.

Such an ambitious project must contain within its horizon both descriptive and prescriptive dimensions. Descriptively, the African-American experience is the ground for reflection. More particularly, the lives of African-American women provide the lenses for focus. The traditionally "good" moral characteristics of personal loss, denial, and sacrifice provide the interpretive framework for elucidating Black women's lives.

The prescriptive horizon is a praxis for the elimination of suffering. The socioethical claim guiding and informing my argument is that womanist ethical reflection rejects suffering as God's will and understands suffering as outrage. From a historical base built on the experience of African-American women, the moral valuing of loss, denial, and sacrifice is questioned. Womanist ethics advocates a renewed emphasis on authority and obedience that will move and guide the contemporary African-American community and its people of faith.

Living in Egypt: A Long and Weary Avenue

African-American women play a functional and autonomous role within the family and Black society due to economic and social conditions, which have devalued and ill-defined the Black woman historically. African-American women are forced, as are other women of color and white women, into images of womanhood imposed by a larger society. Black women also know that they will never reach this model due to the constraints of race and class. One aspect of racism is that it has structured dominant and subordinate roles and relationships between African Americans and whites, and placed Blacks within a relatively closed system while blaming deviant behavior on them.

African-American women have been called matriarchs, Sapphires, and castrators. This is due in large measure to the active role many Black women have had to play in the support of children, husbands, and African-American society. All have usually *assumed* the Black woman's capabilities. This legacy differs considerably from where the majority of white women begin. White culture does not assume that white women are capable.[1] African-American women who have the legacy of clearing the fields, caring for the children of others as well as their own, and functioning in marginalized roles—while being called on to provide the backbone of Black values—are considered a deviation from the norm and an anomaly in United States society.

A majority of the African-American male community has come to believe in the ideal in the United States that they are to be the providers for their families and *their* women. The few leadership roles allowed Black men by the dominant oppressive culture are guarded jealously with little regard for the psychological, theological, ethical, and economic damage done to the African-American community and African-American female and male interpersonal relationships.

How did we get to this state of affairs where loss, denial, and sacrifice are elevated to ethical ideals at the expense of emotional and spiritual health—female and male? I begin my answer to this question in West Africa.

The family unit was extremely important in precolonial West Africa. It consisted of a distinct structure and clearly designated roles for men and women. Marriage was not only between two individuals, but also between all the members of each person's extended family. Marriage was a binding together of two people who represented different families as well as the mutual duties and obligations they were to carry out for each other.

The role of women was political, social, and economic. Politically, women were important to the administration of tribal affairs. Lineage was often matrilinear with women assuming significant duties in the tribe. Joyce Ladner notes a recurring theme in many African legends and mythology:

A woman who is the founder and the mother of the tribe . . . is either a queen or the daughter of a king. She is an aristocratic lady who is involved in politics. For example, the creation myths of the Hausa people in Northern Nigeria or of Niger or Chad begin with a woman who goes out and founds a kingdom. She is the Black Moses of her people into the promised land which is an area near the water where communication is relatively free. She settles down and establishes the traditions of her people.[2]

Women had a close bond with children and this was crucial to the life of the tribe. There was a high regard for the mother's function as child-bearer and perpetuator of ancestral heritage. Economically, women were traders and the West African market woman is an institution even today in West African society. This is not to suggest that African women did not and do not still live under rigorous prescriptions for their behavior with curtailed access to decision making and public life.

Within the internal African slave trade, women were in higher demand than men. This internal market was larger than any of the other markets in slave trading. Women consistently brought higher prices and performed most of the agricultural work as well as the craftwork in most slave-owning African societies and households.[3]

In the significantly smaller Atlantic slave market, men were in greater demand. There is increasing speculation among anthropologists and ethnographers that the slave woman received such harsh treatment in the United States and colonial America because of the greater expectation placed on her within the internal African slave market.[4] Although men received greater value in this country's slave system, the women were to work in all male slave tasks. In addition, they provided a home life for children and performed childbearing duties. Let me hasten to add there was not at any time the savagery or brutality present in the internal African slave trade that was common fare for the Atlantic slave trade.

Legal marriage was denied to African slave men and women. Men were denied their traditional role of family patriarch. Women were forced into autonomy as men were no longer allowed to be the economic provider, disciplinarian, and teacher as they had been in Africa. Slave women suffered economic and sexual exploitation. They had to nurse white babies instead of, or in addition to, their own. The dynamics of northern and southern white culture demanded that the image of African-American women be antithetical to the image of white women. The Black slave woman was the primary outlet for the sexual passion of the white master.

Slave women practiced forms of resistance to this onslaught upon the humanity of African-American people. They practiced abstinence in refusing or attempting to avoid intercourse with white masters. In this vein, they also delayed marriage to a slave male with the hope that childbirth would happen in freedom.[5] Abortion and infanticide were also methods of resistance, but were less common than abstinence. Their resistance to sexual exploitation had political as well as economic implications. By using resistance, women negated, through individual or group action, their role in the maintenance of the slave pool.

Out of this heritage of what Zora Neale Hurston called "the mules of the world," Black women faced Reconstruction and the cult of womanhood. The shift from an agrarian economy (in which work had nonsexual connotations) to one of industrialization and urbanization (where work became largely male-identified and located away from the home) helped to fortify the cult. The subordination of African Americans into the ideology of the Black savage and confinement of white women to the cult of womanhood were interdependent. White southerners and northerners curtailed any political or economic gains African Americans made — controlling the image of Black people was one strategy used. African-American women were promiscuous and evil. White women were the paragons of virtue and purity. Women were to be domestic, modest, and delicate. They were exalted as moral guardians of the home and radiant sources of purity in the new industrial order.

> She sits, she walks, she speaks, she looks — unutterable things! Inspiration springs up in her very paths — it follows her footsteps. A halo of glory encircles her, and illuminates her whole orbit. With her, man not only feels safe, but actually renovated.[6]

Men dominate due to their participation in public life and the relegation of women to the private or domestic sphere. This relegation gives rise to universal male authority over women and a higher valuation of male over female roles. The public realm contains the institutionalized rules and practices that define the appropriate modes of action. It is the political, economic, legal, cultural, and social institutions in which we live as a society. In addition, it is the wide range of actions and practices covered by law. The public realm is the arena of paid work and ideas. It is the world of men. This country's laws, values, education, and morality are debated and shaped in this sphere. Men, not women, are the primary participants.

The private realm is that place of individual actions and interpersonal relations. It is the home. It is the arena where the dominant cultural norms of our society place women.

Each woman — African-American and white — lives with this split and participates in its existence *and* maintenance. We begin to take separate paths when we reach the juncture of the systematic exclusion of Black men (and all men of color) from the public sphere of the dominant white culture. This exclusion suggests that sex-role relationships between people of color cannot be explained fully by the structural oppression between the domestic and public spheres or the differential participation of men and women in the public sphere. Hence it is necessary to distinguish between the public life of the dominant and the dominated societies. The public life of the dominated society is *always* subject to the stresses put upon it by the dominant society. The private life of the dominated society suffers even more so than that of the dominant society.

During Reconstruction, the image of the African-American woman as mammy became a dominant theme. This puzzling image of the Black mammy who was able to care for and be mother to white babies and children was the same woman who was lower than a human being and morally bereft and licentious. White writers portrayed the Black mammy as contented, self-sacrificing, and loyal. She was also the object of white male sexual needs as she was in a condition of moral degradation and promiscuity. This bizarre dichotomy was the fulcrum for the balancing of reality and the irreal image of white women.

African-American women debunked this image through the Black women's club movement. African-American women of the nineteenth century *and* contemporary Black women resist the notion that morality and worth are bound to race, sex, and class. Both groups argue that external circumstances determine morality and worth in an individual, a race, and a class group. Both groups stress that African-American women are not responsible for their degradation.

The contemporary Black woman is called a matriarch. The thesis of the African-American matriarch has its origins in a perversion of the early works of W. E. B. DuBois and the actual theories of E. Franklin Frazier.[7] This thesis posits that Black women have had and continue to have an unnatural dominant role in African-American families and that this role has had tragic effects on Black society.

This peculiar image of the matriarch for the contemporary African-American community arises out of a situation in which many of the women who head poverty households were poor before they became mothers and household heads. This calls into question the concept of feminization of poverty. This phrase implies that these households are poor because of their female heads. In reality, family breakup may merely reshuffle the female poor from one classification to another.

The fact that a household is headed by a woman does not mean that it will be poor. However, in African-American society (as is the case for the majority of people in the United States) many families are kept above the poverty line because there are two employed adults. A single-parent family is more likely to be poor because there is only one wage earner. This becomes deadly if the household head is a woman. Women, on the average, earn much less than men. The sad reality of statistics and facts means that single-parent families with a female head are much more likely to be poor than those with a male head.

Coupled with this, young Black women who are the largest category composing the female-headed single-parent families often lack the skills needed for high earnings. With the absence of relatively inexpensive day care, many single mothers of young children cannot earn enough from outside employment to justify working. By definition, matriarchy means decision-making power; it is the power of women over their own lives and the power over the lives of others. In a society and in a church that has white men in overwhelming positions of power, women in positions of economic and social subservience, and the African-American community fragmented, the notion of an African-American matriarchy is ludicrous.

No one family structure fully represents the diversity of familial arrangements found in the historic and the contemporary African-American community. Although legal marriage was prohibited among slaves, two-parent families were not an uncommon occurrence during slavery and survived the vicissitudes of poverty, migration, and urbanization. Two-parent Black families were common among farm laborers, sharecroppers, tenants, and northern and southern Blacks in the great migration to the North.

Poverty and high mortality among Black men caused a greater proportion of female-headed families among Blacks than whites. After the Great Depression, in 1940, nearly three-fourths of Black families with children under eighteen were headed by two parents. There was no significant increase in male-absent households after the Great Migrations to the urban North. Until the 1960s, 75 percent of Black households with children under eighteen included husband and wife.

The image of the Black matriarch became dominant during the dramatic changes of the 1960s. By 1986, 49 percent of Black families with children under eighteen were headed by women. Black nuclear families and kin-related households remained intact through slavery, Great Depression, migration, urban life, ghettoization, and poverty. It is unlikely that any one of these conditions or their combinations can fully explain the large changes in marriage and family since 1960. Economic and social status differences must be taken into account in any analysis of present-day Black families and the roles African-American women and men play in them. The interaction and intersection of race, gender, and class become key to understanding loss, denial, and sacrifice in the role of Black womanhood.

Traveling to the New Jerusalem: Why This Suffering?

Black women theorists have moved from an embrace of the ideology of the cult of true womanhood and a later romantic notion of how the African-American woman has survived under adversity to one that is more pragmatic.[8] The reality is that most African-American women work outside of their own homes out of necessity and the majority do not control the source of their income. More than 40 percent are heading single-parent households and nearly 36 percent are below the poverty line. The Black woman joins her people in suffering as a state of being—choice is often not an option.

A womanist ethic rejects suffering as God's will and believes that it is an outrage that there is suffering at all. Although the details of analyses may differ, a womanist ethic must be dedicated to eliminating suffering on the grounds that its removal is God's redeeming purpose.

The Black church in this country has paid serious attention to the Hebrew Bible. The suffering of the children of Israel is likened to the suffering of African-American people. It identifies heavily with the Exodus and the journey through the wilderness. Many Black folk in the church grew up with stories of Moses, Abraham, Ezekiel, Ruth, and Esther. Suffering is the entry key to the kingdom. The inevitability and desirability of suffering needs to be challenged.

Within any oppressed group, the members of that group are prevented from acknowledging their anger and frustration at the system and at the tensions under which they must live. But if we believe God is a just God and a loving God, then African-American people of faith must allow and challenge ourselves to search for the roots of our suffering, which exists in our lives and threatens our existence.

Audre Lorde makes a distinction between pain and suffering.[9] For Lorde, suffering is unscrutinized and unmetabolized pain. Suffering is the inescapable cycle of reliving pain over and over again when it is triggered by events or people. It is a static process which usually ends in oppression. Pain is an experience that is recognized, named, and then used for transformation. It is a dynamic process pointing toward transformation.

Suffering is sinful because we do not choose to act through our finite freedom on behalf of our liberation from sin to justice. If, as most African-American women in the church do, the African-American religious community takes the resurrection event seriously, true suffering has been removed through the redemptive event of the resurrection. Through the Suffering Servant, God has spoken against evil and injustice. The empty cross and tomb are symbols of the victory. The oppressed are set free to struggle against injustice, not out of their suffering, but out of their pain that can be recognized and named as injustice and brokenness. The resurrection moves humanity past suffering to pain and struggle. The resurrection is God's breaking into history to transform suffering into wholeness—to move the person from victim to change agent. The gospel message calls for transformation.

The challenge for the African-American community is to work in partnership with the intention of moving from suffering to pain, individually and communally. Within the framework of Lorde's model, suffering is a way of being that prevents effective action and denies individual Black women and men or the African-American community the right and ability to say "no" to their oppression. African-American women have suffered with death-dealing images designed to keep Black women and men in a reactive stance, which does not allow for creative change or challenge to the present conditions. A womanist ethic is never content to merely react to the situation: it seeks to change the situation.

Black women have historically taken the opportunity to redefine suffering for other women, the Black church, and society. Ida B. Wells-Barnett did so in a radical and exciting way for her time. She was unwilling to accept the world as interpreted through the eyes of those who would not challenge the power structure or who chose to acquiesce to the sociopolitical circumstances of her time.

The Fellowship Herald newspaper later echoed her refusal to accept the living conditions of African-Americans in the early twentieth century. Again expressing concern about the vagrancy rates in Chicago among young African-American men, Wells-Barnett offers through the pages of the *Herald*:

> What is to be done? This is the question every law-abiding citizen should ask himself. "What can I do to make conditions better" should be the next question he should ask himself. The ministers, professional men, leaders of organizations should ask themselves: "what have we done to help this situation?" Surely with all the forces that make for good citizenship at work, some solution of this grave problem can be formed.[10]

To live and work through pain acknowledges our human ability to effect change in individual lives and in the lives of others. We must learn to move from the reactive position of suffering to that of the transforming power of pain, to use it as a critical stance and refuse to accept the "facts" handed to us.

The roots of this stance are grounded in the liberating message of the empty cross and the resurrection. God has taken suffering out of the world through the resurrection of Jesus. Because God loves humanity, God gives all peoples the opportunity to embrace the victory of the resurrection. The resurrection moves the oppressed past suffering to pain and struggle and from pain and struggle to new life and wholeness.

Suffering, and any discussion that accepts suffering as good, is susceptible to being shaped into a tool of oppression. Pain allows the victim to examine her or his situation and make a plan for a healthy future. A position of pain encourages an examination of the past and the recovery of the truth. Pain promotes self-knowledge, which is a tool for liberation and wholeness. The pain of the *reality* of contemporary life can give us the power to question what was written about Black womanhood and African-American people in light of the *truth* found in our lives.

Pain assumes that the individual is a loved and cared for child of God and that he or she is blessed with the ability to survive and struggle regardless of the circumstance and oppression. In short, a womanist social ethic *cannot* dodge the question of God's goodness for it is drawn to question continually the inordinate suffering of the oppressed. This ethic is challenged to new dimensions of awareness of God's presence within humanity as a liberating event. The revelation of God's love manifests itself in work to end oppression. We may not always be successful in our agitation for social change, but we must maintain an awareness that every strategy to defeat sin may not be successful but this is not a sign of God's judgment. It may be a sign of incomplete praxis on our part or on the part of others.

A contemporary womanist ethic would understand this as a signal for the need to reevaluate and try different strategies to bring in the just kingdom. Ida B. Wells-Barnett's words to twelve African-American men jailed unjustly in Elaine, Arkansas, reveal the depth of her belief in God's liberating love and her critique of inadequate or incomplete praxis.

> I have been listening to you for nearly two hours. You have talked and sung and prayed about dying, and forgiving your enemies, and of feeling sure you are going to be received in the New Jerusalem ... But why don't you pray to live and ask to be freed? ... let all of your songs and prayers hereafter be songs of faith and hope that God will set you free; ... Quit talking about dying; if you believe your God is all powerful, believe he is powerful enough to open these prison doors, and say so ... Pray to live and believe you are going to get out.[11]

The critical skills evident in pain are crucial for all victims and survivors of oppression. Pain is used by the person who is coming to wholeness *and* concerned about the oppressive conditions of those she joins in partnership. Pain allows the person to critique her individual circumstance and that of her community of partnership.

Christian mission must be done in the context of authority and obedience — not out of a sense of suffering and its goodness. The definitions of authority span two paradigms: authority as domination and authority as partnership. The latter is the paradigm that reflects community, partnership, and justice. The former is primarily a means of subjugation. I enter the discussion of authority with the understanding that authority is legitimated power or shared power.

The traditional concept of power is a natural consequence of an authoritarian model of obedience based on submission. The world is separated into entities with little or no interrelationship. Power becomes the property of these separated entities and is identified with domination. This notion of power involves the notion of invulnerability.

The concept of power that comes from decision and responsibility is one that entails the ability to effect change and to work with others. This power requires openness, vulnerability, and readiness to change. It is dynamic and concerned with the responsibility we have as moral agents for personal and social transformation.

Power as domination is dysfunctional to society because it inhibits diversity and growth. Power as domination restricts vision and movement and reduces flexibility and responsiveness. Power as cooperation and mutual respect is power in process that happens through us. We experience it when we engage in interactions that produce value. Power as cooperation and mutual respect summons us to develop our capacities for nuturance and empathy as well as our interconnectedness. Its project is justice.

The concept of authority that arises out of this understanding of power is shared authority. The key here is partnership that begets coalitions. Shared authority is a dynamic process in which the openness to the future evident in power as cooperation and mutual respect is manifest in the actual living out of movements for change and transformation. Shared authority recognizes the plurality in United States culture and is attentive to the various leadership styles and structures intrinsic in this diversity.

Authority becomes a contextualized commitment based on accountability to God through the risen Christ. This commitment is also grounded in a mutual accountability to those in my immediate community, as well as those representative of the diversity in which I live and must be in coalition and community. My context informs me of a segment of the world, and I must be in dialogue with others who are not members of my specific context. Authority becomes the tool for dialogue within partnership. Each participant is recognized and valued as a cocreator of God's kingdom on earth. The views, the experience, the analysis of each person receives full weight, as strategies of transformation and community are constructed and enacted.

A careful consideration of obedience is necessary when considering shared power and authority in partnership for African-American women and womanists who remain committed to the Black church and Christianity. African-American women in ministry must be aware of and articulate an analysis of female inequality that is cogent to the repressiveness of traditional notions of power as well as obedience. Black women have suffered under triple jeopardy and *must* be thorough and systematic in their analysis.

The authoritarian model of obedience depicts obedience as a self/other relationship exclusively. A general definition is one in which the relationship is that in which there is an imbalance of power. There is a fear of the strength of the person who is asserting superiority. Religious and sociological thought forms have been inseparably intertwined in this model: God and establishment, God and ordinances, God and country. Obedience in this model is not a standard, but a behavioral technique. One never asks the question why.

When obedience concentrates itself completely on a higher and guiding other, it becomes blind to the world. Obedience that is blind to the world and only follows directions has divested itself of all responsibility for what it is commanded to do. Responsibility implies willingness to engage in freedom. This kind of "world blindness" formalized conception of Christian obedience leads to voluntary obedience as an end in itself. This in turn leads to easy manipulation by the authority figure(s) for its own purposes. The Bible, tradition, and experience are used as tools of repression. The individual or group is told what to think and does no independent interpretation.

Discriminating obedience recognizes that the worldview of the authoritarian model is more Greek than Hebraic. Greek thought stressed order and did not tolerate continual change. The biblical worldview is that of movement toward a goal. The authoritarian model cannot adequately express the will of God for the world because this model is interested in the preservation of order and has a hostility toward the future.

In the Hebrew Bible, obedience is always related to justice. It is requested of people directly concerned with shaping the world entrusted to human beings. Obedience implies responsibility: a decision that first discovers God's will and then decides what must be done. Neither the situation nor the will of God can be determined in advance. The person can make the decision in the now only. Jesus requires an obedience that has its eyes wide open as we accept responsibility for the order of the world and engage in transforming that order. The distinction I wish to make in these two models of obedience is one of obedience as religious decision versus obedience as mindless submission. God is a sustaining God who has proclaimed life over suffering and is willing to do battle with the forces of sin and evil to proclaim the good news of a just society.

Living in the New Jerusalem: Jeremiah as a Subtext

A womanist ethic cannot accept mindless violence, conditional justice, destructive life-styles, or complacent inertia. Discriminating obedience trusts and values anger and indignation rather than victimization of injustice. This means that a prophetic womanist ethic may demand going it alone but prefers to be active in a community of faith and witness. Like Wells-Barnett's response to those who were amazed that "no leading people of the race" were active in the Negro Fellowship League, a womanist ethic of the new Jerusalem would reply,

> Neither did Jesus Christ have any of the leading people with him in his day when he was trying to establish Christianity. If I remember correctly, his twelve disciples were made up of fishermen, tax collectors, publicans, and sinners. It was the leading people who refused to believe in him and finally crucified him.[12]

To live and work through pain acknowledges the human ability to effect change in individual lives and in the lives of others. One must learn to move from the reactive position of suffering to that of the transforming power of pain. Wells-Barnett lived her life through the critical stance of pain. African-American women and men must refuse to accept the "facts" handed to us.

We must practice a thorough hermeneutic of suspicion and investigate the conditions and circumstances of daily life. Our discoveries free us from the misconceptions that promote injustice and social, political, and theoethical control. We must sharpen our critical tools, which are necessary to examine the oppressive conditions under which a Black woman or any oppressed individual or group must live.

The new Jerusalem is a horizon for us. A horizon to which we must ask, "What is this society we are trying to create? What does it look like? Is there a common vision? Have we become so overwhelmed by the process that we have lost sight of the end?"

Horizon is an ornery image for the new Jerusalem. It comes from the Greek word *horos*, which means boundary or limit. The horizon describes the edges of our living spaces — it is also the place of sunrises and sunsets. Horizons are very personal, and we each have our own. Our horizons are different, not because the sky and earth change, but because we change, we are different. We can define what a horizon is, but we cannot capture one, we cannot even capture our own. When we are committed to justice and decency our horizons are moved further and further away. When we take seriously the need for change, we can sometimes stand in the same place and discover new horizons we have never noticed.

Again, what is the society we are trying to create? What does it look like? Is there a common vision? Have we become so overwhelmed by the process, that we have lost sight of the end? These are questions a womanist ethic to combat evil takes on individually and collectively. Any discussion of evil and injustice that does not keep these questions in mind easily degenerates to theory and prospect rather than as a blueprint for justice.

The horizon a womanist ethic works toward is a society that respects the rights and humanity of all peoples and nature. It is a society that provides adequate education, health care, and income opportunities. The society that is part of the new Jerusalem respects and cares for the young and the elderly. It is a society that is rich in diversity through its cultural, racial, and ethnic groups. It is a society in which women and men learn to build healthy relationships with one another. It is a society that does not dwell on sexual orientation or life-style. It is a society that addresses the roots of its problems instead of building prison after prison as a vain panacea. It is a society that is uncompromisingly rooted in justice and fueled by people who use their hope to construct and enact meaningful and significant social change.

With such a challenge and such a vision, the Black church, like the people of Israel in Jeremiah,[13] is called to make a new covenant, which is really an ancient one. African-American society is at risk. Womanist ethical reflection insists that the Black church move beyond a ritualized, a sterilized, a codified, and a magnificently vacuous faith to one that comes from the heart, soul, and intellect.

The covenant of Jeremiah, which frames womanist ethical reflection, is one so dynamic, so challenging that the cut of a stone cannot hold it and the script on parchment cannot capture its essence. From this covenant, this faith, this challenge, we craft a community of witnesses and discipleship. This community holds within its bounds women, men, and children of faith with varied life-styles and abilities, different political and theological agenda, and folks from all levels of the class structure.

A covenant that reaches for the horizon of the new Jerusalem demands that the Black church do no less than teach and preach the Bible, witness through our spirituality and our sense of justice, search for pithy Christian religious education, demand the best of who we can be as a church, refuse to accept easy answers to tough questions, realize the danger of blind obedience, and celebrate the joy and challenge of true Christian obedience.

Living in the new Jerusalem means knowing God firsthand. When we feel God's presence and warmth, then the Black church is able to witness out of God's grace-filled forgiveness. Even in the midst of our iniquity, we can reach out to the poor, the dispossessed, the lonely, the rejected as brothers and sisters and not as a mission project. We must never forget that the covenant God makes with us in the testament of Jeremiah is one to be lived from the inside out—to be lived from our center, our soul, our hearts.

The new Jerusalem, and our lives there, means that if we err in our witness as a community of faith, it is to be on the side of trying to reach beyond what we thought possible and not because we settled for less than what we are capable. We attempt an ornery discipleship with the knowledge that God holds us together, gives us the pith of our community, and graces us with relentless love. This love is so total that all are invited to the welcome table, all are challenged to accept the eternal promise, all are called to service, all affirmed. God's covenant with us overwhelms sepulchral faith operating on tiny motives, meager objectives, belittling goals, silly prejudices, and partial successes.

Our witness is framed in our willingness to name injustice and rejoice in the joy of new life and the resilience found in a true community of hope built not on the sands of suffering, but on the bedrock of the cross. This witness is one of prayer and action. It holds the spiritual and the active witness in dynamic relationship.

Loss, denial, and sacrifice, if used, must be reinterpreted and reimaged if the vision of society and the nature of the Black church are to provide more than impotent security. Rather than desirable norms, they must be challenged as hegemonic tools that serve to maintain African Americans in positions of less than. Such "virtues" assume choice. For the African-American male, loss can mean joblessness, violence, prison, and early death. For the African-American female, denial can mean terror and battering. For African-American children, sacrifice can mean poor education and a cycle of poverty. There may be no choice involved—only survival.

Suffering is outrageous. Suffering does not ennoble, enable, or equip this generation or future generations of Black people. A life based on survival and reaction does not produce healthy minds, bodies, or souls. The fragmentation of the spirit and the witness prevents the Black church from living in the new Jerusalem. Rather than rest on counterfeit virtues, womanist ethics challenges the African-American community and the Black church to be the true people of God and hang tougher.

NOTES

1. David Bradley, "Novelist Alice Walker Telling the Black Woman's Story," in *New York Times Magazine* (8 January 1984), 36.

2. Joyce A. Ladner, "Racism and Tradition: Black Womanhood in Historical Perspective," in *The Black Woman Cross-Culturally*, ed. Filomena Chioma Steady (Cambridge: Schenkman Publishing Co., Inc., 1981), 273 n. 8.

3. Claire C. Robertson and Martin A. Klein, eds., *Women in Slavery in Africa* (Madison: University of Wisconsin Press, 1983), 3–37.

4. Ibid.

5. Darlene Hine and Kate Wittenstin, "Female Slave Resistance: The Economics of Sex," in Steady, *The Black Woman*, 291.

6. Ann Douglas, *The Feminization of American Culture* (New York: Avon Books, 1977).

7. W. E. B. DuBois, *The Negro American Family* (New York: Negro Universities Press, 1969). E. Franklin Frazier, *The Negro Family in the United States* (New York: Dryden Press, 1948).

8. The analyses of Joyce Ladner and bell hooks are representative of this shift. In the early 1980s, Joyce Ladner notes that much of the current focus on being liberated from the constraints of society being proposed by white women liberationists in the late 1960s and early 1970s never applied to African-American women. She posits that Black women have always been "free" and able to develop as individuals under the most harsh circumstances. She believes that this accounts for a female personality rarely described in scholarly journals. Joyce Ladner, "Racism and Tradition: Black Womanhood in Historical Perspective," in Steady, *The Black Woman*, 247.

Ladner's image of the African-American woman is one of obstinate strength and survival. This is not the epitome of the U.S. model of femininity. Ladner's view of the strong Black woman contains elements of truth, but is overly optimistic in its assessment. She is equating survival and perseverance in the face of oppression with health.

bell hooks notes, "Usually, when people talk about the 'strength' of black women they are usually referring to the way in which they perceive black women coping with oppression. They ignore the reality that to be strong in the face of oppression is not the same as overcoming oppression, that endurance is not to be confused with transformation." bell hooks, *Ain't I A Woman* (Boston: South End Press, 1981), 6.

9. Audre Lorde, "Eye to Eye: Black Women, Hatred, and Anger," in *Sister Outsider* (Trumansburg, NY: Crossing Press, 1984), 171–72.

10. *The Fellowship Herald* (22 June 1911).

11. Ida B. Wells, *Crusade for Justice*, ed. Alfreda Duster (Chicago: University of Chicago Press, 1979), 403.

12. Ibid., 357.

13. Jeremiah 31:31–34 NRSV (New Revised Standard Version).

6

Using Power from the Periphery

An Alternative Theological Model
for Survival in Systems

Rosita deAnn Mathews

Biblical texts resound with paradoxes that may disrupt our preconceptions and cause us to reconsider a long-held position on an issue. The words of Jesus often provoke another look at our beliefs or assumptions on perplexing existential and theological concerns. Statements that Jesus may have uttered with ease can perplex us if we are attempting to inculcate his directives into our value system and personal ethic. Consider the paradoxical directives involved in telling his followers that in order to gain life they must lose it.[1] In order to be great we must be a servant.[2] The surface simplicity of Jesus' statements disguises the difficulty inherent in living this paradox.

Similar difficulties are raised in the passage where Jesus says that we are not to resist our enemies.[3] The Greek word *anthistemi*, meaning *do not resist*, suggests passivity. Traditionally, it has been preached that resisting enemies by turning the other cheek is an act of passive acceptance of whatever abuse may be directed at the receiver. Rather than responding to the attacks of the aggressor with violence, it was assumed that Jesus meant for us to passively accept the aggression directed toward us without resistance. By responding in this manner, we would exemplify a Christian posture. Far from alleviating the aggression or stopping the advance of evil, this interpretation of the passage promotes self-negation and a refusal to claim personal power in the face of an outside threat. Allowing oneself to be abused by a person or a system does not change the person or the system. Rather it gives the offender permission to continue such onslaughts.

There is another hermeneutic that raises an alternative approach to this passage, and more accurately captures the spirit of Jesus' intent. It also has implications for African-American women working in corporate, political, or ecclesiastical systems. Resisting evil can take on more shapes than merely one of violent resistance or passive submission. Walter Wink suggests that resistance also means utilizing actions toward the aggressor on terms other than those which the aggressor defines.[4] Resisting evil Jesus' way requires that the resister say no to the threat, yet remain true to her sense of ethics despite the repercussions, perceived or real. Resisting evil does not support the use of physical or emotional violence because that would perpetuate the evil itself in a wider framework by validating the attacker's methods. Instead, one resists evil by utilizing alternative action. The response is not one of passivity but of denying the aggressor the opportunity to define our method of resistance. Resisting evil still requires one to fight evil, but not on its terms. Do not use the weapons of the oppressor to counteract the oppressor's systems. Do not use evil to fight evil.

Within these guidelines, resisting evil may entail using power from the periphery. Power from the periphery means using one's power to resist a threat by maintaining or establishing ethical principles and moral standards, and refusing to employ the aggressor's methods. Instead, the person chooses to redefine her involvement with the threat by establishing alternative ground rules within a larger framework than the immediate aggression, and avoiding the use of practices utilized by those in power, even though it may jeopardize her own success. It is a refusal to respond in kind to aggression that violates basic human respect and decency.

The implications of using power from the periphery are particularly dangerous within the framework of corporate politics. Certain acceptable behaviors, which are normative within a corporate setting, may challenge a personal ethic of work and relationship. Correctly interpreting and applying this practice as informed by the Matthew passage can cause personal conflicts. Choosing to retain an ethical framework when others are playing "dirty politics" can clearly damage career advancement. The temptation is to play the same game by fighting fire with fire. Yet by acting within guidelines in which one refuses to respond to others in ways that are incongruent with Jesus' spirit, dignity may be maintained while resisting the aggressor in a manner that upholds us rather than destroys us. Power from the periphery employs a method that forces us to think through all of our actions within the framework Jesus suggested. Simply accepting the system within which we presently function becomes an unacceptable option. By choosing our form of resistance to those who may be aggressors toward us, we retain our dignity by resisting the efforts of those who wish to reinvent us in their image instead of God's.

The decision to use power from the periphery is not only supported by the New Testament directive of Jesus in Matthew, it can also be seen in the Old Testament account in 1 Samuel 24 and 26. In these passages Saul is pursuing David in order to kill him. But in a turnaround, David has an opportunity to kill Saul when Saul pauses in the same cave where David is hidden. Though David's supporters encourage him to kill Saul, David refuses to do so. He refuses to incur "bloodguilt" by killing the servant of the Lord.[5] The act of murder, no matter how justified on the grounds of self-defense, would have been contrary to this ethic. Not only does David allow Saul to live, he experiences remorse for having even considered taking his life.[6] He has refused to use any method of confrontation that is antithetical to his beliefs and values. For him, the end does not justify the means.

At times, our careers will take on such importance to us that we will be tempted to act in a shortsighted manner. The political realities of our vocations can cause us to transcend our moral sphere and cross the line into a gray area, if not into the darkness. If we choose to align ourselves with systems that debilitate others rather than to stay on the periphery and refuse to give away our souls, then we may find our hands also stained with bloodguilt.

Corporate, Political, and Ecclesiastical Systems

Succeeding in a corporate, political, or ecclesiastical system is a difficult task, particularly given the levels of discrimination inherent in them. This discrimination, which is a system's form of evil, is preserved through a corporate culture that often institutionalizes certain injustices by looking the other way or even encouraging them. For example, sexual harassment in the workplace, unless directly addressed, will multiply and harm many people. By refusing to harass others on the basis of gender, race, or cultural background, one is stepping outside of the system's method of functioning. In so doing, the critic is taking a prophetic stance that names the action for what it is and criticizes its existence.

Entering corporate or denominational environments and acquiescing to them without questioning their assumptions can do more harm than we realize. We may be jeopardizing our very souls. Evil is often housed in systems, be they corporate, denominational, or congregational. This evil is the type that dehumanizes the individual, perpetuates profits at any cost, reinforces unethical behavior as policy, and demands total allegiance.[7] We must step out of the grasp of the system and its demands of our allegiance. Unless we consider an alternative strategy, we may have to use the political framework authorized by the system, not letting it own our spirits, yet also exercising power wherever possible to change it.

In stepping outside of the center of power and operating from the periphery, one is setting limits as to the quality of interaction one will have with the system if it chooses to abuse its power against others. These limits can override the ethical temptations that inevitably will be encountered. When we do not use the oppressor's weapons, we momentarily interrupt the system and cause it to become unbalanced. Through the denial of its power over us, we find that we become more powerful. It is difficult to accept that power from the periphery is more powerful than the system's power. But those in the center of an abusive system become symbiotically tied to the system and dependent on its power for their life. Those on the periphery of the system gain strength from other places of power in order to exist. Feeding on the system will eventually prevent the person from being able to distinguish what is actually good from what is not. By remaining on the periphery, one is able to remain objective. It requires more stamina and wisdom to refuse the inducement to join in systemic evil, but by the very act of refusing temptations, strength is gained.

An illustration of the conflict between remaining separate or joining in with systemic corruption can be seen in this illustration. An assistant minister worked in a congregation where the pastor had acquired and maintained political power within the denomination, as a result of information he had obtained on the improprieties of his superior. The assistant minister, likewise, was privy to that same information and had to make the ethical choice of also utilizing this information for her advancement or ignoring it and acquiring political power based on her merits and relationships. Resisting evil in this situation meant refusing to use the information obtained, although within this system it was appropriate to do so. Using power from the periphery would move her from the inner circle position she had earned but put her in a more ethical place.

There are other reasons why she should refuse to use this information to her advantage. By resisting the temptation to abuse someone, she is creating a new spirit. She is interrupting acceptable practices based on the system's allowances and the systemic evil that pervades it. She is creating a new consciousness, even if it is at the expense of her career. Most importantly, by not acting as her pastor did, she is saving her soul from invasion, for when we compromise our morals and ethics, we mount the slippery slope that hands over our soul to something less than God.

There is not much support for choosing alternative methods of resistance to the injustices often perpetrated by systems. The proliferation of information written for women entering corporations includes books and articles that focus on working your way up the ladder, office politics, and how to "make it" in a corporate system. The advice is similar. Dress a certain way (conservatively, in suits), talk about certain things in conversations (like sports), and understand that the business world is like war (which is usually waged by men). If a woman follows simple rules such as these, she is assured success in business. Of course, it is also important to work hard and make the job your life. In other words, if women conduct business along these parameters, that is, if they only conform to the way things are, they can feel assured of being accepted and promoted and flourishing in the system.

A popular magazine geared to African-American women recently presented strategies for becoming a "corporate star."[8] "Being the best you can be," "realizing where the power is," "knowing the corporate culture," "making your boss look good" and "saying nice things about people" were listed as essentials for corporate success. The assumption is that if you follow these simple rules you can be successful in any corporation. What these books and articles do not allude to are the deeper issues of "making it" in a setting where not only the corporate culture but also hiring and promotion are controlled by white men. This makes it difficult for women and minorities to progress through systems.

Furthermore, these books did not explain the consequences of offering total allegiance and conformity to companies, particularly when the culture, that is, the values according to which the company operates, are not conducive to accepting anyone other than white males. "Getting ahead" requires a conformity to the values of a system and its priorities. bell hooks reinforces this in *Talking Back*:

> One of the clear and present dangers that exist when we move outside our class of origin, our collective ethnic experience, and enter hierarchical institutions which daily reinforce domination by race, sex and class, is that we gradually assume a mindset similar to those who dominate and oppress. We lose critical consciousness because it is not reinforced or affirmed by the environment.[9]

Why shouldn't the rules and priorities of a system be accepted? Why should we, African-American women, challenge the bureaucracy that has been in place long before our acceptance into the structures and systems that now dominate our country? Every system has not only a "culture" but its own persona, its own demons. Inculcated within it are certain barriers, temptations and evils, which militate against those within it as well. To survive and succeed in these systems, then, one has to ingest its behaviors and attributes—one has to become an appendage of it. Those who do not are called troublemakers because they do not support the inconsistencies and oppressiveness that it perpetuates. The danger of totally accepting the givens and practices of congregational polity, denominational polity, corporate systems, and the political system is that these systems require that we lose ourselves within them. They require that we perpetuate their agenda, abide by their rules and become a clean slate for the embracing of its values.

When African Americans were brought into this country, they immediately entered a system. That system was slavery. The atrocities were clear beginning with the middle passage across the waters. The sufferings inflicted by plantation owners were evil and not acceptable for any human being. African Americans were pawns in this system, only chattel to be used to further the economic exploitation of those in power. Despite the cruelties, African Americans survived. They retained their creativity, their survival spirit and their faith in God, even though they had to worship that God within a new framework.

Systems today may have changed in some respects but barriers remain. Today we are not chained by shackles and forced to work against our will. Instead, we are expected to inculcate the ideologies and cultures of systems that have denied cultural diversity and excluded the presence of women. No longer denied the right to education and employment, we are now denied access to the inner sanctums through the existence of glass ceilings, which limit our progress.

Fighting to acquire acceptance into these systems, we may forget that we must fight to survive from within the system as a player, just as we had to fight the system that treated us as a pawn. When we forget that imperative, we are in danger of losing ourselves and becoming, again, something to be exploited and discarded. There is a danger that now that we have gained entrance into the doors of corporate America, we may be duped into believing that we are actually a part of it and other systems, rather than realizing that, once again, we are being used to perpetrate practices, values, culture and systems of persons who do not work for our interests, or perhaps even work to our detriment. Unlike slavery, where the practices that abused us were clear, the injuries that we incur upon entering mainstream corporate America may not be as apparent. The hemorrhages we experience may be internal and have no visible physical manifestation. But just as a blood clot may not manifest itself visibly, if it reaches the heart or the brain, it is still deadly.

Survival Strategies

What are the strategies for surviving in these systems, given the evil that may be embedded in their practices? One obvious way is to change them. When one has amassed a certain level of power, rank and influence, one may be able to make certain changes that can partially counteract some of the oppressive nature of these environments. Clearly, African-American women have been able to do just that. Many women have entered managerial positions of power and influence and have been able to work changes that may have alleviated the evils of sexism and racism. I have had the opportunity to make changes in the system by hiring African-American women to work in systems that had previously been inaccessible.

But progression through the system threatens to make one a carrier of its practices. Due to the investment that must be made to reach a certain level, minorities can become just like the oppressor about whom they previously complained. Although power, the ability to effect a change, is something that is useful, it can also work to the detriment of the one seeking it. When it is attained, it may require that you become the same monster you fought by reproducing the oppression of the system.

I have seen women who, after serving as assistant pastors, have so emulated their male mentors as to have developed the same idiosyncracies and shortcomings. In order to attain their goals of ordination or placement, they have so patterned themselves after their pastors, that they took on the demons that they had been fighting and became a breeding ground for the same inadequacies.

Another option in confronting systems is to simply not enter them. Instead, one could stand apart from the system and live marginally to it. But marginality is a place of impotence and fear. Not entering systems, not speaking truth against power allows it to thrive unchallenged. It allows a system space and time to continue to grow and damage society and individuals who are fighting from within it. Marginality is also never safe, for one lives in fear that the power from the center will come to the margin to consume it.

A colleague recently confided that she finally realized that, although she had found favor with her supervisor who had made excessive demands on her time, whittled away her power, and caused her physical distress, she would nonetheless lose her standing if this supervisor left. She said that if he transferred to another agency, she would attempt to transfer with him. Rather than realizing that she was an expert in her field and quite capable, she felt her status was dependent on pleasing him. She had become dependent on his assessment because she had sold her soul for his approval. Her dependency had rendered her powerless and afraid.

I had to decide whether to enroll in a clinical chaplaincy program offered for seminary students training for vocations in hospital ministry. It was a difficult choice for the training is based on very subjective factors and is evaluated by supervisors. These supervisors are either white or male. There were no African-American women who had completed this training. Taking the training meant exposing myself emotionally and vocationally to white men and women and African-American men, few of whom could mirror my experience or affirm it. Yet choosing to omit this training, as did many African-American seminary students, would have been a great loss to my career and my personal growth. Involving myself in it marginally would have been impossible. I chose to take the training and was the target of much subtle racism and blatant disregard for my culture as an African American. On one occasion during a difficult job search, my white female supervisor stated that it would be easier for me to find a position after the white students had done so. I progressed through this training at great personal expense, and despite the system's insistence on not recognizing my efforts and contributions.

Another approach to dealing with systems is to work prophetically within the system. It is likely that a prophet in an institution will become the scapegoat that is driven out, just as those who were allegedly demon-possessed were driven away from the towns in biblical times. Prophets are seen as threats to the system. Their presence and voice state that the system is not acting ethically and responsibly to those within its responsibility and who are its constituents. Prophets become bacteria for which an inoculation must be found and utilized.

The presence of an outsider can be prophetic in itself. In my first semester preaching class, where I was the only woman, none of the white male students spoke to me for the entire semester. Near the end, one student turned to me and declared: "You aren't in this class to become a minister, are you?" Just my presence there had stirred his emotions.

Prophets also become a unifying target for the evil in the system. When an outsider attempts entry into a system, the players within it strategize to remove the new entrant. That is why it is so difficult for new members to be assimilated into congregations. This is also what happened to Jesus. His presence caused former enemies Herod and Pilate to ban together against him.[10]

How can African-American women work within systems? Should we avoid them? Should we embrace them and hope to change them? Should we accept their premises and assume they will work on our behalf? Should we develop eclectic skills and vacillate in our approaches? Jesus' ministry and interactions with the religious system of his day provides the basis for a paradigm by which to operate in institutional life. Jesus often encountered the established religious leaders of his day. As an itinerant preacher outside of the system's control, his popularity and power became dangerous to them. He became a threat. Within the framework of the system, he had to be eliminated. Yet he still persisted in his ministry. He neither ran from it or acquiesced to the demands of the religious leaders or their practices. Instead, Jesus exercised his power from the periphery. He limited his involvement in the religious structure of his day and took a peripheral posture to the establishment. He did not sell his soul or give his allegiance to them. He maintained his character and call within a larger framework, which was important for retaining his personal and professional integrity. That larger framework was to bring the freedom and responsibility of the kingdom of God. Jesus chose his methods intentionally. Limiting his power to and exercising his power from the periphery did not imply that he was powerless. Even his detractors, the scripture states, were aware of his authority. By remaining on the periphery of the system, he was able to utilize his power to change the system and not perpetuate it.

Should we work in these systems and accept their premises and practices as normative for us? If not, how can we work within them and not acquiesce to them? And if we choose to utilize peripheral power rather than playing the accepted power games, what consequences will result?

A Personal Example of Power from the Periphery

For over ten years I have worked in various corporate businesses and systems. In most of these, I have served as a chaplain in medical settings, which, by the nature of my vocation, has placed me on the edges of the setting. Although my power was limited because I was not a physician, I did not function peripherally to the system. I have had the task and obligation of functioning as a vital part of the medical team. Yet in the highly technocratic environment of a hospital, where science is the traditional framework within which health is based and evaluated, I have invented a strategy to address the requirements of my vocation as minister and to work within the system.

Rather than assigning a less important status to my function, I have exercised my pastoral authority in my work. I have attempted to provide a place for the divine-human encounter that can often happen when one is placed at the edge of health and, ultimately, of life. Within those moments, I journey with those who are asking questions about the deeper meanings of life and existence.

Using this pastoral authority has put me at odds with physicians whose call is to preserve life at all costs. They can find it difficult to inform the patient of consequences of surgery or medical treatment or even make patients clearly aware of their impending death. That is when I must step in from the periphery and use my authority and power intentionally.

I have had the added burden of also being the first African-American woman or African-American person in many of these settings, which also increased the difficulty inherent in the position. Not only would I enter a technocratic secular environment as a pastoral authority, I would enter the setting as a woman in a male environment and as an African American in a white environment. Of necessity, I had to develop a way to exercise my call within these oppressive environments.

I also had to sustain myself without many mentors. When I entered these environments, there were few women or persons of color in them to share strategies for surviving within these settings. Although all of the "how-to" books emphasize the importance of locating mentors, none of my mentors have been African-American women chaplains, because I was one of the first.

When I began seminary in the South in the mid-1970s, I was the only African-American woman studying for the ministry at my seminary. After graduation, I became the first African-American woman to work as a clinical resident in a chaplaincy program in New York City. Through this program, I worked at some of the leading hospitals in the world.

After finishing this residency program, I became the first African-American woman to fill a chaplaincy position in a hospital in the city of New York. Next I became the first African-American woman to work as a chaplain in a veteran's hospital in New York. After a few years in this position, I attained the position of director of pastoral services at a veterans' hospital. In so doing, I became the first African-American woman in the country to work in this position out of almost 200 hospitals. As a pioneer, I did not have the luxury of having a mentor to guide me through these systems.

Yet pioneering compelled me to do my own reflection and investigation as to how I would conduct business as I interacted with some of the most powerful professionals in their fields. Certainly, it was important to be skilled and knowledgeable in my field. Yet as a minority person, I encountered prejudices often, because this was the first time many other professionals had worked with people who were not white males. More importantly, when I entered a system that had not made a place for me as a minority, I questioned whether I perpetuated the system by following its written and unwritten values and culture. Was I in conspiracy with the system to oppress others by my actions or inactions?

My concern was to identify a protocol for working within a system without succumbing to its lies of omnipotence and without handing over my soul or self-esteem. This would entail utilizing my power in a way that did not enmesh me in the politics of a system and yet allowed me to function within it.

I was able to deal with this tension by exercising power from the periphery. Without selling my allegiance to a system that demanded total acceptance and without acting in ways I felt were unacceptable to my sense of business ethics, I was able to navigate around obstacles and find places to harbor. In so doing, I have attained the highest position in my field.

Exercising Power from the Periphery

How does one exercise power from the periphery? It is done by refusing to employ destructive tactics when one works from within a system. It is refusing to fight evil with evil. It is using one's position to further the greater good and speak truth on behalf of the individual. It is choosing to operate within an ethical framework and to nurture personal spirituality. It is choosing to do what is right or, at least, what is best. Using power from the periphery also means accepting the consequences of not doing politics according to the system's rules. If you play by your own rules, the paradigm that calls for a high level of living, then you must accept that the system will not usually reward you. Yet we have been asked to transform the world and not conform to it.[11]

African-American women have been the targets of unjust systems, from slavery to higher education. If we accept the operative principles of these organizations without evaluation, we become part of the oppression. We cannot wrestle with the demons and exorcise them if we are also supporting them. However, if we avoid corporations and other institutions, we allow their reign to continue unchallenged. On the other hand, if we choose to use our power from the periphery, utilizing our own "weapons," we can make a difference in the system.

We can exorcise systems and their demons only through practicing integrity. That is the weapon that annihilates. Integrity, competence, and truth, as ineffective as they may seem, establish a foundation upon which evil cannot stand. Integrity builds structures that become impervious to demonic penetration. The refusal to retaliate in kind causes disarray to the forces that attempt to control through infighting. Power from the periphery does not encourage passivity. It is not for the timid. The timid acquiesce and embrace the system. It is a method of responding in a stronger fashion to the onslaughts of the dehumanizing nature of institutions and systems. It is a way to stand. It is a way to speak to its demons as we utilize a personal power and practice that calls the assumptions into question and refuses to accept its generalizations.

To do this successfully, we must realistically assess our need for power, promotion, and acceptance. We must redefine success and not let the system define it for us. The system recognizes our need for approval and will reward us if we accept its teaching, that the only success worthy enough is the success the system awards. When we exercise our power from the periphery, we demonstrate that we have a higher sense of success and we transcend its limitations and constrictions. By exercising power from the periphery, we maintain our soul.

It is the responsibility of those on the periphery to accept that, from this position, the person on the periphery becomes the prophet. Very often this prophet will then find others who are not paying total allegiance to the whims and demands of the system's culture, but who, by necessity, perhaps still remain a part of it. It is then the task of the prophet, the person who has said "no" to the temptation to abuse power, to create new alternatives and provide a method of hope within the system. The prophet does not just criticize but also creates within and energizes the system where possible.[12]

Guidelines for Working with Systems

Designing a protocol for action is not difficult when the principles are finally established. The following is my personal credo for working with systems:

- My actions within a system will be guided by my integrity and not by personal or professional expediency.

As African-American women, we must realize that when we engage in unethical or questionable practices, we become another channel for evil. Ultimately, we discover that evil's rewards do not gratify us. Gains won through practices as this are not as sweet as we would think, because they demand something of us as well. We become a host to the evil rather than a channel through which it can be eliminated. Despite the losses or the costs, we must give careful consideration to the way we will proceed in any environment.

Although at times the decision to act ethically may be made at the loss of professional acceptance or advancement, I can often justify my choice based on objectively viewing the persona of the person who is creating the dilemma. Do I really want to attain advancement in an organization that would allow the promotion of such people who commit these acts?

- I will not compromise my dignity for any achievement, advancement or recognition.

A male friend advised a mutual female friend (both African-American) that in the first year of her new position, she should do whatever she is told to do. If she does, the system will reward her. The reality is that if the system does reward her (which is unlikely, since she is neither male or white), it will demand that she relinquish so much of herself so as to lose her identity, culture, and self-esteem.

A colleague discussed with me the dilemma of applying for a vacant staff position in her congregation. She was sure that climbing farther up the ecclesiastical ladder would also require her to "politic" and operate on a level that was unacceptable to her and devastating to her spiritual health and professional ministry. Although accepting a position farther into the bureaucracy of the institution may have provided an opportunity to influence it, she was also aware that the system would have its own impact on her and could exact a heavier toll. She reasoned that she could have a much more effective impact on the system by retaining a position of lesser privilege and authority, while exercising her power from a position of integrity and dignity.

The issue of retaining one's dignity is an important one. As the only African-American female student at a northern seminary in its doctor of ministry program, I proposed to my colleagues during a presentation that womanist theology is a valid approach. Colleagues who had been very supportive of me and my work suddenly became antagonistic because they saw my exploration as a challenge to their system. I was ostracized by them for the remainder of the term. A Black professor there even attempted to deny my contribution and deter my endeavor by calling me "a bitch" in front of my colleagues. When I asked him why he would use a term like that, he replied that I reminded him of his wife whom he also thought of in that manner. Despite his assessment of my work and the consequences, I refused to take a subservient stance in the seminars. I would not let this professor take my dignity at any cost.

- I will respond to my need for community and my responsibility to it.

As a repeated "pioneer" in several places of employment, one of the most dangerous aspects of entering communities and systems that are homogeneous and segregated is the absence of other minorities. Even when other minorities are present, there can be a reticence to gather together for support. While African Americans in slavery bonded together by singing and worshiping together, some contemporary African Americans tend to discount the importance and necessity of this activity. Consequently, one of the dangers of being a pioneer in a system is that of succumbing to the isolation that often results. Aware of the importance of community, I organized an African-American women's group that has flourished for two years. In time it will develop into a more issue-oriented group, but presently fulfills its purpose of providing a place for these women to "see" each other regularly. All of them are from communities where something as simple as meeting together as African-American women is a rarity.

- I will maintain my commitment, despite forces which try to deter me.

A colleague who was the pastor of a congregational parish spoke at length about a congregant who was disruptive in her parish. She even thought this congregant was demonic. The congregant would sway the power of the ruling board through intimidation and coercion. Consequently, the parish did not grow and was facing a sure and imminent death. Rather than use the same politics the congregant used, the pastor used her power in a different manner. She first showed the congregation that she would not be owned by this parishioner. She did not allow the parishioner the power over her spirit. Instead, the pastor began to work around the congregant by speaking with members about broader topics, such as congregational life and authority. In so doing, she empowered them to use their authority and gifts as congregational leaders rather than engaging in a frontal battle alone with the divisive congregant.

It is difficult for some women to stand in these situations, particularly because they have been socialized to get along at all costs. One way I chose to counteract this learned acquiescence was by studying karate for several years, entering tournaments, and earning high ranks. In one tournament I had to spar against three African-American men, whom I beat. In becoming proficient in this sport, I was more able to hold my ground in my professional and personal life as well.

- I will not compromise my pastoral authority or Christian commitment in any system.

By using power from the periphery and maintaining my integrity, I have been able to also utilize my pastoral authority and the power that comes from living ethically. By choosing not to accept the values of system politics, I have the option of developing standards and principles that are more conducive to my framework. By being clear about my purpose and goals, I can more easily accept the consequences of my choices. Those consequences may at times limit my advancement or acceptance. It has been my experience that by being clear about my position, I have become more respected within the system and seen by some as less of a threat. I have learned to live with not being swept up in the surge of political gameship and have set about doing the work of the Creator as a healer, particularly for those whom the system has injured or abandoned.

Conclusion

The choices I have made to use power from the periphery and resist the temptation to abuse power has resulted in successes in my professional career and ministry as well as in my personal life. I still have my sanity, despite the system's determined efforts to destroy it. And I have pride in knowing that I have exhibited integrity at many crucial junctures. Attempting to live by a set of moral guidelines can ultimately grant some success.

To avoid the temptation to accept the dogmas of unjust systems, African-American women must approach all institutions with suspicion and investigation. Although the system affirms us by allowing us entry, that does not mean it is acting responsibly in its action.

Black women live out a moral wisdom in their real-lived context that does not appeal to the fixed rules or absolute principles of the white oriented, male-structured society. Black women's analysis and appraisal of what is right or wrong and good or bad develops out of various coping mechanisms related to the conditions of their own cultural circumstances.[13]

Womanist theology affirms this position of power from the periphery by encouraging the necessity of retaining one's sense of dignity despite the system's advances and demands. Certainly whenever or wherever possible, African-American women should utilize power from the center to make change. When that cannot happen, power from the periphery will at least allow us to maintain our sanity, culture, and vision despite the onslaughts. By acting ethically and with integrity, we will survive. We must, therefore, approach all systems with suspicion and distrust and then evaluate the role we can have in affecting the system. Finally, we must choose a place within it where we can maintain ourselves and not sell our souls for acceptance into the tenuous security of a system or a promotion. It is never worth losing your soul to gain the world.

Throughout my life, my grandmother told her grandchildren a story. As a teenager in South Carolina in the early 1900s, she worked in the home of a white family as a domestic. The wife had a habit of dropping money on the floor to see if my grandmother would take it. Her action was consistent. She would always leave the money on a nearby table or return it to the wife. She never considered keeping it for herself.

More than a story about honesty, I now view my grandmother's actions as using power from the periphery. Although she was no doubt underpaid for her services, she refused to capitalize on these opportunities by violating her sense of morals and ethics. She refused to adjust her values as a response to any injustice she may have experienced. She refused to capitulate her beliefs.

My mother, too, retained her values and ethics while also paving the way in her career. Being a pioneer in her occupation, she also was enmeshed in the difficulties of retaining her personhood and Christian commitment, yet succeeded in remaining a person of integrity throughout her life.

As our numbers increase, perhaps we can move to the center of systems and purge them of their sinfulness, their despair. That can happen if we do not repeat the same errors that others have committed when confronted by the lies that evil perpetuates and the idolatry it demands. More wisely, we should create new systems based on alternative interactions and power sharing, always being aware of the need to have fresh winds blowing through any system, or deal with the very real possibility that the evils of the system will again rear their ugly heads. It always takes courage to stand within the system, even from its edges. That is the courage that is found within the African-American women's experiences. It is the courage that we need for the future.

NOTES

1. Mark 8:35 NRSV (New Revised Standard Version). All scriptural references are from the NRSV.

2. Matthew 20:26.

3. Matthew 5:39.

4. Walter Wink, "On Not Becoming What You Hate," *Sojourner* (November 1989), 22–24.

5. Walter Brueggeman, *Power, Providence and Personality* (Louisville: Westminster/John Knox Press, 1990), 53–57.

6. 1 Samuel 24:5.

7. Wink, *Unmasking the Powers: The Invisible Forces that Determine Human Existence* (Philadelphia: Fortress Press, 1986), 78–82.

8. Charles N. Jamison, Jr., "So You Want to be a Corporate Star," *Essence* 21 (March 1991).

9. bell hooks, *Talking Back* (Boston: South End Press, 1989), 78.

10. Luke 23:12.

11. Romans 12:1.

12. Brueggemann, *The Prophetic Imagination* (Philadelphia: Fortress Press, 1978), chap. 3.

13. Katie Cannon, *Black Womanist Ethics* (Atlanta: Scholars Press, 1984), 4.

PART III

LOVE'S THE SPIRIT

7

"Wading through Many Sorrows"

Toward a Theology of Suffering
in Womanist Perspective

M. Shawn Copeland

Suffering is universal, an inescapable fact of the human condition; it defies immunities of all kinds.[1] Suffering despoils women and men irrespective of race or tongue, wealth or poverty, learning or virtue; disregards merit or demerit, reward or punishment, honor or corruption. Like sun and rain, suffering comes unbidden to the just and the unjust alike.

Suffering always means pain, disruption, separation, and incompleteness. It can render us powerless and mute, push us to the borders of hopelessness and despair. Suffering can maim, wither, and cripple the heart; or, to quote Howard Thurman, it can be a "spear of frustration transformed into a shaft of light."[2] From some women and men, suffering coaxes real freedom and growth, so much so that Thurman insists we literally see the change: "Into their faces come a subtle radiance and a settled serenity; into their relationships a vital generosity that opens the sealed doors of the heart in all who are encountered along the way."[3] From other women and men, suffering extracts a bitter venom. From still others, suffering squeezes a delicious ironic spirit and tough laughter. Consider the Gullah [woman's] proverb: "Ah done been in sorrow's kitchen and ah licked de pots clean."[4]

As a working definition, I understand suffering as the disturbance of our inner tranquillity caused by physical, mental, emotional, and spiritual forces that we grasp as jeopardizing our lives, our very existence. Evil is the negation and deprivation of good; suffering, while never identical with evil, is inseparable from it. Thus, and quite paradoxically, the suffering caused by evil can result in interior development and perfection as well as in social and cultural good. African Americans have encountered monstrous evil in chattel slavery and its legacy of virulent institutionalized racism and have been subjected to unspeakable physical, psychological, social, moral, and religious affliction and suffering. Yet, from the anguish of our people rose distinctive religious expression, exquisite music and song, powerful rhetoric and literature, practical invention and creative art. If slavery was the greatest evil, freedom was the greatest good and women and men struggled, suffered, sacrificed, and endured much to attain it.

This essay is a theological meditation on "the maldistribution, negative quality, enormity, and transgenerational character" of the suffering of Black women.[5] Such particularizing of suffering requires neither qualification nor apology. However, there can be no ranking of oppression or suffering; no men or women are excluded from the canon of anguish. Indeed, the historic suffering of the Jewish people and the oppression of the hundreds of thousands of indigenous peoples of the lands of the Americas weigh heavily in any discussion of ethnic suffering.[6] Further, the specificity of this essay neither discounts the humiliating racism Black men suffer, nor does it undermine the grievous sexism women of all races and cultures endure. Rather, I hope that the reader shall situate this particularizing of suffering within the ongoing Christian theological effort to respond to the human condition in new and graced ways.

The focus of this three-part essay is not the formal, self-conscious and bold contemporary articulation of womanist theology for an authentic new world order, but rather its roots in the rich historic soil of Black women's experiences of suffering and affliction during the centuries of chattel slavery. In the first section of the essay, enslaved or fugitive Black women speak for themselves.[7] Scholars estimate that Black women wrote about 12 percent of the total number of extant slave narratives, although none of these is as well known as the narratives by fugitive and emancipated men.[8] Mary Helen Washington observes that male slave narrators often render Black women invisible or relegate them to subordinate roles. When Black women are referenced in men's narratives, they are depicted as "the pitiable subjects of brutal treatment, or benign nurturers who help the fugitive in his quest for freedom, or objects of sentimentality."[9] Black women slave narrators offer a stiff antidote to the (hegemonic) cultural stereotypes that Black men seem to have imbibed. As Hazel Carby points out, when these women relate and interpret their experiences on their own terms, they disclose a very different sense of themselves:

> In the slave narratives written by black women the authors placed in the foreground their active roles as historical agents as opposed to passive subjects; represented as acting their own visions, they are seen to take decisions over their own lives. They document their sufferings and brutal treatment but in a context that is also the story of the resistance of that brutality.[10]

Only by attending to Black women's feelings and experiences, understanding and reflection, judgment and evaluation about their situation, can we adequately challenge the stereotypes about Black women – especially those stereotypes that coalesce around that "most popular social convention of female sexuality, the 'cult of true womanhood'."[11]

The centerpiece of this first section is the story of emancipated fugitive slave Harriet Jacobs [Linda Brent], *Incidents in the Life of a Slave Girl*.[12] Jacobs' controversial narrative is quite likely, "the only slave narrative that takes as its subject the sexual exploitation of female slaves – thus centering on sexual oppression as well as on oppression of race and condition."[13] Here, we apprehend not only the intersection of gender and race and class, but a most excruciating form of the suffering of enslaved Black women.

Womanist theology claims the experiences of Black women as proper and serious data for theological reflection. Its aim is to elucidate the differentiated range and interconnections of Black women's gender, racial-ethnic, cultural, religious, and social (i.e., political, economic, and technological) oppression.[14] Hence, a womanist theology of suffering is rooted in and draws on Black women's accounts of pain and anguish, of their individual and collective struggle to grasp and manage, rather than be managed by their suffering. Drawing from these narratives, the second section discusses those resources that support Black women's resistance to evil and the third section sketches the basic elements of a theology of suffering from womanist perspective.

Black Women's Experiences of Suffering

Composite narratives and interviews with emancipated men and women, as well as their children and grandchildren, have given us a picture of daily plantation life.[15] These include chronicles of the horrors and anguish they endured under chattel slavery: the auction block with its rupture of familial bonds, the brutalization of human feeling, savage beatings and mutilation, petty cruelty, and chronic deprivation of human physical and psychological needs. But accounts of the rape and sexual abuse of enslaved Black women are told reluctantly, if at all. James Curry, after his escape, recounting some of the "extreme cruel[ties] practised upon [some] plantations" around Person County, North Carolina, asserted "that there is no sin which man [sic] can commit, that those slaveholders are not guilty of." And Curry lamented, "It is not proper to be written; but the treatment of females in slavery is dreadful."[16] Still, some men and women dared to write and speak about that dreadful treatment – the coarse and vulgar seduction, rape, abuse, and concubinage of Black women under chattel slavery.

Lizzie Williams, who had been held on a plantation near Selma, Alabama, relayed the fear and resignation that overtook so many Black women. "Many de poor nigger women have chillen for de massa, dat is if de massa mean man. Dey just tell de niggers what to do and dey know better dan to

fuss."[17] The following reports are bitter reinforcements:
One former slave repeated this story:

> Ma mama said that a nigger 'oman couldn't help herself, fo' she had
> to do what de marster say. Ef he come to de field whar de women
> workin' an tell gal to come on, she had to go. He would take one
> down in de woods an' use her all de time he wanted to, den send her
> on back to work.[18]

And another former slave told this plaintive account:

> My sister was given away when she was a girl. She told me and ma
> that they'd make her go out and lay on a table and two or three white
> men would have sex with her before they'd let her up. She was just a
> small girl. She died when she was still in her young days, still a girl.[19]

Fourteen-year-old Louisa Picquet escaped from the sexual advances of
one slave owner, only to be sold to another with similar intentions. Years
later in an interview, the emancipated Picquet recalled:

> Mr. Williams told me what he bought me for, soon as we started for
> New Orleans. He said he was getting old, and when he saw me he
> thought he'd buy me and end his days with me. He said if I behave
> myself he'd treat me well: but, if not, he'd whip me almost to death.[20]

Compelled to serve as Williams' housekeeper, caretaker for his sons from
a former marriage, and his mistress, Picquet also bears four children by
Williams. When the interviewer questions her about her life with Williams,
Picquet reveals her innermost anguish: "I thought, now I shall be committin' adultery, and there's no chance for me, and I'll have to die and be lost.
Then I had this trouble with him and my soul the whole time."[21] Picquet
tells her interviewer that she had broached these concerns with Williams
often. But his response, she says, was to curse and to argue that her life
with him was not an impediment to her religious conversion. Picquet continues:

> But I knew better than that. I thought it was of no use to be prayin',
> and livin' in sin. . . . I begin then to pray that he might die, so that I
> might get religion; and then I promise the Lord one night, faithful,
> in prayer, if he would just take him out of the way, I'd get religion
> and be true to Him as long as I lived.[22]

Sometime later, Williams became ill and died.
In what is most likely the first female slave narrative from the Americas,

Mary Prince describes her anger at a slaveholder's lewd intentions and her own efforts at personal modesty:

[Mr. D----] had an ugly fashion of stripping himself quite naked, and ordering me then to wash him in the tub of water. This was worse to me than all the [beatings]. Sometimes when he called me to wash him I would not come, my eyes were so full of shame. He would then come to beat me. One time I had plates and knives in my hand, and I dropped both plates and knives, and some of the plates broke.[23]

Mr. D---- struck her and Mary Prince declares, "at last I defended myself, for I thought it was high time to do so. I then told him I would not live longer with him, for he was a very indecent man—very spiteful, and too indecent; with no shame for his servants, no shame for his own flesh."[24] With that, she walked out and went to a neighboring house. And although Mary Prince is compelled to return the next morning, the slaveholder hires her out to work. Her daring gains her some small measure of relief.

Under the pseudonym Linda Brent, Harriet Jacobs gives us a detailed presentation of the psychological and sexual torment to which she was subjected. Like other fugitive female narrators, Jacobs writes her story neither "to attract attention" to herself, nor "to excite sympathy for [her] own sufferings." Rather, she seeks "to arouse the women of the North to a realizing sense of the condition of millions of women in the South, still in bondage, suffering what I suffered, and most of them far worse."[25]

Born in 1818 to an enslaved mulatto couple, Jacobs describes a childhood in which she and her brother were "fondly shielded" from the harsh reality of their condition. Neither dreamt that they were like "merchandise, [only] trusted to [their parents] for safe keeping, and liable to be demanded of them at any moment."[26] Jacobs' father's reputation and skill as a carpenter earned him unusual privileges and a substantial income, a portion of which he paid annually to the woman who owned him. Allowed to manage his own affairs, her father provided a relatively comfortable home and living for his wife and two children. "His strongest wish," Brent writes "was to purchase his children; but, though he several times offered his hard earnings for that purpose, he never succeeded."[27] The little girl's happiness is marred irrevocably by the death, first of her mother, then that of the female slaveholder, who was also her mother's foster sister. Family and friends had expected the woman to emancipate the children; after all, their mother and grandmother had been trusted family servants and she had promised Jacobs' dying mother that "her children should never suffer for any thing." Yet, the slaveholder's will bequeathed Linda to a five-year-old niece. Looking back more than thirty years, Jacobs wrote mournfully and sagely that "the memory of a faithful slave does not avail much to save her children from the auction block."[28] It is this broken promise that consigns twelve-year-old Linda and her ten-year-old brother William to the household of Dr. and Mrs. Flint.

At fifteen with the onset of her puberty, like Louisa Picquet and Mary Prince, Harriet Jacobs' Linda Brent is confronted by the persistent, unwelcome lewd advances by the male head of the household.

> I now entered my fifteenth year—a sad epoch in the life of a slave girl. [Dr. Flint] began to whisper foul words in my ear. Young as I was, I could not remain ignorant of their import. I tried to treat them with indifference or contempt. . . . He tried his utmost to corrupt the pure principles my grandmother had instilled. He peopled my young mind with unclean images, such as only a vile monster could think of. I turned from him with disgust and hatred. But he was my master. I was compelled to live under the same roof with him—where I saw a man forty years my senior daily violating the most sacred commandments of nature. He told me I was his property; that I must be subject to his will in all things. My soul revolted against the mean tyranny. But where could I turn for protection? No matter whether the slave girl be as black as ebony or as fair as her mistress. In either case, there is no shadow of law to protect her from insult, from violence, or even from death; all these are inflicted by fiends who bear the shape of men. The mistress, who ought to protect the helpless victim, has no other feelings toward her but those of jealousy and rage.[29]

Flint sought not only to satiate his lust, but to wreak his twisted will-to-power, to conquer Linda Brent's body and defile her spirit.

> My master met me at every turn, reminding me that I belonged to him, and swearing by heaven and earth that he would compel me to submit to him. If I went out for a breath of fresh air, after a day of unwearied toil, his footsteps dogged me. If I knelt by my mother's grave, his dark shadow fell on me even there.
>
> When I succeeded in avoiding opportunities for him to talk to me at home, I was ordered to come to his office, to do some errand. When there, I was obliged to stand and listen to such language as he saw fit to address to me.[30]

Brent's revulsion and repulsion are unshakable, even as the physician is consumed by a life of revenge. Flint refuses to sell Brent to the freeborn colored man who wishes to marry her. Flint's insults, taunting, and physical abuse force Brent to break off her engagement.

> [The doctor] had an iron will and was determined to keep me, and to conquer me. My lover was an intelligent and religious man. Even if he could have obtained permission to marry me while I was a slave,

the marriage would give him no power to protect me from my master. It would have made him miserable to witness the insults I should have been subjected to. And then, if we had children, I knew they must "follow the condition of the mother." What a terrible blight that would be on the heart of a free, intelligent father! For his sake, I felt that I ought not to link his fate with my own unhappy destiny.[31]

Flint has a small house built in a secluded place, a few miles outside of town — away from his wife and home. He intends to keep Brent as his mistress; but she vows "never [to] enter it." Brent writes, "I had rather toil on the plantation from dawn till dark; I had rather live and die in jail, than drag on, from day to day, through such a living death."[32] Emotionally distraught, feeling "forsaken by God and man [sic]," Brent acquiesces emotionally and sexually to the sympathy, romantic overtures, and eloquence of the white unmarried gentleman, Mr. Sands.[33]

So much attention from a superior person was, of course, flattering; for human nature is the same in all . . . It seemed to me a great thing to have such a friend. By degrees, a more tender feeling crept into my heart . . . Of course, I saw whither all this was tending. I knew the impassable gulf between us; but to be an object of interest to a man who is not married, and who is not her master, is agreeable to the pride and feelings of a slave, if her miserable situation has left her any pride or sentiment. It seems less degrading to give one's self, than to submit to compulsion.[34]

Brent describes her decision as "a headlong plunge into the abyss," and admits a mixture of motives: "Revenge and calculations of interest were added to flattered vanity and sincere gratitude for kindness. . . . [A]nd it was something to triumph over my tyrant even in that small way."[35] Jacobs' Brent is convinced that the physician will be so outraged at her sexual and emotional choice of Sands that he will sell her. She is just as convinced that Sands will buy her and that she easily can obtain her freedom from him. When Flint orders Brent to move into the completed cottage, she adamantly and triumphantly refuses.

I told him I would never enter it. He said, "I have heard enough of such talk as that. You shall go, if you are carried by force; and you shall remain there."

I replied, "I will never go there. In a few months I shall be a mother."

He stood and looked at me in dumb amazement, and left the house without a word. I thought I should be happy in my triumph over him. But now that the truth was out, and my relatives would hear of it, I felt wretched. Humble as were their circumstances, they had pride in my good character. Now, how could I look them in the face? My self-respect was gone! I had resolved that I would be virtuous, though I was a slave. I had said, "Let the storm beat! I will brave it till I die." And now how humiliated I felt.[36]

Brent used her body, her sex, to gain some measure of psychological freedom from Flint. Although she wounds her grandmother in this process, she is never completely alienated from this good woman, even when she bears her second child by Sands. When Brent hears that her newborn is a girl, she is pained. "Slavery is terrible for men; but it is far more terrible for women. Superadded to the burden common to all, *they* have wrongs, and sufferings, and mortifications peculiarly their own."[37]

Flint is relentless; Brent takes the only and hazardous course open to her. She runs away, resolving "that come what would, there should be no turning back," staking her future on liberty or death. Concealed, first by a friend, then by the wife of a prominent slaveholder, Brent eludes meticulous search for some weeks. Then, following a carefully devised plan involving Brent disguising herself as a sailor, hiding for a few days in a swamp, and darkening her face with charcoal, friends and relatives hide Brent beneath the sloping crawl space of her grandmother's house. For nearly seven years, Linda Brent lived undetected in this garret — nine feet long, seven feet wide, three feet high, accessible only through a carefully constructed and hidden trapdoor that led to a storeroom. Deprived of light and air, with no space to stand or move about, Brent is assailed by insects and heat in the summer and frostbite in winter. But she insists, she was not without comfort: brief conversations with her relatives, the discovery of a small gimlet that she uses to bore three small holes to increase light and air, and the voices — and most importantly the purchased freedom — of her son and daughter. Only her grandmother, aunt, uncle, brother, and a trusted friend knew her whereabouts. During those nearly seven years, Flint threatened and harassed her family and traveled three times to New York to search for Linda Brent who was "practically in his own back yard."[38]

Huddled in her cramped garret, observing the street through a tiny hole in the boards, Brent is an invisible, yet recording witness to the pathos of the world the slaveholders made. One day she notices an enslaved woman passing her grandmother's gate weeping and muttering to herself. This woman, Brent's goodly grandmother tells her later, had been turned out by the mistress of the house and forbidden to return. The wife of the slaveholder had seen the slave woman's baby for the first time, "and in the lineaments of its fair face she saw a likeness to her husband." The very next day this nineteenth-century Hagar and her child were sold to a Georgia trader. On another occasion, Brent sees another enslaved woman "rush wildly by, pursued by two men" and records her affliction. The "wet nurse of her mistress's children," the woman had committed some offense and subsequently was "ordered to be stripped and whipped. To escape the degradation and the torture, she rushed to the river, jumped in, and ended her wrongs in death."[39] Such treatment is corroborated by both Mary Prince and Mattie Jackson. Prince relays her own experience: "To strip me naked — to hang me up by the wrists and lay my flesh open with the cow-skin, was an ordinary punishment for even a slight offence."[40] And Mattie Jackson tells of the similar brutish behavior of slaveholder Benjamin Lewis: "He used to extend his victim, fastened to a beam, with hands and feet tied, and inflict from fifty to three hundred lashes, laying their flesh entirely open, then bathe their quivering wounds in brine."[41]

Mary Prince remembers the brutal death of Hetty, an enslaved woman who was especially kind to her in her youth. She and the other slaves of this plantation believe that Hetty's premature death was caused by a beating she received during her pregnancy.

One of the cows had dragged the rope away from the stake to which Hetty had fastened it, and got loose. My master flew into a terrible passion, and ordered the poor creature to be stripped quite naked, notwithstanding her pregnancy, and to be tied up to a tree in the yard. He then flogged her as hard as he could lick, both with the whip and the cow-skin, till she was all over streaming with blood. He rested, and then beat her again and again. Her shrieks were terrible. Poor Hetty was brought to bed before her time, and was delivered after severe labour of a dead child. She appeared to recover after her confinement, so far that she was repeatedly flogged by both master and mistress afterward; but her former strength never returned to her. Ere long her body and limbs swelled to a great size; and she lay on a mat in the kitchen, till the water burst out of her body and she died. All the slaves said that death was a good thing for poor Hetty; but I cried very much for her death. The manner of it filled me with horror. I could not bear to think about it; yet it was always present to my mind for many a day.[42]

Prince is forced to take over many of Hetty's duties, including the care of the cows. Once again, a cow slips its tether. The cow wanders into a garden, and eats some sweet-potato slips; Prince is blamed. Capt. I-----, the slave master, finds Prince milking a cow. He takes off his boot and strikes her with it in the small of the back. The frightened cow kicks over the pan, spilling the milk. The accident is the slaveholder's fault, but it fuels his rage at Prince and he beats her. "I cannot remember how many licks he gave me then, but he beat me until I was unable to stand, and till he himself was weary." Prince runs away to her mother who is held on a nearby farm. Her mother, Prince tells us, "was both grieved and glad" to see her: "grieved because [Prince] had been so ill used, and glad because she had not seen [her daughter] for a long, long, while." Prince's mother hid her in a hole in nearby rocks and brought her food late each evening. But her father takes her back to the slaveholder. Not surprisingly, Prince is fearful of return. When they arrive, her father entreats Capt. I----- "to be a kind master" to his daughter in the future. But Prince speaks up boldly:

> I then took courage and said that I could stand the floggings no longer; that I was weary of my life, and therefore I had run away to my mother; but mothers could only weep and mourn over their children, they could not save them from cruel masters – from whip, the rope, and the cow-skin. [Capt. I-----] told me to hold my tongue and go about my work, or he would find a way to settle me. He did not, however, flog me that day.[43]

For five years Prince remained a slave in this household, flogged and mistreated almost daily, until she was sold and shipped away from her parents and siblings.

Harriet Jacobs, Mary Prince, Louisa Picquet, Mattie Jackson and all the many thousand women gone were caught in the vicious nexus spawned in chattel slavery – full and arrogant self-assertion of white male power and privilege, white female ambivalence and hatred, the subjugation of Black women and men. These and so many other women were caught, but not trapped. To be sure, these are narratives of staggering affliction – human lives are seized, uprooted, and attacked directly and indirectly, in psychological, intellectual, cultural, social, physical dimensions.[44] Clearly these narratives expose maldistributed suffering, for Black women endured torments precisely because they were Black women and all Black women – enslaved or free – were potential victims. Neither is the suffering disclosed here pedagogically motivated, nor is it some form of spiritually beneficial asceticism. And since such suffering was meant to break, not temper, the spirit, it is of negative quality. Not infrequently, the beatings and abuse these women withstood ended in death. And, finally, their suffering extended for more than three hundred years, striking mother, daughter, granddaughter, great-granddaughter, great-great-granddaughter. Again: These are narratives of affliction, but not narratives of despair; the women may be caught, but they are not trapped. These Black women wade through their sorrows, managing their suffering, rather than being managed by it. In the next section, we turn to look at their resistance, a characteristic feature of their suffering and struggle and potent element in a theology of suffering in womanist perspective.

Resources of Womanist Resistance

Almost from its emergence, Christianity has been described as the religion of slaves.[45] Space does not allow me to elaborate here the nature and character of the psychic moments, spiritual experiences, preaching and teaching, rituals of passage and praise, spirituals and shouts and dance, visions and vocations that signify the distinctive Afric appropriation, if not reception, of biblical revelation by the enslaved Africans in the Americas. From their aural appropriation of the Bible and critical reflection on their own condition, these men and women shaped and "fitted" Christian practices, rituals, and values to their own particular experiences, religio-cultural expectations, and personal needs.[46] The slave community formed a distinctive image of itself and fashioned "an inner world, a scale of values and fixed points of vantage from which to judge the world around them and themselves."[47]

Christian religion was a fundamental resource for womanist resistance. Many women drank from its well, yet selectively so. Harriet Jacobs was critical of religious hypocrisy speaking of the "great difference between Christianity and the religion of the south."[48] Slaveholders who beat, tortured, and sexually harassed slaves prided themselves on church membership. The planter class held one set of morals for white women, another for white men, and assumed that enslaved women and men had little, if any, capacity for real moral experience, moral agency, and moral virtue. All too often, Christian preaching, teaching, and practice complied. Black women's narratives counter these assumptions and stereotypes as well as discern and embrace a religious standard that exposes the moral hypocrisy of the planter class. Moreover, these women are living witnesses to the power of divine grace, not merely to sustain men and women through such evil, but to enable them to turn victimization into Christian triumph.[49] Jacobs records the lines of this old slave hymn that sings the distinction between a pure or true Christianity and that poisoned by slavery: "Ole Satan's church is here below/Up to God's free church I hope to go."

The attitude of the master class toward worship by slaves was not uniform. On some plantations slaves held independent, and sometimes, unsupervised services of worship; on other plantations, they attended white churches, sitting or standing in designated areas; on still others, they were forbidden to worship at all and they were punished if found praying and singing. Yet the people persisted. Christian biblical revelation held out formidable power. It offered the slaves the "dangerous" message of freedom, for indeed, Jesus did come to bring "freedom for the captive and release for those held in economic, social, and political bondage."[50] It offered them the great and parallel event of Exodus, for indeed, it was for a people's freedom that the Lord God chose, called, and sent Moses. Christian biblical revelation provided the slaves with material for the singular mediation of their pain. The spirituals, "forged of sorrow in the heat of religious fervor,"[51] were an important resource of resistance. In and through these moaned or sung utterances, one woman's, one man's suffering or shout of jubilation became that of a people. The spirituals reshaped and conflated the characters and stories, parables and pericopes, events and miracles of the Hebrew and Christian scriptures. These songs told the mercy of God anew and testified to the ways in which the enslaved people met God at the whipping post, on the auction block, in the hush arbor, in the midnight flight to freedom. The maker of the spiritual sang: "God dat lived in Moses' time/Is jus' de same today." The spirituals served as coded messages, signaling the arrival of Moses in the person of Harriet Tubman or other ex-slaves who went back into Egypt to "tell ole Pharaoh, Let My People Go." "Steal away," sang the maker of the spiritual, "the chariot is comin'." And, if the makers of the spirituals gloried in singing of the cross of Jesus, it was not because they were masochistic and enjoyed suffering. Rather, the enslaved Africans sang because they saw on the rugged wooden planks One who had endured what was their daily portion. The cross was treasured because it enthroned the One who went all the way with them and for them. The enslaved Africans sang because they saw the result of the cross—triumph over the principalities and powers of death, triumph over evil in this world.

The slaves understood God as the author of freedom, of emancipation, certainly. Harriet Jacobs recalls Aggie, an old slave woman and neighbor to her grandmother. When Aggie hears the other old woman weeping, she hurries to inquire. But, when told that the grandmother is weeping because her grandson has escaped North, Aggie's joy admonishes Jacobs' grandmother.

Is dat what you's cryin fur? Git down on your knees and bress de Lord! I don't know whar my poor chillern is, and I nebber 'spect to know. You don't know whar poor Linda's gone to; but you do know whar her brudder is. He's in free parts; and dat's de right place. Don't murmur at de Lord's doings, but git down on your knees and tank him for his goodness.[52]

For the slaves, "the God of the fugitive is a God who offers immediate freedom and deliverance to his [sic] chosen people," even if this deliverance sometimes entails trial and fear.[53]

Even as Linda Brent joins in thanks for her brother's safety, she does not hesitate to question God. Brent's experience of oppression forced her "to retain the right, as much as possible, to resist those things within the [dominant] culture and the Bible that [she found] obnoxious or antagonistic to [her] innate sense of identity and to [her] basic instincts for survival."[54] In the following passage, Brent speaks for so many who puzzled and would puzzle at the maldistribution, enormity, viciousness, and recrudescence of this peculiar suffering.

I tried to be thankful for my little cell, dismal as it was, and even to love it as part of the price I had paid for the redemption of my children. Sometimes I thought God was a compassionate Father, who would forgive my sins for the sake of my sufferings. At other times, it seemed to me there was no justice or mercy in the divine government. I asked why the curse of slavery was permitted to exist, and why I had been so persecuted and wronged from youth. These things took the shape of mystery, which is to this day not so clear to my soul as I trust it will be hereafter.[55]

Harriet Jacobs' Linda Brent has made a space for Alice Walker's Celie. Tormented in heart and mind and body, Celie declares: God "act just like all the other mens I know. Trifling, forgitful, lowdown . . . If he [sic] ever listened to poor colored women the world would be a different place, I can tell you."[56]

For the enslaved community, memory was a vital and empowering act. Remembering gave the slaves access to "naming, placing, and signifying,"[57] and thus the recovery, the reconstitution of identity, culture, and self. Memory, then, was an essential source of resistance. As a young girl, Lucy Delaney's mother, Polly Berry, was kidnapped from Illinois and sold into slavery. Like Harriet Jacobs, Polly Berry's emancipation is bound up in a slaveholder's will that an executor disregards. Delaney writes: "my mother registered a solemn vow that her children should not continue in slavery all their lives, and she never spared an opportunity to impress it upon us, that we must get our freedom whenever the chance offered."[58] Delaney's mother kept alive for her children the memory, promise, and possibility of freedom. Fugitive and emancipated slave narrators remember and recall for us, not only their own experiences and suffering, but those of other enslaved women and men as well. Mary Prince explained her own commitment to their memory simply and eloquently: "In telling my own sorrows," she declared, "I cannot pass by those of my fellow-slaves — for when I think of my own griefs, I remember theirs."[59]

Linda Brent, her grandmother, Mary Prince, and Polly Berry all use language to defend themselves from sexual and physical assault and to gain psychological space and strength. *Language* was a crucial form of resistance. In these narratives, women model audacious behavior: wit, cunning, verbal warfare, and moral courage. These Black women *sass*! *The Random House Dictionary of the English Language* defines sass as impudent or disrespectful back talk. Enslaved Black women use sass to guard, regain, and secure self-esteem; to obtain and hold psychological distance; to speak truth; to challenge "the atmosphere of moral ambiguity that surrounds them," and, sometimes, to protect against sexual assault.[60]

Joanne Braxton explores the West African derivation of the word *sass*, noting its association "with the female aspect of the trickster." Sass comes from the bark of the poisonous West African sassy tree. Deconcocted and mixed with certain other barks, sass was used in ritual ordeals to detect witches. If the accused survives the potion, she is absolved; if not, the sass poisons, it kills. For enslaved women, sass is a ready weapon; it allows them to "return a portion of the poison the master has offered."[61] There is strong sass in the lines of a song women cutters sang in the Louisiana cane fields:

"Rains come wet me/Sun come dry me/Stay back, boss man/Don't come nigh me."[62] An emancipated slave recalls Sukie, an enslaved Black woman who used her fists and sass to protect herself from the sexual assault of a Virginia slave master. In revenge, he sells her to traders who, the narrator reports, "'zamined her an' pinched her an' den dey open her mouf, an stuck dey fingers in to see how her teeth was. Den Sukie got awful mad, and she pult up her dress an' tole old nigger traders to look an' see if dey could fin' any teef down there."[63] Strong sass!

Linda Brent uses sass to ward off Flint's sexual and psychological attacks. When the physician mocks her marriage plans, calling her fiancé a "puppy," Brent sasses: "If he is a puppy, I am a puppy, for we are both of the negro race ... The man you call a puppy never insulted me." Infuriated, Flint strikes her. Brent sasses again: "You have struck me for answering you honestly. How I despise you!" "Do you know," Flint demands, "that I have a right to do as I like with you—that I can kill you, if I please?" Unbowed, Brent sasses yet again: "You have tried to kill me, and I wish you had; but you have no right to do as you like with me." At this, Flint is enraged, "By heavens, girl, you forget yourself too far! Are you mad?"[64] Indeed, sass is Linda Brent's means of physical and psychological resistance. Brent is *not* mad. Of course, thinking that Brent may be mad makes it is easier for Flint to dismiss her behavior—and salvage his ego. Rather, Brent and her sassing sisters are naming their own standards, claiming their own bodies, their own selves.

An Outline for a Theology of Suffering in Womanist Perspective

It is ironic, perhaps, that a theology of suffering is formed from resources of resistance. It is not womanist perspective that makes it so, but the Christianity of the plantation. In its teaching, theologizing, preaching, and practice, this Christianity sought to bind the slaves to their condition by inculcating caricatures of the cardinal virtues of patience, long-suffering, forebearance, love, faith, and hope. Thus, to distance itself from any form of masochism, even Christian masochism, a theology of suffering in womanist perspective must reevaluate those virtues in light of Black women's experiences. Such reevaluation engages a hermeneutic of suspicion and a hermeneutic of resistance; but that reevaluation and reinterpretation must be rooted in a critical realism that rejects both naive realism and idealism as adequate foundations for a theology of suffering.

Chattel slavery disclosed the impoverished idealism that vitiated the Gospels, left Christianity a mere shell of principles and ideals, and obviated the moral and ethical implications of slavery—for master and slave alike. Likewise, a naive biblicism is impossible: "the Bible has been the most consistent and effective book that those in power have used to restrict and censure the behavior of African American women."[65] Womanist Christian realism eschews naive biblicism, dogmatic moralism, and idealism distantiated from critical knowledge of experience, of human reality—of Black women's reality. Thus, a theology of suffering in womanist perspective begins with the acknowledgment of Black women's critical cognitive practice and develops through their distinctive Christian response to suffering.

Recalling her father's stories of slavery, Ruth Shays reflected: "The mind of the man and the mind of the woman is the same. But this business of living makes women use their minds in ways that men don' even have to think about. . . . it is life that makes all these differences, not nature."[66] As a mode of critical consciousness and emancipatory struggle, Black women's critical cognitive practice is glimpsed in the earliest actuated meanings of resistance by captured and enslaved African women in North America. This practice emerged even more radically in the patterned operations of seeing, hearing, touching, smelling, tasting, inquiring, imagining, understanding, conceiving, formulating, reflecting, marshaling and weighing the evidence, judging, deliberating, evaluating, and deciding, speaking, writing. As a mode of critical self-consciousness, Black women's cognitive practice emphasizes the dialectic between oppression, conscious reflection on the experience of that oppression, and activism to resist and change it. The matrix of domination is responsive to human agency: the struggle of Black women suggests that there is choice and power to act—and to do so mindfully, artfully.[67]

A theology of suffering in womanist perspective grows in the dark soil of the African-American religious tradition and is intimate with the root paradigms of African-American culture, in general, and African-American women's culture, in particular. Such a theology of suffering attends critically and carefully to the differentiated range of Black women's experiences. It holds itself accountable to Black women's self-understandings, self-judgment, and self-evaluation.

A theology of suffering in womanist perspective repels every tendency toward any *ersatz* spiritualization of evil and suffering, of pain and oppression. Such a theology of suffering seeks, on behalf of the African-American community whose lives and struggles it honors and serves, to understand and to clarify the meaning of the liberating Word and deed of God in Jesus of Nazareth for all women and men who strive against the principalities and structures, the powers and forces of evil. A theology of suffering in womanist perspective is characterized by remembering and retelling, by resisting, by redeeming.

• A theology of suffering in womanist perspective remembers and retells the lives and sufferings of those who "came through" and those who have "gone on to glory land." This remembering honors the sufferings of the ancestors, known and unknown, victims of chattel slavery and its living legacy. As Karen Holloway indicates, this "telling . . . is testimony that recenters the spirits of women, mythic and ancestral, into places where their passionate articulation assures them that neither geography nor history can separate them from the integrity of the essential Word."[68] And that "recentering" revives the living as well. Black women remember and draw strength in their own anguish from hearing and imitating the strategies adopted by their mothers, grandmothers, great-grandmothers, great-great-grandmothers to handle their suffering. These stories evoke growth and change, proper outrage and dissatisfaction, and enlarge Black women's moral horizon and choices.

• A theology of suffering in womanist perspective is *redemptive*. In their narratives, Black women invite God to partner them in the redemption of Black people. They make meaning of their suffering. Over and over again, Black women under chattel slavery endured pain, privation, and injury; risked their very lives, for the sake of the lives and freedom of their children. Praying in her garret, Linda Brent offers her suffering as part of the price of the emancipation of her children. Mattie Jackson recounts that during their escape, her mother fasted for two days, saving what food she had been able to carry away for Mattie and her sister. And, by their very suffering and privation, Black women under chattel slavery freed the cross of Christ. Their steadfast commitment honored that cross and the One who died for all and redeemed it from Christianity's vulgar misuse.

• A theology of suffering in womanist perspective is *resistant*. With motherwit, courage, sometimes their fists, and most often sass, Black women resisted the degradation of chattel slavery. Sass gave Black women a weapon of self-defense. With sass, Black women defined themselves and dismantled the images that had been used to control and demean them. With sass, Black women turned back the shame that others tried to put on them. With sass, Black women survived, even triumphed over emotional and psychic assault.

Moreover, in their resistance, Black women's suffering redefined caricatured Christian virtues. Because of the lives and suffering of Black women held in chattel slavery—the meanings of forebearance, long-suffering, patience, love, hope, and faith can never again be ideologized. Because of the rape, seduction, and concubinage of Black women under chattel slavery, chastity or virginity begs new meaning.

Harriet Jacobs' sexual liaison with Mr. Sands causes her great remorse and she experiences a loss of self-esteem. Indeed, for Jacobs, this spiritual and existential agony shadows the remainder of her life. A theology of suffering in womanist perspective ought offer her comfort: Does not the sacrifice of her virgin body shield and preserve the virginity of her spirit and her heart? And, of what importance is a virgin body if the spirit and heart are violated, raped, crushed? And can we not hope that in the life of death, Harriet Jacobs has found "god in [her]self and loves her/loves her fiercely?"[69]

NOTES

1. The title of this chapter is taken from "The Memoir of Old Elizabeth, a Coloured Woman" (1863) in *Six Women's Slave Narratives*, The Schomburg Library

of Nineteenth-Century Black Women Writers, gen. ed., Henry Louis Gates, Jr. (New York: Oxford Paperbooks/Oxford University Press, 1988), 13. For some Christian theological explorations of suffering, see Ladislaus Boros, *Pain and Providence* (New York: Seabury Crossroad Press, 1966); Rosemary Haughton, *The Passionate God* (Ramsey, NJ: Paulist Press, 1981); Arthur C. McGill, *Suffering: A Test of Theological Method* (Philadelphia: Westminster Press, 1982); Dorothee Sölle, *Suffering*, trans. Everett R. Kalin (Philadelphia: Fortress Press, 1975); Simone Weil, "The Love of God and Affliction," in *Waiting for God*, trans. Emma Craufurd (1951; New York: Harper Colophon Books/Harper & Row Publishers, 1973), *Gravity and Grace*, trans. Arthur Wills (New York: G. P. Putnam's Sons, 1952).

2. Howard Thurman, *Disciplines of the Spirit* (1963; Richmond, IN: Friends United Press, 1977).

3. Ibid., 76.

4. Quoted in Mary Helen Washington, "Zora Neale Hurston: A Woman Half in Shadow," in Zora Neale Hurston, *I Love Myself When I Am Laughing . . . And Then Again When I Am Looking Mean and Impressive: A Zora Neale Hurston Reader*, ed. Alice Walker (New York: Feminist Press, 1979), 19.

5. William R. Jones, *Is God A White Racist: A Preamble to Black Theology* (Garden City, NY: Anchor Press/Doubleday, 1973), 21-22. Twenty years ago, Jones sought to provide the new emerging Black theology with what he considered to be a much needed preamble. Black theology, Jones asserted, lacked a viable theodicy. What had Black theology to say about divine justice and vindication after centuries of chattel slavery, murder, lynching, rape, and persistent discrimination? How was Black theology to affirm a God of love, of compassion, of mercy, of care? How could Black theology operate as if the goodness of God toward all humankind were an unimpeachable theological axiom? What had Black theology to say about the maldistribution, negative quality, enormity, and transgenerational character of Black suffering? Provocatively to some and blasphemously to others, Jones asked, "Is God a white racist?" He took his title from a line in a poem written in 1906 by W. E. B. DuBois, "Litany at Atlanta," in *The Seventh Son: The Thought and Writings of W. E. B. DuBois*, vol. I, ed. Julius Lester (New York: Random House, 1971), 422-426. In frustration and anguish, DuBois exclaimed:

Keep not Thou Silent, O God!
Sit not longer blind, Lord God, deaf to our prayer and dumb to our dumb suffering. Surely Thou, too, art not white, O Lord, a pale bloodless, heartless thing! (425)

DuBois' work is part of an often overlooked strand in the African-American theological and literary tradition that puts God on trial because of the nature and character of Black suffering and that ridicules efforts to legitimate and rationalize that suffering on the grounds of divine intervention — future release and vindication. For some representative religious and theological examples, including those suspect of Christianity's value for the enslaved, see Nathaniel Paul, "An Address Delivered on the Celebration of the Abolition of Slavery in the State of New York, July 5, 1827," in *Negro Orators and Their Orations*, ed. Carter G. Woodson (New York: Russell and Russell, 1969); David Walker, "An Appeal" (1829) in *Walker's Appeal/Garnet's Address* (New York: Arno Press & The New York Times, 1969); Frederick Douglass, "On the Union, Religion, and the Constitution," (1847) in *Frederick Douglass: The Narrative and Selected Writings*, ed. Michael Meyer (New York: Modern Library College Editions/Random House, 1984); Daniel A. Payne, *A Recollec-*

tion of Seventy Years (Nashville: Publishing House of the A. M. E. Sunday School Union, 1988). For some representative literary examples, see Georgia Douglas Johnson, *Bronze* (Boston: B. J. Brimmer Company, 1922), 32; Countee Cullen, *Color* (New York: Harper & Brothers, 1925), 3, 20-21, 36-41; idem., *The Black Christ* (Harper & Brothers, 1929); Nella Larsen, *Quicksand and Passing*, ed. Deborah E. McDowell (1928; New Brunswick, NJ: Rutgers University Press, 1986), especially 109-130, 133-36; Jessie Redmond Fausett, *Plum Bun* (New York: Frederick A. Stokes Company, 1928), 308, 309; Langston Hughes, "Goodbye Christ," *Negro Worker* (November-December 1932); Benjamin E. Mays, *The Negro's God, As Reflected in His Literature* (1938; New York: Atheneum, 1969), 189-244; Zora Neale Hurston, *Dust Tracks on a Road: An Autobiography*, 2d ed., ed. Robert E. Hemenway (1942; Urbana and Chicago: University of Illinois Press, 1984), 266-279; and Alice Walker, *The Color Purple* (New York: Harcourt Brace Jovanovich, 1982), especially, 164-168.

6. For some discussions of Jewish suffering, especially the Holocaust, see Hannah Arendt, *The Origins of Totalitarianism* (London: Allen & Unwin, 1962), *Eichmann in Jerusalem: A Report on the Banality of Evil* (New York: Viking Press, 1964); George L. Mosse, *Toward the Final Solution: A History of European Racism* (London: J. M. Dent & Son, 1978); Henry Friedlander and Sybil Milton, eds., *The Holocaust: Ideology, Bureaucracy, and Genocide* (Millwood, NY: Kraus International Publications, 1980); Alex Grobman and David Landes, eds., *Genocide: Critical Issues of the Holocaust* (Los Angeles: Simon Wiesenthal Centre, 1983); Zygmunt Bauman, *Modernity and the Holocaust* (Ithaca, NY: Cornell University Press, 1989). For some discussion of the suffering of the indigenous peoples of the Americas, see Lewis Hanke, *The First Social Experiments in America: A Study in the Development of Spanish Indian Policy in the Sixteenth Century* (Cambridge, MA: Harvard University Press, 1935); Roy Harvey Pearce, *Savagism and Civilization: A Study of the Indian and the American Mind* (1953; Berkeley: University of California Press, 1988); Vine Deloria, Jr., *Custer Died for Your Sins: An Indian Manifesto* (London: The Macmillan Company/Collier-Macmillan Limited, 1969), *God is Red* (New York: Grosset & Dunlap, 1975); Francis Jennings, *The Invasion of America: Indians, Colonialism, and the Cant of Conquest* (1975; New York: W. W. Norton & Co., 1976); Octavio Paz, *One Earth, Four or Five Worlds*, trans. Helen R. Lane (1983; New York: Harcourt Brace Jovanovich, 1985).

The oppression and violence endemic to white racist supremacy has been a characteristic feature of Black life since the advent of modernity and shows little abatement in the postmodern age. In the United States, white women and men endure no such protracted, intentional, and institutionally authorized spirit numbing affliction, induced merely by their pigmentation. See David Hume, *Essays and Treatises on Several Subjects*, 2 vols. (Edinburgh, 1825), I, 521-22; Immanuel Kant, *Observations on the Feeling of the Beautiful and Sublime* [1764; ET: *Beobachtungen über das Gefühl des Schönen und Erhabenen*], trans. John T. Goldthwait (Berkeley: University of California Press, 1960), 111, 78-79; David Mermelstein, ed., *The Anti-Apartheid Reader: South Africa and the Struggle against White Racist Rule* (New York: Grove Press, 1987); David Theo Goldberg, ed., *Anatomy of Racism* (Minneapolis, MN: University of Minnesota, 1990); Dominick Lacapra, ed., *The Bounds of Race: Perspectives on Hegemony and Resistance* (Ithaca, NY: Cornell Paperbacks/Cornell University Press, 1991).

7. "The History of Mary Prince, a West Indian Slave" (1831), and Lucy Dela-

ney, "From the Darkness Cometh the Light or Struggles for Freedom" (ca. 1891) in Gates, ed., *Six Women's Slave Narratives.* Sources regarding autobiographical narrative and literary criticism that I have found useful in preparing this essay include Robert B. Stepto, *From Behind the Veil: A Study of Afro-American Narrative,* 2d ed. (1979; Urbana and Chicago: University of Illinois Press, 1991); Charles T. Davis and Henry Louis Gates, Jr., eds., *The Slave's Narrative* (New York: Oxford University Press, 1984); Hazel Carby, *Reconstructing Womanhood: The Emergence of the Afro-American Woman Novelist* (Oxford: Oxford University Press, 1987), Joanne M. Braxton, *Black Women Writing Autobiography: A Tradition Within a Tradition* (Philadelphia: Temple University Press, 1988); and Karla F. C. Holloway, *Moorings and Metaphors: Figures of Culture and Gender in Black Women's Literature* (New Brunswick, NJ: Rutgers University Press, 1992).

8. John Sekora and Darwin T. Turner, eds., *The Art of Slave Narrative: Original Essays in Criticism and Theory* (Macomb, IL: Western Illinois University, 1982).

9. Mary Helen Washington, "Meditations on History: The Slave Woman's Voice," in her edited *Invented Lives: Narratives of Black Women, 1860–1960* (Garden City, NY: Anchor Press/Doubleday & Co., 1987), 8. Washington points up the example of Frederick Douglass—whose narratives omit information about his first wife, Anne Murray Douglass. Washington reports that Douglass' silence is countered by the testimony of his eldest daughter who reveals her mother's hand in his escape.

10. Carby, *Reconstructing Womanhood,* 36.

11. Ibid., 21.

12. Harriet Jacobs [Linda Brent], *Incidents in the Life of a Slave Girl* (1861; New York: Harcourt Brace Jovanovich, 1983).

13. Jean Fagan Yellin, "Texts and Contexts of Harriet Jacobs' *Incidents in the Life of a Slave Girl: Written by Herself,*" in Davis and Gates, eds., *The Slave's Narrative,* 263. Only within the last decade has the slave status and racial heritage of the author of *Incidents in the Life of a Slave Girl* been verified. Many interpreters and historians viewed the story as too horrific to be true. Yellin discovered a cache of letters written by Harriet Jacobs about matters narrated in her autobiography and has been able to establish the truthfulness and substantive accuracy of her account.

14. For a definition of womanist theology, see Toinette Eugene, "Womanist Theology," in *The New Handbook of Christian Theology,* ed. Donald Musser and Joseph Price (Nashville: Abingdon Press, 1992).

15. The earliest major projects to collect and preserve the eyewitness accounts and experiences of the men and women who had been enslaved were begun in the first quarter of the twentieth century at Hampton Institute in Virginia, Southern University in Louisiana, and Fisk University in Tennessee. The Hampton Project resulted in *The Negro in Virginia,* Virginia Writers' Project (New York: Hastings House, 1940). At Southern, interviews were conducted under the direction of John B. Cade and culminated in his "Out of the Mouths of Ex-Slaves," *Journal of Negro History,* 20 (July 1935): 294-337. The two volumes of the Fisk University study have been included in George P. Rawick, ed., *The American Slave: A Composite Autobiography,* 19 vols. (1941; Westport, CT: Greenwood Publishing Co., 1972). These initial efforts to preserve the life stories of our ancestors were given focus and support with the establishment of a comprehensive program of interviews inaugurated and carried through under the auspices of the Federal Writers' Project of the

Works Project Administration (WPA) during the years 1936 to 1938. This project began on the local and regional levels and under the directorship of John Lomax evolved into a systematic national endeavor. Approximately 2 percent of the total of emancipated African peoples in the United States in 1937 were interviewed. The Slave Narrative Collection consists of more than 10,000 pages of typescript and contains 2,000 interviews.

16. John W. Blassingame, ed., *Slave Testimony: Two Centuries of Letters, Speeches, Interviews, and Autobiographies* (1977; Baton Rouge: Louisiana State University Press, 1989), 138, 128; also, 157-158.

17. Norman R. Yetman, ed., *Voices from Slavery* (New York: Holt, Rinehart and Winston, 1970), 317.

18. Dorothy Sterling, ed., *We Are Your Sisters: Black Women in the Nineteenth Century* (New York: W. W. Norton, 1984), 25; also see Gerda Lerner, ed., *Black Women in White America: A Documentary History* (New York: Random House/Vintage Books, 1973), 45-51, 149-163; also Rawick, ed., *The American Slave*, 174-175.

19. Sterling, ed., *We Are Your Sisters*, 25, 26-31.

20. Bert James Loewenberg and Ruth Bogin, eds., *Black Women in Nineteenth-Century American Life: Their Words, Their Thoughts, Their Feelings* (University Park and London: Pennsylvania State University Press, 1976), 58.

21. Ibid.

22. Ibid.

23. "The History of Mary Prince," 13.

24. Ibid.

25. Jacobs, *Incidents in the Life of a Slave Girl*, xiii-xiv.

26. Ibid., 3.

27. Ibid.

28. Ibid., 6.

29. Ibid., 26-27.

30. Ibid., 27, 30.

31. Ibid., 41.

32. Ibid., 54-55.

33. Ibid., 55.

34. Ibid.

35. Ibid., 54, 56.

36. Ibid., 57.

37. Ibid., 79.

38. Ibid., 101, 97-151; also, Braxton, *Black Women Writing Autobiography*, 32.

39. Jacobs, *Incidents in the Life of a Slave Girl*, 124.

40. "The History of Mary Prince," 7.

41. "The Story of Mattie J. Jackson," in *Six Women's Slave Narratives*, 37.

42. "The History of Mary Prince," 7.

43. Ibid., 8, 9.

44. Weil, "The Love of God and Affliction," 119.

45. See Sölle, *Suffering*, 151-178; Weil, "The Love of God and Affliction," 117-136; Friedrich Nietzsche, "The Antichrist," in *The Portable Nietzsche*, selected and translated, with an introduction, preface, and notes by Walter Kaufmann (New York: Viking Press, 1954), 565-656.

46. Albert Raboteau, *Slave Religion: The 'Invisible Institution' in the Antebellum South* (New York: Oxford University Press, 1975), 213.

47. C. Johnson and A. P. Watson, eds., *God Struck Me Dead* (Philadelphia and New York: Pilgrim Press, 1969), vii.

48. Jacobs, *Incidents in the Life of a Slave Girl*, 77.

49. On a Roman Catholic systematic theological reading, Katie G. Cannon, in her *Black Womanist Ethics* (Atlanta, GA: Scholars Press, 1988), in fact, presents a prologomenon to a womanist ethics. In her dissertation, Cannon researches historically and concretely the social and cultural contexts in which Black women's moral agency dares emerge—thus, the conditions that provoke womanist ethics. Most importantly, Cannon's research allows her to identify categories for women's expression of that agency: invisible dignity, quiet grace, and unshouted courage. See Washington, "Meditations on History," 8; Deborah Gray White, *Ar'n't I a Woman? Female Slaves in the Plantation South* (New York: W. W. Norton & Co., 1985), 119.

50. Thurman, *Deep River and the Negro Spiritual Speaks of Life and Death* (Indianapolis, IN: Friends United Press, 1975), 16.

51. James Weldon Johnson, ed., *The Book of American Negro Spirituals* (New York: Viking Press, 1925), 20. For a comprehensive discussion of the making and history of the spirituals, see John Lovell, Jr., *Black Song: The Forge and the Flame—The Story of How the Afro-American Spiritual Was Hammered Out* (1972; New York: Paragon, 1986).

52. Jacobs, *Incidents in the Life of a Slave Girl*, 135.

53. Melvin Dixon, "Singing Swords: The Literary Legacy of Slavery," in Davis and Gates, *The Slave's Narrative*, 313.

54. Renita J. Weems, "Reading Her Way through the Struggle: African-American Women and the Bible," in *Stony the Road We Trod: African American Biblical Interpretation*, ed. Cain Hope Felder (Minneapolis, MN: Fortress Press, 1991), 63.

55. Jacobs, *Incidents in the Life of a Slave Girl*, 125-126.

56. Walker, *The Color Purple*, 164.

57. Holloway, *Moorings and Metaphors*, 38.

58. Lucy Delaney, "From the Darkness Cometh the Light or Struggles for Freedom," 15-16.

59. "The History of Mary Prince," 12.

60. Braxton, *Black Women Writing Autobiography*, 30.

61. Ibid., 30, 31; see Amanda Smith, *An Autobiography: The Story of the Lord's Dealings with Mrs. Amanda Smith, the Colored Evangelist* (Chicago: Meyer and Brothers, 1893), 386-89.

62. Sterling, *We Are Your Sisters*, 26.

63. Ibid., 27.

64. Jacobs, *Incidents in the Life of a Slave Girl*, 38-39.

65. Weems, "African American Women and the Bible," 62.

66. John Langston Gwaltney, *Drylongso: A Self-Portrait of Black America* (New York: Vintage Books/Random House, 1980), 33.

67. Patricia Hill Collins, *Black Feminist Thought: Knowledge, Consciousness, and the Politics of Empowerment* (Boston: Unwin Hyman, 1990), 52.

68. Holloway, *Moorings and Metaphors*, 187.

69. Ntozake Shange, *For Colored Girls Who Have Considered Suicide/When the Rainbow Is Enuf* (New York: Macmillan, 1977), 63.

8

A Womanist Perspective on Sin

Delores S. Williams

Womanist theology, like most Christian theology, is sourced by a community, in this case the African-American community.[1] To be sourced by a community means that womanist theology is informed not only by African-American women's religious and social experience but also by the entire community's faith — its beliefs developed over time about sin, salvation, grace, and so forth.

As sociologist Elsa Barkley Brown claims, womanist consciousness is thinking/acting simultaneously in two related contexts: the context of the oppressed Black community's concerns and struggles and the context of women's struggle for liberation and well-being.[2] Womanist thought cannot provide notions of women's experience that separates community concerns (e.g., racial struggle) from women's rights struggle. Separating this experience splits Black women's experience — comparable to the body/mind split or the nature/history split so characteristic of oppressive Western thinking.

Brown's notion of womanist consciousness provides guidelines for the method used in this essay. This notion suggests that exploration into aspects of Black women's Christian belief system necessitates simultaneously giving some attention to aspects of the Christian belief system of the African-American community (males included) in which Black women's understanding of sin, salvation, and grace emerged. Therefore, this essay explores two related areas. It provides an historical perspective on sin as this perspective has developed in the African-American community. Then it examines some nineteenth-century African-American women's ideas about sin reflected in their individual narratives. The final section of the article is constructive. It begins to develop a womanist notion of sin informed, in part, by the Black female and Black male sources explored earlier in this essay.

To arrive at notions of sin as they developed historically in the African-American community, I examine three deposits of the community's religious culture. These are the spiritual songs contained in *Slave Songs of the United States*;[3] and the autobiographical statements of more than one hundred ex-slaves interviewed by writers in the Fisk University Social Science Foundation and in the Federal Writers' Project. The autobiographical statements consulted for this essay are contained in two texts: *Voices from Slavery* (material collected by writers of the Federal Writers' Project) and *God Struck Me Dead* (material collected under direction of Fisk's Social Science Foundation).[4] The third deposit of Black religious culture examined is Black theology. Attention is given to James H. Cone's understanding of sin as it is presented in his book *A Black Theology of Liberation*.[5]

To arrive at Black women's concept of sin, the following narratives were consulted: *Memoir of Old Elizabeth A Coloured Woman*; *The Life and Religious Experience of Jarena Lee, A Coloured Lady Giving Account of Her Call to Preach the Gospel*; *Memoirs of the Life, Religious Experience, Ministerial Travels and Labours of Mrs. Zilpha Elaw*; *A Brand Plucked From the Fire: An Autobiographical Sketch by Mrs. Julia A. J.Foote*; *Incidents in the Life of a Slave Girl*; *The Story of Mattie J. Jackson*; Lucy Delaney's narrative *From the Darkness Cometh the Light or Struggles for Freedom;* and Kate Drumgold's *Slave Girl's Story*.[6]

Review of Black Community Ideas about Sin

Of the 129 spiritual songs in English in *Slave Songs of the United States* (Allen collection), only about twelve mention the word "sin" or "sinner(s)."[7] The references to sin often occur in the company of what appear to be some unrelated themes, thereby making it extremely difficult today to arrive at definite ideas about the understanding of sin held by the songs' creators. For instance, the song "Hear From Heaven To-day" refers to sin as forgiven and ". . . my soul set free."[8] The allusions to heaven in the song suggest an eschatological context (". . . I yearde from heaven today . . ." and "De trumpet sound in de oder bright land . . ." and "De Bell is a-ringin' in de oder bright world"). But there are also themes of birth ("A baby born in Bethlehem . . ."), and themes of movement and invocation ("Hurry on my weary soul . . . hurry on . . . ," and "My name is called and I must go . . ."). The song does not reveal an obvious connection between these themes and the reference to sin. The emphasis of the song is upon communication, hearing ". . . from heaven today . . ." not upon sin. Yet due to the association of sin with forgiveness and freedom ("My sin is forgiven and my soul set free") in the first stanza followed immediately by the line "And I heard from heaven today," one might ask whether hearing from heaven depended first upon forgiveness of sin and freedom of the soul? *Or,* since the chorus comes before the stanzas in this song, are the song's creators suggesting that because they heard from heaven today, their sins are forgiven and their souls set free? (The chorus says "Hurry on, my weary soul, And I yearde from heaven today, hurry on, my weary soul, and I yearde from heaven today.") Are they suggesting that the forgiveness of sin is the necessary prelude to the realization of some kind of freedom? Though the emphasis of the song is not upon sin, perhaps the community's understanding of the character of personal sin figures into whatever meaning the eschatological context intends to convey to the slave community.

Because of the coded messages that scholars agree are hidden in the songs, one can never answer such questions with any degree of certainty. And the collective consciousness out of which the slaves operated cautions today's interpreters against understanding singular pronouns like "my" and "I" as indicating a single individual rather than the entire slave community. But the speculation can be made that this particular spiritual song refers to sin couched in some kind of eschatological experience in which Jesus' birth, the authors' identities,[9] traveling, and audio communication had a relational meaning only the slave community understood. However, it is not difficult to discern the freedom motif present in this song, for it is present in many other songs in the Allen collection.

These songs in the Allen collection present a variety of contexts in which sin and the sinner(s) are mentioned. In addition to the eschatological context of the songs' references to sin, there are apocalyptic and communal-care contexts, confessional contexts, and contexts of struggle, victory, and redemption. Thus in the song "Turn, Sinner, Turn O!" the sinner is warned that the world is going to end or she or he may die before turning away from sin. In "The Sin-Sick Soul" the slave community is reminded that some of its members have gone "... to glory ... "; therefore, it is the responsibility of the (remaining?) community members to take care of those who need it, the sin-sick souls. Another song, "You Must Be Pure and Holy," confesses that the authors were once "... wicked an'-a prone to sin ... ," but they were "... born again." Some of the songs speak of struggle, of "... wrestle with Satan and wrestle with sin, stepped over hell ..." and got the victory to "... come back again."[10] They speak of redemption because "... de Lamb done been down here an' died ... Sinner won't die no mo'."[11]

Two songs in the Allen collection contain interesting bits of theology (with reference to sin) that have not, to date, become significant in any written theology issuing from the African-American Christian community. In the song "Go in the Wilderness" there appear to be two deities with two distinct functions in relation to sin. The first is "... de Lord, my God ..." who exercises the gigantic task of taking "... away de sin of the world." Then there is "... Jesus ... de Lord ..." who meets the slaves in the wilderness. It is Jesus who attends to the suffering of "... weepin' Mary" and the ailments of " 'Flicted sister." It is Jesus who helps the slave become a Christian, get religion, reaffirm commitment (e.g., "... backslider ... ")

and ". . . get converted." For Jesus waits to meet the slave in the wilderness.[12]

Then there is the song suggesting what might be a conflict between ". . . de Lord's [will] . . ." and the individual's or community's actions in relation to the eradication of sin. The song's creators are concerned about ". . . de trouble ob de world . . . ," and they ". . . ask de Lord how long I hold 'em." Evidently "de Lord" said "Hold 'em to de end." But the slaves respond "My sins so heavy I can't get along." (I suppose the "sins" here have reference to "de troubles of the world" since the nature of the sins is not specified.) Then the "I" in the song (i.e., the community that created the song) takes the initiative and ". . . cast my sins in de middle of de sea." Contrary to the emphasis upon obedience to God, which usually prevails in the spiritual songs, this one defies ". . . de Lord" and acts contrary to what ". . . de Lord" has apparently willed, that is, that the community hold its burdens forever.[13]

An additional song retells the story of the fall so that the consequence seems to be placed on Adam rather than Eve. Consider these lyrics:

O Adam, where are you? Adam, where are you? Adam where are you? O what a trying time. 2) Lord, I am in the garden. 3) Adam, you ate that apple. 4) Lord, Eve she gave it to me. 5) Adam, it was forbidden. 6) Lord said, walk out de garden.[14]

An intriguing thing here is that neither Adam nor Eve receive the harsh punishment for their action that Adam and Eve received in the biblical account. While disobedience constitutes the wrongdoing in the song, Adam's only punishment is that he must leave the garden. God speaks no word of chastisement to Eve. Perhaps the brutal treatment and near-death beatings that the slaves often received for disobeying their slave owners discouraged them (the slaves) from believing God could be as cruel and vindictive as their slave masters. In other sources (e.g., their narratives), the slaves are very clear about the cruelty of their masters in relation to slaves and about the brutal floggings that permanently scarred the slaves' flesh. (I do not know of any slave narratives, lyrics or lore that project an image of a cruel, brutal God.)

Finally with regard to the notions of sin in *Slave Songs of the United States*, the following claims can be made:

1. Sin has something to do with the trouble and burdens the slaves have to bear, but there is no notion that sin will be passed down from generation to generation because of Adam's sin in the garden.
2. In relation to sin, sometimes the deity (or deities) functions in two ways: (a) to rid the entire world of sin, and (b) to meet the slave in a special context where the deity [e.g., Jesus] attends specifically to the sins of the slave community; this context is often referred to as

"the wilderness." Thus some of the songs express the belief that God attends to sin in both a universal and an existential context.

3. As a way of dealing with sin, slaves seem more concerned about a process of moving toward positive transformation and destination than with identifying individual acts as sinful.

4. The spiritual songs in this collection seem to reflect more a social sense of sin than a personal one, and this social sin is done by one group against another group.

However, the personal narratives by some of the ex-slaves speak openly about sin. Usually, their speech about sin is more general than specific — though there are some intimations that dancing, attending dances, and playing cards constitute wrongdoing often caused by Satan.[15] As in the spiritual songs, freedom and deliverance are still major themes in the religious experience recounted by the ex-slaves.

Sin in Ex-slaves' Autobiographies

An ex-slave testified that "The darkest hours of my life as a slave came just before freedom, and in the same way, my trials with sin, when everything seemed lost I was delivered."[16]

Another person, recounting a conversion experience, tells of hearing a voice from the east singing "Your sins are all washed away, free, free my Lord. Your sins are all washed away, free, free, my Lord, Your Father's don' set you free."[17] Like the spiritual songs, most of these autobiographical accounts do not reveal the specific nature of the sin over which the authors get the victory.

In some of their descriptions of their conversion experiences and some of their testimonies about everyday life-experience, the ex-slaves mention sin in accord with literal biblical references. For instance, in the narrative "Souls Piled Up Like Timber," the author reports that she had a vision, and "a voice spoke to me saying, go tell your husband that the wages of sin is death but the gift of God is eternal life."[18] Yet there are references to sin that are nonbiblical and may have been original to slave culture. For instance, several of the ex-slaves speak of having been "sin-sick" prior to their conversion encounter with God. This kind of illness was described as a general debilitation that affected both the body and the spirit. Getting rid of this sin involved what the ex-slaves called "spiritual death" — that is, becoming metaphorically "dead" to an old way of being, acting, and thinking and taking on a "new existence," a new way of being, acting, and thinking without actually experiencing death in a literal sense. This "spiritual death" came to a person as the result of a visionary experience in which God, Jesus and/or angels guided the recipient to the new and higher way of life. Graphic descriptions of the experience of "spiritual death" abound in the autobiographical statements. One ex-slave says "God struck me dead"; another one declares "I was split from head to foot."

Like some of the lyrics by creators of the spiritual songs, the ex-slaves' autobiographical statements put sin, Satan, and hell on the side of their former owners and overseers. There is no doubt that many ex-slaves believed the slave masters and overseers were hell-bound because of their sins against innocent, powerless victims. Many of the autobiographical statements are quite clear in their description of the specific sin of which the slave master was guilty. One ex-slave presents this picture of a "white devilish slave master":

> On the farm adjoining ours was another plantation . . . old man F. [the plantation's owner] had a lot of slaves . . . he was a devil on earth . . . He used to walk or ride through the fields and take his foot and kick poor women . . . with child and cause them to have miscarriage right there in the field. Then he would call the Negro foreman to bring a cart and haul away this damn − −.

Continuing the description, the ex-slave reports that

> A woman had better not stop to suckle her baby [while working in the field] else she would be beat almost to death. I actually saw old man F. walk through the field and seeing a baby crying, take his stick and knock its brains out and call for the foreman to come and haul off the nasty, black rat.[19]

Thus the ex-slave concludes that "I don't believe a just God is going to take no such man as that into his kingdom."[20] Another ex-slave, Richard Caruthers, described a Black overseer as "rough. His temper born of the devil, himself. His name Tom Hill but us call him 'Devil Hill.' "[21]

Stealing was thought to be a devilish act taught to slaves by their owners. An ex-slave reports that "Many . . . slaves were taught to steal from neighboring plantations. They would slip out at night . . . steal a cow or hog . . . and bring it home and lock it up in the smokehouse. . . . If a neighbor came to inquire about anything missing, the slave master would deny any knowledge of it." She says "Now these white folks are always talking about the Negro stealing. If they steal, it is mostly because they were taught to do it in slavery time."[22] There is indication that some of the ex-slaves questioned whether stealing by slaves was "stealing" when the slave was hungry and destitute. Recounting his slave experience, ex-slave Richard Carruthers says:

> If they [slave owners] didn't provision you 'nough, you just had to slip round and get a chicken. . . . grabbin' a pig . . . You had to catch him [the pig] by the snoot so he wont squel, and clomp him tight while you knife him. That ain't stealin', is it?[23]

On the basis of data in *God Struck Me Dead* and in *Voices from Slavery*, one can suggest that the former slaves' new experience of freedom gave them the opportunity to express religious beliefs they had not been able to express openly in slavery. Time and again, in their autobiographical accounts of their conversion experiences, ex-slaves speak of their deliverance from sin in relation to an idea of election by God. In a vision, one former slave hears God say "I've chosen you before the dust of the earth."[24] Another person has a visionary encounter with God who says, "You have been chosen out of the world, and hell can't hold you."[25] To an anxious seeker "trying to hurry him [sic God] and get a religion," God said, "Behold, I am a time-God . . . I work after the counsel of my own will, and in due time I will visit whomsoever I will."[26] Later, God chooses this suppliant to visit. And, of course, deliverance from sin was the gift God gave all those God chose to undergo "spiritual Death." It is clear many ex-slaves did not believe that their former slave owners were among those God had chosen.

Some interesting comparisons and contrasts can be made between notions of sin in the spiritual songs in the Allen collection and the talk about sin in the statements of the ex-slaves in *God Struck Me Dead* and *Voices from Slavery*. Similar themes appear in the spiritual songs and in the autobiographical statements. In both instances, "sin" indicates an undesirable state from which the slave is set free. Thus, after slavery was over, arriving at a state of freedom is still a major aspiration connected with the former slaves' notion of sin.

Words and images related to sin that appear in the spiritual songs in the Allen collection also appear in the ex-slaves' autobiographical statements about their lives and conversion experiences. The phrase "sin-sick" soul appears in the data from both sources. The image of a "white, marble stone" appears in data from the two sources as do the images of mourners and burdened people. The color "white" appears in all the data and usually indicates something positive. In spiritual songs Jesus rides a white horse. His adversary rides a grey horse. In some of their autobiographical statements about their visionary experience, the ex-slaves picture Jesus, the liberator of their sins, as white and heaven is sometimes said to be constructed of white materials. Angels are often clad in white.

There are also definite contrasts between the notions of sin in the spiritual songs and those in the autobiographical statements. Inasmuch as references to sin occur in their descriptions of their conversion experiences, the ex-slaves make it absolutely clear that they are alluding to experience internal to their individual psyches. Thus sin is discussed more in terms of individual victory than in terms of community burdens, aspirations, and victories. A new linguistic term emerges in some of the ex-slaves' narratives as they describe the psychic and physical condition they experienced prior to their individual visions of transformation which victory over sin accomplished. Former slaves speak of feeling and being "heavy" just before they experience the vision. (Perhaps in the psychological terminology of our time, this condition would translate as depression. Or, perhaps this is similar to the abyss Karl Barth describes where the person receives the gift of faith.) An important difference to be reiterated here is that the ex-slaves have a much more individualistic story to tell about sin than do the spiritual songs, which seem more concerned about the Black community as a whole.

Several reasonable speculations can be advanced about this apparent move toward individualism. After slavery, the slaves became responsible for their individual, economic welfare—providing for their own clothes, their own food, their families, finding their own jobs, and their own shelter. In a sense, the collectiveness that had structured slave consciousness was, after slavery, impacted by the new need to be conscious of one's responsibility for one's self. This is not to suggest, however, that the slave lost all sense of collective consciousness after the Emancipation. There is enough evidence in African-American social and literary history to demonstrate that the reentrenchment of economic bondage, segregation, and white racism after Reconstruction welded the newly freed slaves into a community in which they shared a common plight. Yet this community or collective consciousness has, since slavery, lived in constant tension with the impulse toward individualism that the dominating culture values, rewards, and encourages Americans to develop. Also, the splintering of the ex-slave religious community into many institutional denominations (churches) stressing personal salvation (from sin) no doubt increased the tension between Black collective consciousness with regard to sin and individualistic awareness and goals.

Taking all these points of similarity and difference seriously, the following statements can be made about the relation between notions of sin in the Allen collection of spiritual songs and the notions of sin in the autobiographical narratives of the ex-slave:

1. Sin in the spiritual songs is often related to trouble and burdens. In the autobiographical statements sin has something to do with trouble, but sin is also related to "feeling heavy" (perhaps a psychological state).
2. Some spiritual songs suggest two deities functioning in two distinct ways, but Jesus seems to have taken over all concepts and functions of the divine in the narratives of the ex-slaves.
3. The ex-slaves are concerned with sin as it relates to their efforts for positive transformation in the community (as was the case in the spiritual songs). But some autobiographical statements also suggest that certain acts are wrong (e.g., going to dances, playing cards).
4. The autobiographies associate Satan and the Devil with white oppressors as the creators of the spiritual songs are also thought to have done; but in one of the autobiographies a Black person, a cruel overseer, is also associated with the Devil. "White," in itself, is not deval-

ued or deemed evil by the ex-slaves. Rather, certain patterns of human relations that yield cruelty and enslavement are thought to be sinful and evil.

5. In the spiritual songs and the autobiographies there are intimations of two kinds of moral action incorporated in the Black understanding of transgression. One can be termed "wrongdoing," which (in some autobiographies) may refer to specific acts like stealing for which the ex-slave does not feel responsible. Rather, the responsibility is put upon the oppressor whose conduct creates the condition making stealing necessary on the part of the slave. And then there is that transgression that involves collective social evil far more serious in its consequence than acts of wrongdoing; this social evil occurs when one dominant group exerts its power in a way that brutalizes another group with less power. The result of wrongdoing on the part of the ex-slave (especially in the autobiographies) was apparently personal, psychic disorder like depression, guilt, and so forth. The result of social sin was consignment to hell.

In the latter part of the twentieth century, some proponents of Black liberation theology have provided a concept of sin apparently built more upon the notions of sin contained in the spiritual songs than upon notions of sin reflected in the autobiographies of the ex-slaves. This is especially true about the idea of sin contained in James Cone's book *A Black Theology of Liberation.*

Sin in a Theology of Liberation

Cone does not speak of individual sin. Rather, he (like the spiritual songs) speaks of sin in a communal or collective sense "inseparable from revelation." And revelation is knowledge of God's involvement in the liberation struggle of the racially oppressed Black community. (This idea of Cone's is strikingly similar to the hope for revelation and liberation expressed in such spiritual songs as "God's Gonna Trouble the Waters.") One cannot grasp the full meaning of sin in Cone's thought without knowledge of his explanation of Black theology's way of understanding "humanness."

What the spiritual songs communicate covertly, Cone can, of course, articulate clearly — i.e., that freedom is an absolutely necessary constituent of the human condition if "humanness" is to prevail in society. Thus, within a liberation context, Cone declares that:

Being human means being against evil by joining sides with those who are victims of evil. Quite literally it means becoming oppressed with the oppressed, making their cause one's own cause by involving oneself in the liberation struggle. *No one is free until all are free.*[27]

But freedom, as the essence of humanity, is not a state of being into which one is born and in which one maintains "peaceful" bliss throughout the stages of one's life. Rather, Cone's freedom means participation in the liberation struggle of racially oppressed people. Associating human nature (as freedom) with the biblical reference to human beings made in the image of God, Cone claims that "the image [of God] is human nature in rebellion against the structures of oppression. It is humanity involved in the liberation struggle against the forces of inhumanity."[28]

Since, in Cone's theology, sin is only spoken of in a collective sense (in terms of a community's rather than an individual's life), he advances notions of sin for the Black community and also for the white community. He asks a rhetorical question: "What . . . does sin mean for whites from the black perspective?" His response is that "The sin of whites is the definition of their existence in terms of whiteness. It is accepting the condition that is responsible for Amerindian reservations, black concentration camps, and the rape of Vietnam. It is believing in the American way of life as defined by its history."[29] Thus Cone concludes that "What we need is the destruction of whiteness, which is the source of human misery in the world."[30]

For the Black community, according to Cone, "sin represents the condition of estrangement from the source of one's being . . . for blacks this means a desire to be white. . . . Sin for blacks is loss of identity." Therefore, sin "is saying yes to the white absurdity—accepting the world as it is by letting whites define African-American existence. To be in sin is to be contented with white solutions for the "black problem" and not rebel against every infringement of white being on black being."[31]

While spiritual songs and autobiographies of ex-slaves do not lend themselves to in-depth comparisons with well-developed theological statements like Cone's *A Black Theology of Liberation*, there are several emphases related to sin that run through all three sources. First, freedom is emphasized as a reality achieved as sin is conquered. All three sources either suggest or express clearly an idea of election in God's relation to the Black American community. Either covertly or overtly, the spiritual songs, the autobiographies and Cone's theology identify those who oppress Black people as sinners; and both God and African Americans "war" against these sinners. In all three sources sin, itself, is associated more with patterns of human relation and patterns of divine and human relation than with individual acts identified as sin—though some autobiographies do identify a few individual acts as sinful.

Yet there are distinctive features, with reference to sin, that each source contributes to the history of African-American Christian thought. The Allen collection of spiritual songs reveals a stage in Black American Christian history when slaves intricately structured language in symbolic and metaphorical patterns to communicate their collective belief that slavery was evil and slave owners were therefore living in sin. In part, the autobiographies of the ex-slaves take a turn inward toward the individual psyche and connect sin with debilitating feelings; then they speak of deliverance from sin in terms of personal renewal. *A Black Theology of Liberation*, written considerably later than the Allen collection of spiritual songs and the ex-slave autobiographies, makes sin and color prejudice synonymous. Using racial oppression as its point of departure for describing African-American reality in the latter part of the twentieth century, this source pictures a Black God unequivocally on the side of Black people struggling to be liberated from the sin of racial oppression.

It is Black women's full-length, autobiographical narratives, written in the nineteenth and early twentieth centuries, that show the development of female consciousness about sin. This development often proceeds from feelings of personal unworthiness to a sense of somebodiness bestowed by an encounter with Jesus. Reaching the level of "somebodiness" amounts to what they see as liberation. Most of the Black women's full-length autobiographies considered in this essay do not identify specific sins. The feelings of personal unworthiness seem to be the result of sin. Liberation from sin often occurs amid visionary experiences apparently precipitated by mental depression or even inclinations toward suicide associated with these feelings of unworthiness.

African-American Women and Sin

Mary Prince, a West Indian slave woman, tells how she became conscious of sin:

> The slave woman who had the care of the place [the plantation] asked me to go with her to her husband's house, to a Methodist meeting for prayer. . . . I went; and they were the first prayers I ever understood . . . one woman prayed; and then they all sung a hymn; then there was another prayer and another hymn; and then they all spoke . . . of their own griefs as sinners. . . . This meeting had a great impression on my mind and led my spirit to the Moravian Church. . . . The Moravian ladies taught me to read in class. . . . I dearly loved to go to the church. . . . I never knew rightly that I had much sin till I went there. When I found out that I was a great sinner I was very sorely grieved, and very much frightened. I used to pray God to pardon my sins for Christ's sake, and forgive me for every thing I had done amiss; and when I went home to my work, I always thought about what I had heard from the missionaries and wished to be good that I might go to heaven.[32]

Before her connection with these Christian denominations, Prince had no conception of sin in relation to herself. It is this connection that brings her a sense of personal unworthiness.

However, Old Elizabeth, a North American slave woman, was born to religious parents who belonged to the "Methodist Society." At an early age, she had a sense of sin as personal unworthiness. In the context of her visionary experience, she says she received personal liberation from sin. Relating the effects of being separated from her mother who was sold, Old Elizabeth says:

> I had none in the world to look to but God, I betook myself to prayer, and in every lonely place I found an altar. I mourned sore like a dove and chattered forth my sorrow, moaning in the corners of the field, and under the fences. ... One evening, after the duties of the day were ended, I thought I could not live over the night ... and my spirit cried within me, must I die in this state and be banished from Thy presence forever? I own I am a sinner in Thy sight, and not fit to live where thou art. ... Just at this season, I saw with my spiritual eye, an awful gulf of misery. As I thought I was about to plunge into it, I heard a voice saying, "rise up and pray," which strengthened me.

Elizabeth continues, telling about a visionary experience in which she saw "a director, clothed in white raiment" who led her to a higher place where she "saw the Saviour standing with His hand stretched out to receive me." Then she says:

> At this moment I felt my sins were forgiven me, and the time of my deliverance was at hand. I sprang forward and fell at His feet, giving Him all the thanks and highest praises, crying, Thou has redeemed me — Thou has redeemed me to thyself. ... I was at this time not yet thirteen years old.[33]

Jarena Lee in her autobiography, published in 1836, claims that she had a sense of her own sinfulness even before she was seriously involved with the Christian religion through one of its denominations. She says that her parents "being wholly ignorant of the knowledge of God, had not therefore instructed me in any degree in this great matter." Even so, Lee believed that "in my early history, the spirit of God moved in power through my conscience, and told me I was a wretched sinner" (because she told a lie). Later, her encounter with the preaching of a Presbyterian missionary gave her the rationale for accepting herself as inherently sinful and unworthy. She says:

> At the reading of the Psalms [by the missionary], a ray of renewed conviction darted into my soul. These were the words, composing the first verse of the Psalms for the service: Lord, I am vile, conceived in sin, Born unholy and unclean. Sprung from man, whose guilty fall Corrupts the race, and taints us all. This description of my condition

struck me to the heart, and made me to feel in some measure, the weight of my sins, and sinful nature.[34]

She often contemplated suicide. But like Mary Prince and Elizabeth, Jarena Lee also had an empowering mystical experience that gave her a sense of having been forgiven for all her sins. These mystical or visionary experiences with God/Jesus seem to have elevated these women's self-esteem and given them a sense of their "somebodiness."

Elizabeth and Jarena Lee apparently understood sin in an ontological sense whereby the flaw or fault is in existence itself. This sense of ontological sin seems to have been imparted to them through Christian teaching they received from Christian parents or through their own encounter with Christian denominations. It is through a personal encounter with Jesus that they are empowered not only to believe that one can gain victory over this flaw in existence called sin. This encounter also empowers Elizabeth and Lee to preach and believe that preaching is a proper vocation for women.

Zilpha Elaw, whose autobiography was published in 1846, was clearer than the other women in her identification of the cause of the sin for which she felt guilty. Though her parents had been very religious, they died when Elaw was young, thus leaving her in the care of a family of Quakers for whom she was a servant. Evidently the Quakers did not practice the form of religious exercises that Elaw thought were beneficial for her. She says, "nor were religion and devotion referred to by them [the Quaker family] in my hearing, which rendered my transition from home the more strange." She goes on to declare that "being very young, and no apparent religious restraint being laid upon me, I soon gave way to the evil propensities of an unregenerate heart, which is enmity against God, and heedlessly ran into the ways of sin, taking pleasure in the paths of folly."[35] Here, Elaw expresses her belief that unreformed emotions (which were thought to reside in the heart) caused her to sin, and this sin had to do with pleasure (the "paths of folly"). Yet Elaw claims never to have experienced "that terrific dread of hell by which some Christians appear to have been exercised; but I felt a godly sorrow for sin."[36] It is clear that Lee and Elaw understand sin related to personal salvation. This idea springs from the Methodist and Moravian beliefs to which they became attached but is also informed by the visions they believed came from Jesus calling them to preach.

We cannot overlook the fact that some nineteenth-century slave women and free Black women were influenced by certain Christian movements. Julia A. J. Foote, an evangelist publishing her narrative in 1879, had an understanding of sin also shaped by the Holiness Movement getting a major foothold in the United States during her time. Most of the women were perhaps influenced by the emphasis of the Second Great Awakening Movement in America. Fostering evangelical forms of Christianity, this movement put stress upon conversion through a spiritual journey. "This spiritual journey began with an acknowledgment of personal sinfulness and unworthiness and ended in an emotional experience of salvation by God through the Holy Spirit."[37] But according to sociologists C. Eric Lincoln and Larry Mamiya, there were great differences between Black and white conversion experiences. Lincoln and Mamiya quote Mechal Sobel who claims that "Analysis of the black visionary experiences indicate . . . that they were very different [from the white] from the outset, and . . . their uniqueness was highlighted as whites grew less concerned with the spiritual journeys."[38]

Some of this uniqueness had to do with Black women's liberation from "unworthiness" (figuring into Great Awakening notions of sin) to a state of "somebodiness," which they felt was granted by their encounter with the sacred in their visions. It was these women's belief in this bestowing of "somebodiness" upon them by the power of the sacred that empowered them to become itinerate preachers and advance fine arguments supporting women's right to ordination.

However, there were also aspects of African-American women's social reality in the nineteenth century that might have helped make the big difference in the nature of their conversion and visionary experience (i.e., different from whites). So much of the American culture "told" the Black woman she was unworthy. She was not worthy of the pedestal position upon which white womanhood had been placed by Victorian standards. She could be sexually abused by any man in the culture without any man ever being punished for this abuse. She could be forced by law or by economic necessity to labor in areas where other women (e.g., white women) were thought too "fragile" to perform the tasks associated with the areas — areas often designated as "men's work." These visionary experiences, and the call to preach contained in them, helped Black women resist the widespread social ideology in America claiming that Black women were by nature sexually promiscuous and immoral (i.e., unworthy to model "true womanhood").

These visions, often providing an encounter with Jesus, healed Black women's consciousness of their "unworthiness" and boosted their self-esteem. Thus Black women could survive and achieve well-being in spite of the devaluation of Black womanhood, which white America incorporated in its social ideology of white supremacy. Perhaps one of the reasons nineteenth-century Black women flocked to the evangelical Christianity of the Great Awakening was that this kind of religion helped them put concepts of unworthiness on the side of sin. Therefore, consciously or unconsciously, Black women's spiritual development — in the context of this particular expression of the Christian religion — helped them rise above white society's assignment of "unworthiness" to Black womanhood.

A Womanist Notion of Sin

Hence we can claim that at least two social sources fed into this "unworthiness" felt by some Black women. One source was the elevation of white womanhood and the devaluation of Black womanhood which was, in actuality, a devaluation of Black women's humanity. The other source was the indifference of the U.S. legal system to the defilement of Black women's bodies—especially through overwork, lynching, and rape of Black women by white men.[39] Defilement here carries the dictionary meaning "to ravish, violate . . . to sully, dishonor."[40] The narratives of nineteenth-century Black women relate many incidents of the rape and violation of Black women's bodies by white male overseers and slaveholders. During slavery, many Black women were also violated through their work; their labor was thoroughly abused.[41] There are narratives in which the white slaveholding class refer to Black women and their progeny as filthy and dirty and therefore "proper" subjects for physical violation and destruction.[42] As early as 1565 John Hammond, in his tract about women's work written during that year, confirmed that servant women (i.e., poor white women) "were not put to work in the fields but in domestic employments." Then he adds: "some wenches that are nasty, and beastly [i.e., Black women] and not fit to be so employed are put into the ground [i.e., put in the fields to work]."[43]

In the construction of a womanist notion of sin informed by the Black community's and Black theology's belief in social sin, it is quite legitimate to identify devaluation of Black women's humanity and the "defilement" of their bodies as the social sin American patriarchy[44] and demonarchy[45] have committed against Black women and their children. Even among the gods of the ancients in Western culture, defilement of the body was considered a most grievous act for which one received severe punishment. In Homer's *Iliad*, the gods become angry with Achilles not because he kills his opponent Hector, but because he defiles Hector's body after he has killed him. Death is humility enough, but to defile a person after death deserves the punishment of being cut off from eternal life—which, of course, was the punishment Achilles received. He loses his invulnerability, and his heel becomes his vulnerable point which, if properly wounded, can lead to his death.

In the context of both the Hebrew Testament and the Christian Testament, defilement was a serious matter yielding grave consequences. Jacob's daughter Dinah (in the book of Genesis) is defiled (raped) by a prince. Her brothers murder the rapist, his father and all the men in the territory over which the prince's father rules. In the Christian Testament, the Pharisees accuse Jesus' disciples of not observing the Jewish laws concerning defilement (Mark 7:1–8). Jesus' message contradicted Jewish laws about defilement related to ritual cleanliness and helped lead to his death (Matt. 15:10–20). Jesus tried to change Jewish traditional association of defilement with physical realities like unclean hands before one eats and with foods designated as unclean. Thus Jesus says "whatever goes into the mouth passes into the stomach, and so passes on. . . . But what comes out of the mouth proceeds from the heart, and this defiles a man [*sic*]. For out of the heart come evil thoughts, murder, adultery. . . . These are what defile a man [*sic*]; but to eat with unwashed hands does not defile a man" (Matt. 15:17–20). In other words, it is atrocious actions against another person that constitute defilement. Inasmuch as womanist theology takes the Bible seriously as a validating tool, a womanist notion of sin claims that defilement of Black women's bodies and the resulting attack upon their spirits and self-esteem constitute the gravest kind of social sin of which American patriarchal and demonarchal society is guilty.

In our own time, this American way of defilement has also reached beyond Black women to nature itself. The powers that be in America have defiled the land with their rapid industrial and technological advancement. The waters are polluted by oil spills and debris from industrial plants. The air is unfit to breath because of industrial smog. The fruit and vegetables from the land are poisoned by the chemical spraying of the land. Certain animals that were once plentiful in the United States are now extinct or nearly extinct because of the male lust for "the hunt" or because of the greedy lust for money to be gained from animal fur. Hence womanist theology can claim a definite parallel between the defilement of Black women's bodies and the defilement of the health of earth's body (the land, air, and water) by the people who own the means of production. The spirit and self-esteem of the land are just as impaired by this defilement as are Black women's spirit and self-esteem injured by defilement of their bodies. All of this constitutes the sin of which our society is guilty.

Like theologian James Cone's way of identifying sin as a society's way of taking away people's humanity, womanist theologians can claim that society's way of devaluing Black womanhood is also sin. For Black women's womanhood is their humanity. To devalue Black women's womanhood is to take away their humanity. This can be illustrated by focusing upon some aspects of Alice Walker's understanding of Black womanhood suggested in her definition of a womanist.[46]

Walker identifies a womanist as Black or of other color. Cone has shown well enough how Black people's color has been the basis upon which many white Americans have judged Black people to be subhuman. Walker lifts up Black women involved in the single-parenting act of passing on advice to the female child. The relationship between mother and child in a single-parent household is not valued as the proper circumstance out of which "normal" and psychologically healthy children can come. These kinds of relationships and family life are devalued. Needless to say, American culture does not value the advice that women give. Walker, in her description of a womanist, challenges stereotypical ideas devaluating Black women. She describes a womanist as "Responsible . . . in charge . . . serious." This challenges the stigma of "childlike," "girlish," and "frivolous," which patriarchal and demonarchal social attitudes assign to Black women. According to Walker, a womanist loves men and women sexually or nonsexually. This challenges those who devalue the humanity of lesbian women. A womanist defines universality in terms of an array of skin colors. This gives intrinsic value to *all* skin color: "brown, pink and yellow" as well as "white, beige and black." Walker describes Black women's love in terms of dance, the moon, the spirit, love, food, roundness, struggle, the folks, and love of themselves as women. This affirms the cultural elements through which Black women express their humanity. To devalue any of this understanding of a womanist is to devalue Black women's womanhood, to devalue their humanity, to be guilty of sin—the sin that denies that Black women's humanity is in the image of God as is all humanity.[47]

In accord, then, with spiritual songs and the theology of James Cone, the womanist understanding of sin in this essay places guilt on the side of society at large. But unlike the spiritual songs, the narratives of ex-slaves and the theology of James Cone, this womanist notion of social sin also extends to the African-American community. There, Black woman's humanity is also devalued and their bodies are defiled by rape and domestic violence. Black lesbian women are the most devalued in the Black community where homophobia abounds. Hence Christian womanist women oppose sin when they make political alliances with liberated feminist forces and *enlightened* males acting to alleviate this kind of social sin in Black, white, and other cultural communities.

A question may be raised at this point. What constitutes individual sin according to womanist theology? And does this definition of sin as devaluation of Black womanhood and as defilement exempt Black women from being sinners? Individual sin has to do with participating in society's systems that devalue Black women's womanhood (humanity) through a process of invisibilization—that is, invisibilizing the womanist character of Black women's experience and emphasizing the stereotypical images of Black women that prevail and are perpetuated in the larger society. These stereotypes image Black women as having "child-like mentality," as being "girlish" in their actions and as being "frivilous and loose" in character. These stereotypical images reflect Black womanhood as unserious and not worthy of serious valuation. Participating in the perpetuation of this kind of understanding of Black womanhood and Black women's humanity constitutes individual sin. Black women also participate in sin when they do not challenge the patriarchal and demonarchal systems in society defiling Black women's bodies through physical violence, sexual abuse, and exploited labor.

There are, then, at least four distinctive features of this womanist notion of sin:

1) Unlike ideas about sin in spiritual songs, ex-slave autobiographies and in Cone's theology, this womanist notion of sin takes the human body and its sexual resources very seriously; the abuse and depletion of these resources amount to defilement which constitutes sin;

2) Black womanhood and humanity are synonymous and in the image of God; Black women's sexual being is also in the image of God; therefore to devalue the womanhood and sexuality of Black women is sin; to devalue

the womanhood and sexuality of Black lesbian women is also sin;

3) Feelings of personal "unworthiness" expressed in the Black women's narratives used in this study indicate problems in women's self-esteem. Unlike the spiritual songs, autobiographies and Cone's ideas about sin, the womanist notion of sin in this essay takes seriously Black women's depleted self-esteem. Thus elevating and healing Black women's self-esteem figures into womanist notions of what constitutes salvation for the oppressed African-American community.

4) In the history of Black Christian thought, this womanist notion of sin is unique in its suggestion of parallels between the defilement of Black women's bodies and the defilement of nature.

The great hope of womanist theology is for Christians to come together and work in concert to alleviate the sin of devaluation and defilement threatening the lives and spirits of Black women as well as the life of the natural environment that sustains all life.

NOTES

1. It should be pointed out that womanist theology is also sourced by the feminist community. However, this sourcing must be the subject of an extensive study and therefore cannot be dealt with in the limited space allotted to this essay.

2. Elsa Barkley Brown, "Womanist Consciousness: Maggie Lena Walker and the Independent Order of Saint Luke," in Micheline R. Malson, Elizabeth Mudimbe-Boyi, Jean F. O'Barr, and Mary Wyer, eds., *Black Women in America* (Chicago: University of Chicago Press, 1988), 173–196.

3. William Francis Allen, Charles Pickard Ware, and Lucy McKim Garrison, eds., *Slave Songs of the United States* (1867; reprint New York: Peter Smith, 1951).

4. Norman R. Yetman, ed., *Voices from Slavery* (New York: Holt, Rinehart and Winston, 1970) and Clifton H. Johnson, ed., *God Struck Me Dead* (Philadelphia: Pilgrim Press, 1969).

5. James H. Cone, *A Black Theology of Liberation*, 20th anniversary ed. (Maryknoll, NY: Orbis Books, 1990).

6. The narratives by Jarena Lee and Julia A. J. Foote are collected in Henry Louis Gates, Jr., ed., *Spiritual Narratives,* The Schomburg Library of Nineteenth-Century Black Women Writers (New York: Oxford University Press, 1988). The narratives by Old Elizabeth, Mattie J. Jackson, Lucy Delany, and Kate Drumgold are in Gates, ed., *Six Women's Slave Narratives,* The Schomburg Library of Nineteenth-Century Black Women Writers, 1988. The narrative by Jarena Lee is collected in William L. Andrews, ed., *Sisters of Spirit* (Bloomington: University of Indiana Press, 1986).

7. Henceforth in this essay *Slave Songs of the United States* will be referred to as the Allen collection. Allen was one of the editors for this work.

8. In these spiritual songs the individual and the collective seem to be one. References to sin and its eradication appear to have more to do with community experience and expectations than with any single person's experience.

9. "Authors' identities" is plural here because the songs were created in a collective, communal context and not by one person. However, the word "personal"

accompanies this plural, collective usage because in the songs creators use the singular pronoun "my" to refer to sin.

10. See "Almost Over," Allen collection, 74.

11. See "Sinner Won't Die No More," in Allen collection, 85.

12. "Go in the Wilderness," Allen collection, 14.

13. In this song, "de Lord" may be a code word for the slave owner. If so, the song puts responsibility for the slaves' trouble, burdens and sin upon the slave owner. By casting their sins in the middle of the sea, the slaves would be expressing the belief that they have the power to relieve themselves of sins (burdens) "de Lord" has willed for them to "Hold . . . to de end."

14. "What a Trying Time," the Allen collection, 74.

15. With reference to dancing, the following testimony appears in the autobiographical statement "Angels Warm Me in My Dreams" in *God Struck Me Dead*: "I remember one night — oh, I used to love good times — I was lying down after a dance. I felt so wicked. . . ." And in the narrative "Waiting for to carry me home," this appears: "Now I was a great dancer . . . and in spite of my praying I went to dances." See pages 121 and 122 in *God Struck Me Dead*. The autobiographical statement "Before the Wind Ever Blew" suggests that playing cards is wrong, 111.

16. "A Preacher From a God-Fearing Plantation," in *God Struck Me Dead*, 73.

17. Ibid., 109.

18. Ibid., 97.

19. "Slavery Was Hell Without Fire," in *God Struck Me Dead*, 161.

20. Ibid.

21. Norman Yetman, *Voices from Slavery*, 53.

22. "Slavery Was Hell Without Fire," *God Struck Me Dead*, 161–162.

23. "Richard Carruthers," in Yetman, *Voices from Slavery*, 53.

24. "Waist-deep in Death," in *God Struck Me Dead*, 165.

25. "More Than Conqueror," in *God Struck Me Dead*, 171.

26. "Hooked in the Heart," in *God Struck Me Dead*, 19.

27. James H. Cone, *A Black Theology of Liberation*, 88.

28. Ibid., 94.

29. Ibid., 107.

30. Ibid.

31. Ibid., 108–109.

32. Mary Prince, "The History of Mary Prince, A West Indian Slave," in Henry Louis Gates, Jr., ed., *Six Women's Slave Narratives*, The Schomburg Library of Nineteenth-Century Black Women Writers (New York: Oxford University Press, 1988), 16–17.

33. Old Elizabeth, "Memoir of Old Elizabeth, A Coloured Woman," in Henry Louis Gates, Jr., ed., *Six Women's Slave Narratives*, The Schomburg Library of Nineteenth-Century Black Women Writers (New York: Oxford University Press, 1988), 5, 6.

34. Jarena Lee, "The Life and Religious Experience of Jarena Lee, A Coloured Lady, Giving an Account of Her Call to Preach The Gospel," in William L. Andrews, ed., *Sisters of the Spirit* (Bloomington: Indiana University Press, 1986. First published by the author in Philadelphia in 1836), 27.

35. Mrs. Zilpha Elaw, "Memoirs of the Life, Religious Experience, Ministerial Travels and Labours of Mrs. Zilpha Elaw, An American Female of Colour," in William Andrews, ed., *Sisters of the Spirit*, 54.

36. Ibid., 55.

37. C. Eric Lincoln and Lawrence H. Mamiya, *The Black Church in the African American Experience* (Durham, NC: Duke University Press, 1990), 6.

38. Ibid.

39. For an account of the lynching Black people, male and female, have experienced in the United States see Ralph Ginzburg, *One Hundred Years of Lynching* (Baltimore: Black Classic Press, 1962). Especially see page 38: "Negro Suspect Eludes Mob; Sister Lynched Instead." Also see this entry that appears on page 36: "HARVARD PROFESSOR FAVORS LEGALIZING LYNCHINGS." Reporting a 1900 newspaper account, the book printed this: "Professor Albert Bushnell Hart, of Harvard College, speaking before the American Historical Association in convention . . . said that if the people of certain States are determined to burn colored men at the stake, those States would better legalize the practice."

40. *Webster's Seventh New Collegiate Dictionary* (Springfield, MA: G. & C. Merriam Co., 1971), 216.

41. For an account of Black women's defilement through their work, see the reference to Hetty in Prince, "The History of Mary Prince, A West Indian Slave," in *Six Women's Slave Narratives*.

42. For instance, see the reference to the physical abuse of a Black woman and the destruction of her child by a white slave owner on page 135 above.

43. Winthrop D. Jordan, *White Over Black* (New York: Norton, 1968), 77.

44. For a discussion of the way in which Black women's experience challenges Christian notions of redemption on the basis of this sin of defilement see Delores S. Williams, "Black Women's Surrogacy Experience Challenges Christian Notions of Redemption," in Paula Cooley, William Eakin, and Jay McDaniel, eds., *After Patriarchy* (Maryknoll, NY: Orbis Books, 1991).

45. Delores Williams coined the term *demonarchy* to name the oppression that white American social institutions, directed by both white men and white women, exert upon the lives of Black women. Contrasting patriarchy and demonarchy, Williams identifies a positive side of patriarchy that white women enjoy but is not extended to Black women. This positive side has merit because it allows white women to get the education it takes to secure for themselves most of the jobs and benefits the American civil rights movement obtains for women. White-controlled social institutions, which feminists have characterized as patriarchal, also intend to preserve and save the lives of the children of white women as long as those children issue from the sexual relations of white men and women together. On the other hand, white-controlled American institutions do not intend to preserve and save the lives of the children of Black women. Rather, these institutions employ demonic government in relation to Black children and Black women which intends to destroy their lives. See Williams' treatment of demonarchy in her article, "The Color of Feminism: Or Speaking the Black Woman's Tongue," in the *Journal of Religious Thought* 43 (Spring-Summer, 1986).

46. See Alice Walker, *In Search of Our Mothers' Gardens: Womanist Prose* (New York: Harcourt Brace Jovanovich, 1983), xi-xii.

47. This womanist notion of social sin as devaluation of humanity also includes racism, sexism, and classism which cannot happen in a society unless one group devalues the humanity and equal worth of another group.

9

African-American Spirituals

Confronting and Exorcising Evil through Song

Cheryl A. Kirk-Duggan

African-American spirituals are the product of a maieutic or midwifery process. These cultural artifacts helped incubate and deliver the souls of Black folk from total despair. Spirituals disclose the reality of and the fight against two evils that helped induce their birth: slavery and racism.[1] People of African descent were not intended for inclusion in the compact, "We, the People ... " The physical presence of both African and Native Americans insured that *the white man*[2] in the United States could always know that he was superior to the slave, whose servitude mirrored the whiteness, freedom, and limitless possibility that were accessible to white men. In response to the institutionalized racism and its idolatrous faith of the seventeenth to nineteenth centuries, Black slaves begot the spirituals. One century later, the civil-rights campaigns adopted many of these spirituals as psychological and spiritual mechanisms to combat anti-Black racism.

These spirituals document the reality of the oppressed and the oppressor and the use of power in the United States of America. They catalog the political and religious Afrocentric experience. Afrocentricity,[3] a holistic ideology central to all analysis involving African erudition, fosters a cultural reconstruction of human transformation. This perspective radically critiques an environment that involves a ruling Eurocentric ideology fused with an Afrocentric social and intellectual milieu. Afrocentricity compels an inquiry of slavery.

Slavery was a massive economic-based U. S. institution that was later justified by prejudicial, biblical, scientific, political, and psychological mythologies. Even after abolition and manumission became law, racism remained a contingency in the myths and rituals of U. S. civil religion. The paradox of institutionalized slavery existing within Christian community is the evil or sin of racism. One of the sins of racism is idolatry because it calls into question the goodness of God's creation and offers a counterdeity, that is, biology or nature, as a fit subject for human adoration. At its core, racism is America's *original sin* against the Holy Spirit.

Racism is original sin since it represents an expulsion from the Garden of Love; it values and devalues life according to its warped sense of the good. Neither racism nor slavery are peculiar to the United States; the spirituals are. More than 6,000 African-American spirituals express African-American relationships to God and narrate Black people's survival in the United States since 1619. Spirituals chronicle the systematic subjugation of a people's legal and moral human rights because of "the color line." Spirituals existentially involve holistic living that demands exorcising, confronting, and reconciling evil. Theodicy, the theology of justice, represents one approach to the paradox posed by the presence or absence of Divine Goodness in the midst of human-perceived evil. Spirituals explore this issue midst a synthesis of the African holistic, religio-musical worldview, and the European Protestant biblical and hymnodical traditions.

The slave-self who sang these spirituals was evident in the womanist participants of the civil rights movement. That spirit remains in womanists, who are "among the women who dare to dream and dare to make their dreams come true."[4] A womanist is a Black feminist or feminist of color who is audacious, willful, responsible, and curious. She loves and commits to human survival and wholeness. Womanists, steeped in an unflinching African-American heritage, have honed memories and stories into the words and music of the African-American spiritual. My reading champions a womanist hermeneutic concerned about liberating the tridimensional victimization of African-American reality via race-sex-class. Such victimization spawned a pregnancy conceived in a racist womb of love and hate.

That pregnancy resulted in the spirituals, a birth child of the African-American experience in the United States. The maieutic or midwifery process included the prenatal African traditions and birth event of institutional slavery. The spirituals are the liberating offspring born of a communal "inspiring fire."[5] That fire recreates the enslaving experience of life and death veiled in hope as African and Eurocentric theological, anthropological, sociopolitical, and literary perspectives fuel the spirituals. Holding such myriad tensions together arouses the dialectic that undergirds African-American life.

This essay argues that the combined text and music of African-American spirituals fashion an Afrocentric concept of theodicy. An Afrocentric, womanist, constructive theodicy via theory and praxis builds on the transformational powers of text and music. This process will unveil a holistic, African-American vision of theodicy that engages my two passions: theology and music. History produced the vehicle: research determines the hermeneutic and methodology.

Context: An Informed Hermeneutic Frames the Quilt of Dialogue

The languages of midwifery, nurturing, and quilting occur throughout the essay. To make a quilt, one *frames* the design, traces the pattern on paper, and then cuts out the pattern. After collecting the fabrics and cutting out the various patterns from the fabrics that form each design, the quilter pieces or sews together the sections of the design to form a block. The individual blocks are sewn together to make the upper layer of the quilt. The final quilt has three layers: the backing, the inner layer of cotton batting, and the top, designed layer. This essay engages a hermeneutic with the following frames: (1) sociohistorical—the background or context of the spirituals; (2) narrative-dialectical—the spirituals' statement about theodicy; (3) rhetorical-musical critical—the dialogue between the two eras; (4) philosophical-theological—the viability of spirituals as channels for theologizing.

The Context: A Sociohistorical Frame

Spirituals are a blueprint of the slave's mind. Spirituals share the folk experience and reflect the religious thought of African-American Christians. Although the spirituals existed prior to the end of the seventeenth century, spirituals remained an oral system until their transcription in 1867 in the William Allen collection, *Slave Songs of the United States* (1867).[6] The Fisk Jubilee Singers, on their first concert tour in 1871, and the Hampton College Choir first brought the arrangements of spirituals to concert halls throughout the world.

Many of the Africans brought to the United States had encountered the Bible and Christianity in Africa. Filtered through North American Christian revivalism and teaching, slave songs became folk-inspired rites of religious feeling. The spiritual evolved into an independent, creative, musical work wherever slaves lived. African *musicking*,[7] under slavery, added new themes to old customs. Slaves in the United States were forbidden to be African and were barred from being American. Although Congress outlawed the importation of African slaves in 1807, large-scale smuggling of slaves into the United States continued until the northern naval blockade of the South during the Civil War. Some former abolitionist groups in the North began to approve of slavery for economic reasons based on biblical interpretations.[8] Yet, African slaves never stopped singing. They changed their language from African dialect to American English.

The language and music of the spirituals reveal that slaves hungered for physical and spiritual freedom. Freedom is a God-given right and the essence of the Age of Revolution.[9] Spirituals, like slave narratives, celebrated the human quest for freedom. Freedom extolled full humanity and life without fear. The refusal to accept enslavement led to personal strategies of accommodation, aggression, and/or insurrection. Singers created coded "freedom" spirituals that immortalized and disguised subversive acts. The 1960s "freedom now" civil-rights "insurrections" involved a therapy of mass nonviolent protest. Both the pre-Civil War and the "freedom now" eras exacted blood sacrifice endemic to struggles against structural malevolence or evil. The juxtaposition of structural malevolence against the exaltation for freedom, along with racism based on economic injustice, are key components of U. S. civil religion.

This civil religion has its own higher judgment, its prophets, its martyrs, its sacred events and places, its rituals, its symbols; and it regulates power. This civil faith views the United States both as a society in perfect accord with the will of God and as a people who are a paradigm to all nations. Grounded in Puritan covenantal theology, this heritage cloaked the malevolent interests and ugly passions of slavery and racism imbedded in U. S. civil religion to the point of dogma.[10]

Racist laws and mores are transmitted through myth and sacralized through ritual. Such parochialism posits the inferiority of others. That perceived inferiority serves to justify exclusion, mistreatment, and genocide. Because some believed freedom sprang from Christianity, some slaveholders did not allow their Africans to practice Christianity. During the latter half of the eighteenth and early nineteenth centuries, domestic technology[11] increased the economic value of slaves. Meanwhile, a religious revival spread Christianity among African Americans. As vehicles of faith and history, the spirituals, then and now, attest to protest and attend to faith. Present-day African-American women use the spirituals to praise their God, to protest in faith, and to seek civil freedom against structural malevolence. Through the spirituals, womanists both express their heritage of communal zeal and demand respect, justice, human freedom, and dignity. Like their ancestors, the 1960s freedom fighters, the 1990s Black womanists proudly rely on a strong African-American heritage reminiscent of the music of the spirituals.

In the 1960s, the spirituals sounded a call to action — uniting African-American history with a contemporary freedom struggle. The freedom songs galvanized parts of the Black community when other forms of communication failed. Adaptations of earlier spirituals inspired all people, Black and white, female and male, together to fight injustice. Spirituals embodied persuasive ideological elements toward holistic human actualization. They exposed the Northern and Southern economic triumphalism that sentenced the enslaved to an existence of living death. Slaves were the scapegoats of the pre-Civil War era just as impoverished African-American women are the Girardian scapegoats of the 1990s.

Scapegoating is a complex and extreme form of violence. Scapegoating involves choosing a victim to bear the punishment for others' conflicts, difficulties, shortcomings, and sins. Victimizers choose their victims because of the latter's membership in a class that is vulnerable to persecution.

Scapegoating feeds on distinctions where "[e]thnic and religious minorities tend to polarize the majorities against themselves,"[12] via the victims' cultural, religious, and physical criteria. A thin line separates scapegoating and revolutionary violence, since only in the destruction of everything that limits a person can he or she find freedom, humanity. Racism and slavery make scapegoats based on economic and racial properties.

Slaves endured and avenged scapegoating via song.[13] Freedom fighters used spirituals and freedom songs to induce inspiration, hope, free speech, and affirmation. The more the freedom fighters sang, the more social reality changed. The jailers' physical threats could not stop the singing. "What they're trying to do is take your soul away. . . . [They] took the mattresses away and people sang as they had never sung before. We thought we were winning the battle, they [the victimizers] were on the run"[14] from the reality of their own evil perpetrations. Spirituals so infiltrated the atmosphere, that in 1964, President Lyndon Johnson ended his personal appearance before Congress seeking successful passage of omnibus civil-rights legislation with the triumphant words of that famous song of the freedom fighters, "We Shall Overcome."

In confronting evil, slaves rebelled and survived the trauma. Afrocentric music, simultaneously religious and secular, aimed toward social well-being. Traditional European music was categorized and separated out as a distinct vocation within a broader society. Africans deemed music to be act and reality, within an oral tradition. Europeans viewed music as object, keyed to accurate performance, from *written* works. Spirituals illuminate how African Americans experience and respond to systemic evil or sin. The spirituals join the litany of freedom songs as calls to just action and communal solidarity. The spirituals are part of the musical tradition that recognizes the emotional fervor and appeal to the masses of the "Marseillaise," "Deutschland über Alles," Verdi's "la Libertad," the "Internationale," José Marti's "Guantanamera," and Woody Guthrie's "This Land Is Your Land." The swell of Black voices empowered those who faced death with a zeal for life. Choosing life unfolds paradoxically as a narrative-dialectic.

The Story: A Narrative-Dialectical Perspective

The slave narratives, and parallel stories of the 1960s civil-rights era, infer that African Americans have never accepted enforced societal subservience. African Americans have always desired freedom, a just verdict rendered upon their betrayers, and a strategy for gaining a more just future. The desire for imminent freedom and justice are the leitmotifs of most spirituals and of Black intellectual thought. The heritage of Black intellectual thought along with sociopolitical and religious activism provided an impetus for nonviolent protest. Up to the 1950s, African Americans remained disfranchised and experienced prejudice in employment and housing. Ironically, the legal success of the National Association for the

Advancement of Colored People (NAACP), which was limited to destroying the "separate but equal" fiction for all public schooling, along with heightened Black self-esteem, and massive resistance led to new expectations culminating in the 1960s student sit-ins and the so-called "civil-rights revolution." Spirituals embraced that revolt. The Bible and life itself provided a living documentary on slave existentialism and ontology and the racist experiences of their progeny. Death threats required that creators and singers of spirituals symbolically and metaphorically mask and code their authentic message.

The DuBoisian metaphor that captured this plight of duality or double-consciousness is the veil.[15] An African American is "born with a veil, and gifted with second-sight in this American world," which affords consciousness of the other, not true self-consciousness. A clear referent of the double-consciousness concerns the bombardment of the African milieu of holistic harmony with the disharmony of racism. The harmony, framed by unity, pervades the oral-aural narratives of traditional storytelling and praise singing retained by those of the African diaspora that emerges in the spirituals. The inherent destruction of slavery and racism jars the existence of one nurtured in harmony. African Americans feel the living contradiction of double-consciousness or "two-ness" of souls, thoughts, and unreconciled strivings. Their hesitant striving is the paradox of double aims: escaping white contempt yet surviving within a white society. Marginalization of the Black community within this larger society, which was caused by protracted, institutionalized racism, forces the African-American experience to remain veiled.

Part of this veiled reality encompasses the human struggle for liberation and cultural and human affirmation. Strong communal values midst a ritualized economic and racist civil religion of oppression recreates daily tensions that require a veiled existence for traditional Black values to remain functional. The spirituals celebrate the retention of transplanted African sociocultural richness in the lives of Black men and women in their preservation of life within the narrative Black aesthetic. That veiled Black reality resides today in the oral-aural-written stories of their own community, notably in the canon of womanist or Black feminist authors.

> Black female writers, as participant-observers, capsulize on a myriad of levels, the insularity of their home communities . . . Black female authors emphasize life within the community, not the conflict with outside forces. In order to give faithful pictures of important and comprehensive segments of Black life, these writers tie their character's stories to the aesthetic, emotional and intellectual values of the Black community.[16]

The study of the narrative-dialectic midst the music reveals how stories are formulas for garnering meaning from chaos. Probing for that dialectic is aided by the musical genre because African-American *musicking* becomes a counter-integrative model that allows one to question and reclaim historical realities. The double-consciousness within the African-American experience, set in narrative, celebrates the aesthetic tradition that remembers communal roots and values the differences that have nurtured survival. The narrative dialectic critique of the spirituals allows one to examine the spirituals in a way that may express the dialectic recognizing the inadequacies of Black/white, either/or language perceptions; make visible the historical baggage of European hegemony and racism; illuminate the themes and variations of multiple relationships within created order; question the complacency of language; and "[u]nveil chaos within the patterns of certainty."[17] The essence of African-American life in stories set to music in the spirituals is revealed by rhetorical and musical criticism.

Creativity: A Rhetorical-Musical Perspective

Afrocentric rhetorical criticism makes African holistic ideology central to all analysis involving African culture and behavior toward a cultural reconstruction of human transformation.[18] Musical criticism surveys the combined textures of sound and silence and performance methods as they meld text and music to create a message. Rhetorical-musical critique affords a literary and aesthetic insight.

Afrocentric rhetorical-musical critique relies on the oral-aural tradition of the spoken word, crucial in Black cultures. The slaves' ideas, often impenetrable to outsiders, are accessible through rhetorical critique. Rhetorical tools employ divine names, metaphors, synonyms, nondeistic major characters, repetition, stimulus-response language, and set the genre. The genre of the spiritual is the *folk song*.

These folk songs communicate by using a complex, distinct language game of family intimacy that applies oral shorthand, values, irony, symbol, accent, and significant silences. Slaves mixed symbolism, mysticism, and irony to orate and interpret their exploited beings.[19] Duality in spirituals relies on a blend of pathos and humor to shape themes that critique a slave's setting. Spirituals vocalize the victimization as messages of desperation or hope. These messages rely on the language of American-biblical-Christian mythology.

Many spirituals drew on biblical texts for concepts, characters, authority, and assurance. The singers talked "face to face" with Old Testament heroes and heroines, and their New Testament cosuffering Jesus. Slaves appropriated basic theological ideas[20] to express their religious cosmology and passion for freedom. The spiritual's core message focused on a protest hermeneutic of survival and hope.[21] A similar religious leaning of exiled peoples and the final triumph of spiritual forces over earthly events was fixed in the psalms.

The psalms and spirituals are poetic pilgrimage songs of faith. Both canons evolved pseudoanonymously over time and share psychologies that related individuals, the community, and their God. In comparison, the psalms rejoice in the punishment of oppressors, but the spirituals forgo vengeance. Rhetorical devices like motivation, repetition, and personification see both as "honest dialogues of faith."[22] The psalms, prophetic materials, and the spirituals champion balance in their mandate for justice. Spirituals relate to a balanced ontology. Biblical texts are optional. Both slave and slaveholder engaged the American-biblical-Christian mythology, but the polarity of their hermeneutics poignantly reiterates the double-consciousness of African-American existence. The Afrocentric mythology and language of the spirituals become more apparent by examining "rhetorical pairs" like response and persuasion or faith and comedy-humor. These motifs temper balance with double-consciousness.

The double-consciousness of faith juxtaposed against comedy-humor among the victimized is healthy. African Americans survived because of therapeutic humor. Humor helps people brave their fate with zest. Classic comedy-humor is an attitude that affords one a holistic life. Paradoxically, comedy ultimately helps one to view any event as light drama; even when reality is painful one can still perceive the comedic side.[23] Comedy corrects and heals society's ills. Such light drama shows the radical, incongruous mix of bodily instinct and rational intellect, expels the scapegoat, and depicts human experiences. Comedy as wit exercises artistic mental agility and linguistic grace. Humor responds to comedy and may evoke laughter. A comedic effect results by joining two frames of reference and infusing a drop of malice.

Spirituals elicit humor via allegory's symbolism, satire's distortions, or parody's destruction of illusion.[24] The music and text combine comedy-humor with faith to foster survival. Humor sensitizes religious persons to the holy, the mysterious, to suffering, and joy. Graced with humor, the slaves' cosmological faith tolerated ambiguities and contradictions because these perimeters were not conclusive. Faith knows laughter and shapes our concept of finitude.

With faith, humor tempers lives and becomes religious through balance and laughter. With faith one receives empowerment to transcend difficulty and move toward inclusivity. With faith, life becomes sacramental and we nurture and affect preservation. Faith inwardly frees us to be creative and loving. *Humor as ritual* and *comedy as myth* become religious. They move toward the faith that exists midst incongruity, absurdity and frustration, and reshape the human condition. Comedy sees (1) the incongruity of the ironic and the ridiculous, and (2) a plot line that leads to the reparation of the hero and a harmonious society. The comedic sense then parallels the serious in many kinds of literature. The story of Job and that of African-American slaves both share a comedic sense. Both epics are comedy because they address incongruities and embrace the riddles of life. Both use ambiguity, irony, and caricature, prefer life over death,[25] and evoke the question of a just, created order. Rhetorical devices inform and persuade the audience and provide a rich text conducive to Afrocentric musicality.

African-American music sprang from socially essential African *musicking*. Performance practices of the spirituals integrated techniques like improvisation, call and response, dance, a variety of intervals and scales,[26] and musical textures like tempo and rhythmic polyphony. Their distinct African qualities sustained the fertile maieutic processes that engendered the spontaneous composition and performance of text and melody. Variations in vocality and style expressed approval or disapproval, defiance, sorrow, joy, fear, and unity. Language and body expressions merged with musical improvisation to convey emotions and coded messages of spirit and hope. Spirituals, a hermeneutical and artistic feat, celebrate life by reciting history and making music. Their unity and integrity protect self-esteem, community, and hope. The communal concern for justice in the spirituals occurs in music's performance and structural design aimed at humanity and God.

God-Talk: The Philosophical-Theological Frame

Spirituals are sorrow songs, "weary at heart . . . the siftings of centuries . . . more ancient than the words, . . . the voice of exile."[27] Spirituals begin with a God worthy of praise, report a crisis, and conclude with praise. Other spirituals instruct. They emphasize themes of blessing, warning, respect of God, daily life, and imply a contrast between the righteous and the wicked.

Traditionally, philosophy and theology explained this contrast by questioning God's existence while viewing evil within the theories of nonbeing, dualism, despotism, and moral theory. The first three theories either negate the historical problem, are antithetical to Judeo-Christianity, or they discount God's freedom-power. Other scholars see the question as a matter of logic, evidence, existence, cognitive theocentrism, unanswered questions, or constructive theory.[28] The African-American religious experience assumes that God exists, but asks whether God cares. This essay assumes God's existence, finds plausible the unanswered questions argument, and critiques the relationship between God and humanity within society. Both God and human beings choose their own behavior. The choice to condone slavery and racism was legitimated through the propagation of mythology and the practice of oppressive ritual.

The American-biblical-Christian mythology nurtures the racism that spirituals combat and transcend. Prejudice may be a universal human sin, but racism is America's sin midst a system of oppression for a socioeconomic purpose.

Slaves *then* and African Americans *today* live within a society that uses power structures to systematically victimize or limit the power of individuals by race-sex-class. Slavery and racism are evil, offensive acts toward God and humanity that abuse the God-given power of freedom. Made effective through incarnation or institutionalization, power ameliorates or annihilates. With an ability to heal or destroy, the dynamics of power penetrate all existence, including language. The entities or powers that depict the slaves' personification of power in the language of the spirituals are the powers known as Satan and the demonic.

Satan symbolizes (1) culture alienated from God, (2) the image of unredeemed humanity's collective life, and (3) knowledge that humanity lives in a world where evil, that is, some irreducible power, cannot be humanized, integrated, or cured.[29] The demonic refers to the capitulation of persons to oppressive power structures and to the results of malfunctions in personal development. Racism and slavery as collective possession occur where the demonic becomes a mass psychosis. The treatment for collective possession is a collective exorcism. Spirituals are ritual components of a collective exorcism where slaves fight evil with the power constructs of freedom and justice through song.

Slaves found power in religious experience as deliverance. They sang about ultimate and immediate power based on passages from Revelation, Matthew, John, Genesis, Exodus, and Isaiah.[30] Jesus symbolizes power now and in the future, and Pharaoh was *the* symbol of earthly, human power.

Freedom, an essential component of theodicy, required divine and human justice. Slaves resisted bondage and prayed for the emancipation resonant in Israel's Exodus and Jesus' resurrection. Internally, Blacks were never slaves, for "before [they would] be a slave, [they would] be buried in [their] grave."[31] For slaves, God's rule or the idea of spiritual afterlife was the ideal for an earthly, eschatological life.

Spirituals embody an inaugurated eschatology that maintains the tension between the *now* and the *not yet*. The slaves' annihilation lay in slavery, their deliverance came through Christ Jesus. The spirituals portrayed heaven on earth before physical death, and heaven as home after death. Singing the spirituals momentarily denied the psychological restraints and the temporal harshness of slavery. The slaves' Christian life was activity, growth, and faith midst blessedness and peace and ended with holiness. Although God's righteous and eschatological judgment inundated victim and victimizer alike, a Christian eschatological life meant the defeat of slavery.

Christian slaves could modify their master's claims, confront despotism with love, and call for obedience only to God. Eschatologically, the spirituals reflect a faith with "the capacity to circumvent obstacles and to find fresh avenues for its expression," but spirituals *do not* withhold the pursuit of worldly pleasure before heavenly joy.[32] In freedom, God is present with slaves and they know the experience of heaven.

God's word of freedom is irreconcilable with slavery. God freely creates human beings as moral agents, able to choose good or evil. The evil or sinful act of slavery severs this relationship with God and with one's neighbor. Accepting that sin is redeemable in Christ, spirituals require a radical

conversion of all relationships and demand a faith that affirms and com-
·municates value. Such a faith is set in time as spatial sequences of habitual
action. Future time for slaves means from the present time up to six months.
A sense of Christ's imminent return and the brutality of slavery intensified
the desire for both imminent and eternal freedom. Slaves saw *true time* as
eternal,[33] and viewed the Christian life eschatologically. A loving Jesus
meant freedom and justice in the noumena. Why an *omni-God*[34] knowingly
makes creatures who can choose evil and permits their evil choices is incongruous, a dilemma of theodicy or justice.

The theology of justice indicts American slavery. The actuality of slavery
and racism requires a Black existential, eschatological theodicy, as religion
sustained the dehumanization of African Americans. Some slaves made no
distinction between true Christianity and that practiced by white slave owners. Others were ambivalent. Many slaves believed in a just God; others
were confused. Slaves differentiated between universal, historically contingent, and applied justice. Universal or eternal justice was the only hope for
society. The lived theodicy of the slaves and the premises of just doctrine
both indict slavery and the repertoire of scholarship that nurtured racist
thought and lineage.

Justice requires historical consciousness and biblical remembrance.
God's covenant of righteousness embodies the just Word to human brokenness. Justice is corrective restoration that incorporates the Exodus
image of liberation, the rainbow image of covenant, the jubilee image of
new beginnings, and the christological image of identification with the poor
and the oppressed. The triumph of justice over racism or ethnic suffering
occurs in the visions of Exodus, Jubilee, and the Magnificat.[35] The Bible,
as a living mythology and memory of a people, provides stories that critique
injustice and illumine justice within the spirituals.

A constructive theodicy, cognizant of prevalent views and tensions, the-
orizes from the spirituals themselves. Such a hermeneutic respects the
ambiguities of life and sees liberation as salvific because oppression results
in suffering. Salvation must first affirm God's benevolence. Liberation must
call into account divine and human responsibilities in the particular social
setting. Scholars have questioned God about observed cruelties against
persons that erase human sensibilities. William Jones argues that if there
is a multievidential Christ-event, divine malevolence would be a necessary
conclusion.

Jones forfeits other options, from atheism to quietism, to suggest a
humanocentric theism.[36] Humanocentric theism seems to support a constructive Black theodicy: it champions human freedom and duty, reshapes
divine powers, negates divine approval of human (ethnic) suffering, avoids
escapism or quietism, and makes human activity decisive for one's salvation
or liberation. Major Jones claims that William Jones posits a limited God.
William Jones finds belief in an unlimited God rife with moral and logical
contradictions: either God is not an *omni-God* or God is a white racist.

While the limited God view attempts to remove the total onus of evil from God and enhances the import of human beings, victimized persons need the assurance of final victory in divine good. Under Black theology, God can be viewed as weak-armed but never "weak in the knees."[37]

African-American spirituals qualify the essence of a constructive theodicy. These songs celebrate an *omni-God*, champion freedom, and hold human choice responsible for personal and institutional evil. The spirituals allow reflection on past and present victimization towards a transforming vision and onus. Most scholars agree that the spirituals assume retributive justice for their masters, but revenge by the slaves is not a governing motif. Spirituals avoid a speculative theodicy that would rationalize the suffering of innocent people. They hold that the law and desire of God commands the good, which sinning slave owners disobey. Slave communication about divine justice parallels biblical apocalyptic language.

Job claims that the suffering by innocents does not negate an *omni-God*, for divine and social justice are inseparable.[38] That is, love transcends and combats systematic social injustice in history. Slaves suffered *physical* bondage in union with God and slave owners suffered *spiritual* bondage while alienated from God. Habakkuk protests that God neither hears nor acts and thus negates law and justice, even as he recalls God's saving acts. Neither Habakkuk nor Job question God's power under God-permitted injustice and suffering. A believer can endure pain without losing faith through divine self-disclosure. Habakkuk's struggle with redemption and righteousness midst evil is the victim's struggle. The books of Job and Habakkuk show that life is a daily series of deaths to human desires and deeds, as faith leads toward perfection within God.

The slave singers assumed God's loving righteousness, justice, and goodness of relationship, not dominance. Jesus gave them relief in confidence and joy. Evil was not eternal but was God's problem. Slaves did not directly challenge God, like Habakkuk and Job, but set the questions in prayers, dialogue, or addresses. The challenge can be heard in the songs the slaves called "seculars," the Blues. The spirituals honor the love of God as compassion in the encounter of suffering.

Spirituals support an argument for a Black theodicy-theology, because social and cultural environment affect personal religious questions. Suffering underscores divine freedom, which allows human choice. Divine versus human freedom relates to a christological, eschatological theodicy: the immediate revelation of divine pathos in Jesus Christ. Slaves prayed with Jesus and adopted Christian symbols but not the Pharisaical practices of Christians in the name of religion. Slaves trumpeted elemental, compassionate justice. Without this triumph, slaves might have rejected Christianity outright.[39] In the spirituals, just as in the Sermon on the Mount, God championed the downtrodden. Spirituals evinced love and praise for God, the slaves' source of unity and mercy.[40] God in Christ gained all hopes and related to all problems and all persons. Incarnate love, as compassion, empowers a person or community to resist subjugation and violence. The pre-Civil War abolitionist movement and the civil-rights Freedom-Fighters' movement confronted and resisted the cruelty of U. S. apartheid.[41] In the heart of confrontation and protest, syncretism logically developed as African religio-musical traditions accompanied exported slaves to the American colonies and merged with like Christian beliefs.

African religion infused every aspect of human existence, sustaining the unity and sacramental nature of life. Africans knew God and devoted their intelligence to learning how to live in the world, not master it. Fully authentic life within society as family was celebrated through communal singing and dancing.[42] The imposed religious behaviors of Christianity, Islam, and indigenous African religions merged with the slave's Reformation-based salvific piety with the Bible as final authority; that is, a Creator God, afterlife, and final judgment. Many scholars coopted biblical sources to justify American slavery, since the New Testament did not overtly call slavery a sin.[43] With biblical warrant and a xenophobic need to control, enslavement for cheap labor was legitimized when the drafters of the U.S. Constitution held that slaves were only three-fifths a person.[44] This was codified when the Supreme Court declared that slaves were property, not citizens, in the infamous Dred Scott Decision.[45]

Many slaves lacked orthodox, Western religious experience because society thought of slaves as incapable of being converted. Many shunned organized worship because American religion was no religion at all. This *religion for profit* created scapegoats of the victimized. Slaves were fed Pauline injunctions of obedience to thwart any empowerment a religious African American might attain. Some churches condoned slavery yet held slaves' souls in trust. The slaves' experience foreshadowed the religious hypocrisy that gripped the United States during the civil rights movement in the 1950s and 1960s. That hypocrisy did not daunt the belief of slaves nor the Freedom Fighters, because Jesus Christ is the Liberator.

In the spirituals, Jesus was God. Jesus' resurrection was the slave's hope for progress and renewal: a hope for liberation of all those enslaved by powers and principalities. Jesus' divinity held because of his supernatural power and atoning work. Jesus' humanity, evinced in his empathy for slaves' situation as one of sorrows, was acquainted with grief. The person of Jesus and the place called heaven meant total freedom. Heaven was the "New Jerusalem," God's throne, a place of endless Sundays, in present and future spatial time. Heaven was the free land with the Prince of Peace. The *slaves' view of God*, not Christian teaching and preaching, *defined their view of divine justice and human freedom.*

Some spirituals viewed God and Jesus as synonyms; in others, Jesus becomes a composite of Christ and Moses; in still others Jesus and the Holy Spirit are coterminous. Scholars argue both for an implicit Trinity and a disregard of the same because of the omission of the term Holy Spirit in many of the spirituals.[46] The spirituals celebrated freedom:

Moses the human liberator; Christ the holy Spirit Jesus, comforter and redeemer of sin; and the transcendent God revealing God's real person in situations of liberation: God the Creator-Revelator (Maker), God the Freedom-Fighter (Christ Moses), God the Redeemer-Comforter (Holy Spirit Jesus) – God the Revelator, Freedom-fighter, Liberator. . . . the godhead [is] one.[47]

The omission within the spirituals of any devotions to the Virgin Mary is unusual, given the social environment[48] and the adaptation by the spirituals of biblical texts. One explanation may be that the spirituals recognized the feminine aspect of Jesus, whereas the traditional Roman Catholic dogma regarded Jesus as wholly masculine. Few of the early spirituals explicity celebrate Jesus' nativity.[49] An exploration of this area of omission is beyond the scope of this essay.

Spirituals affirmed that Christ, the King, enabled African-Americans to transcend the limitations of slavery. White instruction avoided any hints of political liberation and the slaves required a vital, timeless God-image, a mature Christ. Slaves confronted a crisis by appealing to the crucified Jesus who judged and liberated humanity from the duel for power, fear, and sin.[50] Many spirituals commemorate the eschatological healing, saving power of Christ in the Eucharist. Meals are times of sharing and reconciliation.[51] The power of the common meal urges the consideration of a multifaceted liberation or messianic motif that includes the Exodus, the Cross, and the Eucharist with an implicit Pentecost!

In the spirituals, the reconciliation symbolized by the Eucharist affirms an existential, subjective-communal, or "*I-Thou*," experience for the slaves. The *It-Thou* – as a subjugated chattel – changes to an *I-Thou* life of total personhood in Jesus Christ. Slaves use the spirituals to explore their existential concerns about freedom and being in life and death. Death is a state of resignation combined with fear and dread, related to suffering and nothingness. Spirituals profess a Christ who defeated death at the cross and assures the faithful of eternal life in states of goodness. Death never conquers life. Life in Christ conquers death. Death is swallowed up in victory. Life is a pilgrimage, a mysterious given. A constructive theodicy accepts the defeat of death on the cross, the gift of life through the resurrection, and celebrates the invitation to the victim and victimizer for reconciliation toward healing presented at the Eucharist. For the enslaved, many new choices become available.

Choosing freedom over slavery means knowing fear and hope. The enslaved put these emotions into coded lyrical expression. Slaves experienced the hardships of daily bondage rather than romanticized plantation life and sang of a harsh and real existence. While many abolitionists and white churches advocated treating slaves paternally according to the Golden Rule, the Black church remained the center of slave culture, nurture, and protest. Slaves fully participated within ambiguous yet defiant

Black religious experience. Spirituals dramatized the themes of Black religion that spanned slavery, rebellion, resistance, and death.[52] The concerns of those earlier slave bards in the antebellum spirituals sustained the Black protest of the 1960s civil-rights era. Womanist insight lends a spirited and enlightened vision to the African American quest for freedom and justice.

Womanist ideology springs from the feminist aspects of the African-American religious folk expression of mothers to their children. A womanist loves, commits to survival and wholeness of all people, has integrity and vision. Womanist insight and critique creates a perspective that is: (1) eschatological; (2) about liberation; (3) historical; (4) based in reality; and (5) transformational. Through African-Christian, biblical womanist vision, identification and healing midst a living God becomes intensified.

With such a womanist reading, people have no hesitation about who God is. God is a personal, powerful, compassionate, liberating God who encompasses masculine and feminine qualities and cares about an individual's circumstances.[53] The liberating dimensions of the Hebrew Bible linked with real, communal experiences of African Americans undergird many spiritual texts. These combined events involve several hermeneutical voices: the voice of suspicion opposes the evangelical veto of the Hebrew Bible's communal salvation; the voice of remembrance connects the prophetic God with modern suffering; the voice of creative actualization involves the listeners. These voices celebrate the essence of a powerful, able God, who is "a mother to the motherless and a father to the fatherless." Together they set a comprehensive reading of powerlessness over against a language of power and survival.[54] The language of power and survival combat the mythologies of Black inferiority, divinely mandated enslavement, and distorted divine will that slave apologists used to legitimize their hermeneutics of oppression.[55] The spirituals embody the language of power and survival that celebrates African Americans as *imago Dei*.

As *imago Dei*, each Black soul is an authentic human being who can be and does act midst the double-consciousness in the two worlds of Black and White, symbolized by the veil. Authenticity resists schizophrenia and moves toward wholeness beyond survival to liberation. The spirituals champion that reality. Spirituals tell the African-American liberation story through the Exodus as they wear the mask of authentic, audacious confrontation, conflict, and revelation. Womanists look at the spirituals and see the distant and recent past, the present and the future. Each existential moment is one of cruelty yet hope, with opportunities for affirmation and liberation. With power and love, womanists know that the wholeness of no person is complete until the African-American woman is no longer the victim of race-gender-class bias and xenophobia. The spirituals challenge African-American women to a life of faith and comedy-humor and transformation. There all meet Jesus face to face and in one another.

Conclusion: Salvific Exorcism

Spirituals proclaim that slaves knew *who they were*, despite the institutionalization of slavery and the related dispersion of ten million Africans to the shores of the United States. These persons of color *knew* they were fully human in God. There was no slave identity crisis. The slaves used their *musicking* to affirm their own being and to survive their predicament. The survival of the spirituals today demonstrates the triumph of life over death, of justice over injustice. The reality of spirituals represents the active grace and mercy of God; that such creativity came out of such tyranny. The spirituals or chants of exorcism embody divine and human compassion and wisdom. These litanies of praise and protest reflect the real merciful justice alive in God, not as a Marxist opiate, but an ontology of the faithful.

The spirituals are committed to a theodicy where God and human beings freely participate together in a society that demands the exorcism of the evils of slavery and racism. These chants cry out for justice and call for accountability, but avoid reductionism at the point of blame and asking *why*. My analysis has as its premise the concept of a liberating *omni-God* and a society made up of individuals who freely make either good, neutral, or evil choices.

A womanist constructive methodology is essential because of: (1) the tridimensional victimization African-American women experience, and (2) African-American women's liberation must stand midst the liberation of all Black families, and ultimately all people everywhere. A womanist vision is critical where the exorcism for Black freedom has often been co-opted by persons who have exploited the Black inclination to be inclusive by recruiting Blacks for their needs and self-interest during the epochs of the Civil War and 1960s civil rights movement.[56] Justice, as embodied in the spirituals, is that of mutuality and empowerment, not usury or manipulation. Mutuality represents the powers of good as compassion, creativity, and wisdom. Those powers foster change and call for a hopeful imagination and an undying faith.

Spirituals call for a faith framed by humor that affords dialogue. The playfulness of love faces evil and suffering with compassionate, redemptive power.[57] These songs remind women and men that God is love. In love, God liberates and calls us all to appreciate the character of Jesus in all persons, through the power of the Holy Spirit. The quest for physical and spiritual freedom is difficult. The physical or flesh is ego-centered, the spirit is God-centered. Yet, God-centered physical life is spiritual and authentic. The spirituals champion authentic physical and spiritual life.

The spirituals call for an eschatological life of vision and integrity. They inspire an existence that celebrates an Afrocentristic holistic life that demands internal and communal unity. The spirituals call for God-given standards of justice and freedom for all persons within one's social matrix.

Although much of the text of the spirituals is dialectical or veiled, spirituals do not defer life. The spirituals afford a view of that duality through the lenses of the Exodus, the Cross, and the Eucharist. Some of these chants arouse a focus toward an internal musing of the Magnificat. The desperation that impregnated Afrocentric cosmology fostered a creative birth of compassionate survival. A sense of immediate historical time – the present – makes the spirituals contingent, yet they remain timeless songs of liberation.

Oppressive systems, minor setbacks in the movement, and human frailty cannot thwart the triumph of freedom. The slave bard and the freedom fighter share that belief. These activists knew the comedic in the satirical distortion of how society enslaves within a creation ordained by divine freedom. The former victim does not have to fear life in freedom or become an oppressor when freedom is attained in the tradition of Isaian justice and righteousness. The spirituals simultaneously claim a compassionate God, realize that evil exists, and demand accountability of themselves, God, and the oppressors. The spirituals realize that apartheid and genocide are unconscionable and can not be vindicated.

Spirituals are a living, vocal commentary on essential Black life that transcends survival and celebrates liberation. That cosmology strongly stands for: (1) a faith in God as Alpha and Omega; (2) a trust in surrendering to the will of the Lord; (3) a life of praise and thanksgiving for everything, knowing that God's judgment and mercy drops as gentle dew upon the just and the unjust alike[58]; (4) dignity, self-respect, and respect for others; and (5) love for self, God, family, and all people.

Agapic love immerses itself in prayer and hope and has no room for hate. This life of agapic love portrayed in these spirituals calls for reshaping the world and redefining and transforming all structures and values toward healing relationships of injustice and victimization. Such healing transformation reflects the goal of the preponderant themes of theodicy in these spirituals: the power of freedom born of agapic love. The question that this life and the spirituals pose for us to answer is: *Can We Love Well Enough?*[59]

NOTES

1. Racism is an idolatrous faith; a by-product of the ideological justification of European political and economic power arrangements over people of color. Racism is a search for self-identity, while seeking to cancel the selfhood of other races by acts of deprivation and words of vilification. Racism is total hate; an inherently brutal system; a pathological will to power. See George D. Kelsey, *Racism and the Christian Understanding of Man* (New York: Charles Scribner's Sons, 1965), 9–11, 19–33.

2. The usage of the term *white man* is purposely racial and gender specific.

3. Molefi Kete Asante, *The Afrocentric Idea* (Philadelphia: Temple University Press, 1987), 4–6.

4. Maya Angelou, "The Jamison Spirit," *Essence* 21 (December 1990), 67.

5. John Lovell, Jr., *Black Song: The Forge and the Flame: The Story of How the Afro-American Spiritual Was Hammered Out* (New York: Macmillan, 1972), 126, 397.

6. William F. Allen, Charles Pickard Ware, and Lucy McKim Garrison, *Slave Songs of the United States* (New York: Peter Smith, 1867).

7. Ibid., 77–92; Christopher Small, *Music of the Common Tongue: Survival and Celebration in Afro-American Music* (London: John Calder, 1987), 50. *Musicking*, the present participle of the verb "to music," means to engage in the activity of creating music by the act of taking part in a musical performance.

8. 1 Pet. 2:18 KJV (King James Version). "Slaves, be subject to your masters with all fear; not only to the good and gentle."

9. Eugene Genovese, *Rebellion to Revolution: Afro-American Slave Revolts in the Making of the Modern World* (Baton Rouge: Louisiana State University Press, 1979), 46.

10. The United States is the only nation founded on a creed in the Declaration of Independence that deals with justice issues, condemns anarchism, and by inference condemns atheism.

11. The inventions of the cotton gin, spinning, and weaving machines.

12. Rene Girard, *The Scapegoat*, trans. Yvonne Freccero (Baltimore: Johns Hopkins University Press, 1986), 13.

13. John Earl Taylor, "The Sociological and Psychological Implications of the Texts of the Ante Bellum Negro Spirituals" (Ed. D. diss., University of Northern Colorado, 1989), 189, 192; Albert Beckham, "The Psychology of Negro Spirituals," *The Southern Workman* 60 (1931): 393. Beckham claims singers languishing in pity relayed their dire plight. Many knew pity, but did something about it. Some of the spirituals were palliative, i.e., they mentally reduced the intense pain of slavery. Some were sorrow songs. Depending upon the text and performer, these categories did not have to be mutually exclusive. Sometimes the emotional context overlapped.

14. Henry Hampton and Steve Fayer, *Voices of Freedom: An Oral History of the Civil Rights Movement from the 1950s through the 1980s* (New York: Bantam Books, 1990), 38, 108, 94–96.

15. W. E. B. DuBois, *The Souls of Black Folk* (1903; reprint New York: Bantam Books, 1989), 2–4.

16. Katie Geneva Cannon, *Black Womanist Ethics* (Atlanta: Scholars Press, 1988), 77–78, 87–90.

17. Terry McMillan, *Breaking Ice: An Anthology of Contemporary African-American Fiction* (New York: Penguin Books, 1990), vii–x.

18. Asante, *The Afrocentric Idea*, 4–6.

19. Russell Ames, "Protest and Irony in the Negro Folksong," *Science and Society* 14 (Summer 1950): 207–12. Wayne McLaughlin, "Symbolism and Mysticism in the Spirituals," *Phylon* 24 (1963): 70. The mysticism embodied mystery, revelation, faith, and the transcendent soul in communion with God. Their symbolism expressed affection, hope, grief, loneliness, regret, toil, struggle, faith, and death.

20. Howard Thurman, *Deep River and the Negro Spiritual Speaks of Life and Death* (Richmond, IN: Friends United Press, 1975), 20.

21. The vocabulary of themes pertained to: 1. Daily life, cultic or worship practice; 2. Death, freedom and hope; 3. Celebration or agony over protest; 4. Black solidarity and Black heroes; 5. The Exodus, escape and deliverance; 6. Praise of God, communion, and King Jesus; 7. Judgment, heaven and hell; 8. Manumission

and African colonization; and 9. The Civil War and slave patrols. Beckham, "Psychology of Negro Spirituals," 392.

22. William H. Bellinger, Jr., *The Psalms: Reading and Studying the Book of Praises* (Peabody, MA: Hendrickson Press, 1990), 16, 73.

23. After hundreds of persons had come to pay their respects to my own family as my father, the late Deputy Rudolph Valentio Kirk, lay in state (with words of assurance, hugs, kisses, and handshakes), I leaned over and asked my mother, the late Naomi Ruth Kirk, if we should wash with Phisohex when we returned home. We all began to laugh in the midst of our bereavement.

24. For example, humor is apparent as (1) satire's distortion in "Ride On, King Jesus," as no one can harm me because Jesus rides on a milk-white horse; (2) as allegory's symbolism in "Ezekiel Saw the Wheel" relates to the movement toward freedom, and (3) as parody's destruction of illusion in "He's Got the Whole World in His Hands" understands that God, not white slaveowners, has ultimate power.

25. Of friends/slave owners as the mockers become a mockery.

26. In the work of Frederick Hall, cited by Lovell in *Black Song*, Hall definitively traced spiritual tunes to Africa. He cited the peculiar use of: pentatonic (5 tones), hexatonic (6 tones), and heptatonic (7 tones) scales; lowered thirds, raised sixths, and lowered sevenths (intervals). Hall found a perpetual rhythmic motion, and recognized that rhythms served the feeling rather than an accurately measured accent. Scales conformed to song, not song to scale.

27. DuBois, 177–81.

28. Alan Richardson and Alan Bowden, eds., *The Westminster Dictionary of Christian Theology* (Philadelphia: Westminster Press, 1983), s.v. "The Problem of Evil," by John Hick. Dualism makes evil coequal with a benevolent God. The few biblical metaphors that imply despotism remain a theological mystery. Moral theory limits God's power by the human concepts of God's character, an epistemic dilemma. The logical argument examines the analytical consistency of claims about the divine and evil. The evidential question deals with the amount and/or kinds of evil that make the existence of God improbable. The cognitive theocentricism argument assumes the existence of God and makes evil abstract. The unanswered questions, argument or problem of theodicy develops when theists need a rational, adequate justification of why God allows evil's existence—possibly abandoning the question of "Why?" while believing God has a morally sufficient good reason for permitting evil.

29. Sharon L. Moore, "Walter Wink On 'The Powers,'" Unpublished Essay (Fall 1989), 15–20; See Wink, *Unmasking the Powers* (Philadelphia: Fortress Press, 1986), 9–68.

30. Blassingame, 145. See Lovell, *Black Song*, 230–35; 550–51. In writing on spirituals and Jewish thought, Lovell cites Paul Laubenstein's "An Apocalyptic Reincarnation," in the *Journal of Biblical Literature*, 1932, which notes that spiritual composers used only certain parts of the Bible. Slaves used the history, narrative, and apocalyptic which Laubenstein credits to the African consciousness.

31. Words from the spiritual, "Oh, Freedom;" Thomas Webber, *Deep Like the Rivers: Education in the Slave Quarter Community, 1831–1865* (New York: Norton, 1978), 140–45.

32. James H. Evans, Jr., "African-American Christianity and the Postmodern Condition." *Journal of the American Academy of Religion* 58 (Summer 1990), 208.

33. McLaughlin, "Symbolism and Mysticism in the Spirituals," 72–73. The dis-

cussion about "time" almost seems contradictory. McLaughlin talks about an immediate and future eschatology, similar to the views of Gayraud Wilmore and this writer. Other times he appears to be more future oriented as in traditional eschatology. A critical reading of McLaughlin notes his view that clock-time (past, present, and future) is an illusion; true time is eternal time. Perhaps true time for the slave occurred at the point when he or she knew the time of heaven, of being fulfilled in God's time. As such, this argument allows for an immediate and future interpretation.

34. I use the term *omni-God* as a referent for an all-powerful, omnipotent, omniscient, infinitely good and loving Creator.

35. See Karen Lebacqz, *Justice in an Unjust World: Foundations for a Christian Approach to Justice* (Minneapolis: Augsburg, 1987) for a thorough discussion.

36. William R. Jones, *Is God a White Racist? A Preamble to Black Theology*, C. Eric Lincoln Series on Black Religion (Garden City, NY: Anchor Books/Doubleday, 1973), vii–25; 185–97. Quietism is a system of religious mysticism that teaches perfection and spiritual peace are attained by annihilation of the will and passive absorption in contemplation of God and divine things. Jones suggests that another way to talk about a quietistic theodicy is Marx's opiate. He argues that eschatological theodicy is not acceptable because it presupposes divine intrinsic benevolence, where a difficult present will be replaced by a future bliss. Such a theodicy involves an unresolved mystery.

37. Major J. Jones, *The Color of God* (Macon, GA: Mercer Press, 1987), 65–67.

38. Alexander Di Lella, "An Existential Interpretation of Job," *Biblical Theology Bulletin* 15 (April 1985): 49, 54; Walter Brueggemann, "Theodicy in a Social Dimension," *Journal for the Study of the Old Testament* 33 (1985): 4–5. One must also recognize that an exploration of the meaning of suffering is also an attempt to reduce God to human understanding, since human beings by definition cannot possess divine understanding. Gustavo Gutiérrez, *On Job: God-Talk and the Suffering of the Innocent* (Maryknoll, NY: Orbis Books, 1987), 88–91.

39. Lovell, *Black Song*, 386–87.

40. Thurman, *The Negro Spiritual*, 77–95; and McLaughlin, "Symbolism and Mysticism in the Spirituals," 72–73. Introducing the word "Hallelujah" signals a call to praise, the contact between singer and God's luminous reality. "Hallelujah" symbolizes the mystic moment of unity, the highs and lows of life. Christa Dixon, *Negro Spirituals: From Bible to Folk Song* (Philadelphia: Fortress, 1976), 3–5. H. H. Proctor, "The Theology of the Songs of the Southern Slave," *Southern Workman* 36 (November 1907): 586–87.

41. Wendy Farley, *Tragic Vision and Divine Compassion: A Contemporary Theodicy* (Louisville: Westminster/John Knox Press, 1990), 117.

42. The family, i.e., the living, the dead, and the unborn, achieved full existence. Dena Epstein, *Sinful Tunes and Spirituals: Black Folk Music to the Civil War* (Urbana, IL: University of Illinois Press, 1977), 63–76. These included celebrations for holidays and rites; and the work, field, and boat songs.

43. R. Laird Harris, Gleason L. Archer, Jr., and Bruce K. Waltke, eds., *Theological Wordbook of the Old Testament*, s.v. "Abad," by Walter C. Kaiser; Gerhard Kittel, ed., *Theological Dictionary of the New Testament*, trans. and ed. Geoffrey W. Bromiley, s.v. "Doulos," by Karl Heinrich Rengstorf; George Buttrick, Thomas Kepler, Herbert May, John Knox, and Samuel Terrien, eds., *The Interpreter's Dictionary of the Bible*, s.v. "Slavery in the Old Testament," by I. Mendelsohn. Hen-

derson Sheridan Davis, "The Religious Experience Underlying the Negro Spiritual" (Ph.D. diss., Boston University, 1950), 337–80, 62, 222; E. N. Elliot, *Cotton is King, and Pro-Slavery Arguments: Comprising the Writings of Hammond, Harper, Christy, Stringfellow, Hodge, Bledsoe, and Cartwright, On This Important Subject* (Augusta, GA: Pritchard, Abbott & Loomis, 1860), 337.

44. The "three-fifths" designation was only for the purposes of national elections and taxation: "Representatives and direct Taxes shall be apportioned among the several States which may be included within this Union, according to the respective Numbers, which shall be determined by *adding to the whole Number of free Persons*, including those bound to Service for a Term of Years, and excluding Indians not taxed, *three fifths of all other Persons*" (emphasis added), U.S. Constitution, Art. I, sec. 2.

45. 60 U.S. 393 (1857).

46. Some of the spirituals talk of the "Spirit movin'." This is a reference to either the human animus, or to the Divinity in general. It may also refer to the Third Person of the Trinity.

47. Jon Michael Spencer, *Protest and Praise: Sacred Music of Black Religion* (Minneapolis: Fortress Press, 1990), 32.

48. Proctor, "The Theology of the Songs of the Southern Slave," 655–56; and C. J. Ryder, "The Theology of the Plantation Songs," *American Missionary* (1892): 15. Although many Blacks belonged to Catholic masters in Louisiana, Ryder never heard nor found any praises sung to the Virgin anywhere in the plantation melodies, despite the prominence of Mariology in the Roman Catholic tradition elsewhere. (A 1990 compact disc, *Black Christmas: Spirituals in the African-American Tradition*, contains fourteen spirituals: four of these celebrate Mary but do not idolize her.)

49. However, stanza 3 of "Go, Tell It on the Mountain" reads,

> Down in a lonely manger
> The humble Christ was born,
> And God sent us salvation
> That blessed Christmas morn.

50. Ibid.

51. In the African-American community, people have come together to share a meal to show love and concern. During lean times the fare may have been "greens, pot liquor and corn bread and hoppin' John, and a few sweet potatoes." The joy and comraderie and nurturing elevated the feast to caviar.

52. Vincent R. Harding, "Religion and Resistance Among Antebellum Negroes, 1800–1860," in *The Making of Black America: Essays in Negro Life and History*, Vol. 1, *The Origins of Black Americans*, ed. August Meier and Elliot Rudwick (New York: Atheneum, 1969), 181. The invisible institution of antebellum days became visible and the chief institution of freed Blacks. After the Civil War and the gradual breakdown of the customary, partially integrated but paternalistic ecclesiastical system of the Old South by 1865, the Black church became the chief agency of social control. The church gave impetus to economic cooperation among African-Americans and was a safe refuge from a hostile world. While there is no empirical entity as *the* Black church, the complex religious institution identified as such serves as a surrogate for nationality, a vital means preserving racial solidarity. The church is a radical, independent yet sometimes divisive body imbued with Afrocentric and Eurocentric mythology and values collectively in the Black community.

53. "He's [God/Jesus] Got the Whole World in His Hands; . . . He's Got the little, bitty baby in His Hands."

54. Cheryl Townsend Gilkes, "Mother to the Motherless, Father to the Fatherless: Power, Gender, and Community in Afrocentric Biblical Tradition," *Semeia: An Experimental Journal for Biblical Criticism* 47 (1989): 58–61, 65. Vincent Wimbush, "Historical/Cultural Criticism as Liberation: A Proposal for an African-American Biblical Hermeneutic," *Semeia: An Experimental Journal for Biblical Criticism* 47 (1989): 45.

55. Katie Geneva Cannon, "Slave Ideology and Biblical Interpretation," *Semeia: An Experimental Journal for Biblical Criticism* 47 (1989): 11–16.

56. Jamie Phelps, "Racism and the Bonding of Women," in *Women's Spirit Bonding*, ed. Janet Kalven and Mary Buckley (New York: Pilgrim Press, 1984), 71–72.

57. Farley, *Tragic Vision and Divine Compassion*, 81.

58. The Gospel of Matthew 5:45; Shakespeare, *The Merchant of Venice*, IV., i.

59. Mary Chrichlow, "The Struggle of a Black Lutheran," and Elizabeth M. Scott, "A Black Woman's Perspective on Racism, Classism, Sexism, and Ageism," in *Women of Faith in Dialogue*, ed. Virginia Ramey Mollenkott (New York: Crossroad, 1987), 90, 168–69.

10

"Soprano Obligato"

The Voices of Black Women and American Conflict in the Thought of Anna Julia Cooper

Karen Baker-Fletcher

For both contemporary and historical women, the silencing or dismissal of women's voices has been a major manifestation of the evil of domination. As womanist writers have all indicated, Black women face a triple oppression of racism, sexism, and classism. Therefore, Black women and other women of color have experienced the suppression or dismissal of their voices in a particularly profound way. Anna Julia Haywood Cooper was a Black woman who addressed this problem boldly in late nineteenth-century America.

Born Annie Julia Haywood in Raleigh, North Carolina, on August 10, 1858, Dr. Anna Julia Cooper was one of the most highly educated and intellectual Black women of the late nineteenth and early twentieth centuries. Her mother, Hannah Stanley Haywood, was a slave and her biological father was her mother's master.[1] In accordance with slave law, young Annie followed the slave condition of her mother. Cooper was five years old in 1863, when Abraham Lincoln's Emancipation Proclamation freed slaves from bondage.

Through education, Cooper escaped the "new slavery" the masses of Black women faced as underpaid, overworked, emotionally and physically abused domestic servants, sharecroppers, or laundry women in a South resistant to change. For Cooper, education was necessary for both Black women and men to come to full voice in a racist society.

Cooper's education began in 1868 at St. Augustine's Normal and Collegiate Institute, a mission school in Raleigh, North Carolina, founded by the Episcopal Church to educate Black Americans.[2] She received her B.A.

from Oberlin College in 1884, graduating with Mary Church Terrell and Ida Gibbs (Hunt), and in 1887 she received an M.A. from Oberlin in mathematics.

Cooper began teaching at the prestigious "M" Street School in Washington, D.C., in 1887, where from 1901 to 1906 she served as principal. When Cooper introduced college preparatory subject matter to the curriculum, the school was accredited for the first time by Harvard University. But from 1904 to 1905, the predominantly white Washington, D.C., school board took measures to oust Cooper from her principalship. They thought Washington's colored high school should emphasize industrial and vocational subjects.[3] Four years later, Cooper was invited to return as a teacher to the "M" Street School by the new superintendent. She had a long teaching career at the "M" Street and Dunbar High Schools.[4]

In 1925, Cooper received her Ph.D. after defending her dissertation on "Attitudes toward Slavery in Revolutionary France" at the Sorbonne. Five years later, in 1930, Cooper was of retirement age and required by Washington, D.C., law to leave her position at Dunbar High School. When Frelinghuysen University, a school for Black working adults in Washington, D.C., elected Cooper to serve as the school's second president she accepted the offer. In dire financial straits, the school eventually relocated in Cooper's home. Cooper was dedicated to Frelinghuysen's service of social, educational, and moral uplift for Black working women and men. She resigned from the presidency of Frelinghuysen in 1939, but continued to work as registrar. She did not retire completely until 1949, at the age of ninety.[5] She died in 1964, at the age of 105.

Born in servitude, Cooper saw freedom as an opportunity to willingly dedicate her life to Christian service.[6] Like her contemporaries in the Black women's club movement, Ida B. Wells, Mary Church Terrell, and Frances Ellen Watkins Harper, Cooper sought to implement a vision of freedom, equality, and justice. She raised her voice as a teacher and lecturer to argue for the education of Black women. Employing the nineteenth-century ideal of true womanhood, Cooper argued that because women inherently possessed moral sympathy and were the earliest educators of children, the Black woman was "the fundamental agency under God" in the development and regeneration of her race.[7] Therefore, Black women's education and the contribution of their voices in the public sphere were necessary for social reform.

In *A Voice from the South*, published in 1892, Cooper audaciously, shrewdly, and courageously questioned, challenged, and chastised the domination of the weak by the strong in Western culture. Originally, Cooper delivered most of the essays in this volume as lectures or speeches. She raised her voice to criticize the evils of racism, sexism, classism, and imperialism in late nineteenth- and early twentieth-century America. Moreover, she lifted her voice against the evil of domination generally, whether against injustices toward Native Americans, violence toward Black women, or the practice of footbinding in China. She argued that it was time for women's voices of every color to be heard.

Anna Cooper's title for her book, "A Voice from the South" is striking. It reveals Cooper's consciousness of the importance of women's voices. Cooper was an author, conscious of the difficulties of creating a narrative voice that would be taken seriously in a world that discriminated against persons based on their gender and the color of their skin. But Cooper stepped out to speak, with the presupposition that freedom and equality were the universal birthright of humanity.[8] In her pamphlet, *Equality of Races and the Democratic Movement,* she metaphorically described God's presence in human beings as a "divine spark," a "shadow mark," an "urge cell," and finally a *"Singing* Something." This *Singing* Something, the progressive movement toward freedom and equality in human beings, rises up against the evil of domination. For Cooper, God acts as a liberating voice and as the author of reform within human beings. Cooper argued for the right of women of every race and culture to make vocal and practical contributions to social reform.

Coming to Voice

Anna Julia Cooper wrote *A Voice from the South* during a period in United States history when Black women were coming to voice. Tired of the silencing effects of slavery on Black women and men, threatened by white backlash through the establishment of Jim Crow and Black codes in the South, Black women organized in unprecedented numbers to write and speak out against segregation.

The South was in the throes of trying to maintain the semblance of a feudal order, to use Cooper's description. It remained grossly and violently segregated. Few Blacks escaped the new slavery to become economically independent. House slaves became house servants, field slaves became sharecroppers who were still tied to overseers and a landowner. Southern chivalry—the protection of female honor—was, as in slavery, reserved for elite white women. Black women were still being raped. Black men were being lynched.

Toilet facilities for Black women and men were inadequate. In her descriptions of her travels back to the South, Cooper cited an incident in which she came to facilities labeled "Women" and "Colored" and pondered which heading she came under. In response to the gross discrimination she and other Black women had experienced, Cooper raised her voice. In the preface to *A Voice from the South*, entitled "Our Raison D'Etre," Cooper wrote:

> In the clash and clatter of our American Conflict, it has been said that the South remains Silent. Like the Sphinx she inspires vociferous disputation, but herself takes little part in the noisy controversy. One

muffled strain in the Silent South, a jarring cadenza has been and still is the Negro. And of that muffled chord, the one mute and voiceless note has been the sadly expectant Black Woman.[9]

Cooper translated her love and knowledge of music into metaphors of the nature of the voices of a diversity of people: the larger conflicted American populace and the people of the South, particularly Black men and Black women. Cooper frequently used musical terminology to poetically describe the importance of the speech of Black and white women as well as of the Black community. Above, Cooper described the voice of the Southern Negro generally as a "muffled strain" or "chord" and a "jarring cadenza" in the silent South. The voice of the Negro, her metaphors suggest, was suppressed. It strained to be heard in the American controversy that the South preferred to withdraw from. And, when it was heard it was a jarring cadenza, a flourish, one might say, that startled those who heard it.

Within this chord, the notes or voices that made up the "voice of the Negro," the Black woman was a mute and voiceless note. The voice of the Black woman, Cooper's metaphor suggests, was suppressed. No wonder this chord that made up the voice of the Negro had a jarring sound, as Cooper described it. The muffled strain of the Negro, startling already to European-American ears with its cry for justice, was and still is an incompletely heard chord without the full vocal presence of Black women.

A Voice from the South is divided into two parts. Cooper entitled "Part First," which is comprised of her essays on womanhood, "Soprano Obligato." She entitled "Part Second," which deals with the question of the problem of race in American culture, literature, and economics, "Tutti Ad Libitum."

The first title describes the voice of the Black woman as obligatory. That is, the voices of Black women must not be omitted. The metaphor also suggests the separateness, the isolation of the voice of the Black woman. In contrast, the second title describes the Black community as a whole, its men and women, as an improvisational movement. There is no set plan, no set ending. Rather, they are in the process of creation even as they are heard by their listeners.

Cooper was sensitive to the problems of voice and audience for both Black women and men. Cooper continued in "Our Raison D'Etre" to describe the "colored man's inheritance and apportionment" as "the sombre crux" or "cul de sac" of the nation, like "a dumb skeleton in the closet." The colored man, she contended, despite his ceaseless harangues was "little understood" and "seldom consulted." Cooper was critical of America's gross misunderstanding of the plea Black men had brought before the bar. Moreover, Cooper criticized America for not consulting Black women for their testimony in the nation's consideration of the race problem:

Attorneys for the plaintiff and attorneys for the defendant, with bun-
gling *gaucherie*, have analyzed and dissected, theorized and synthe-
sized with sublime ignorance or pathetic misapprehension of counsel
from the black client. One important witness has not yet been heard
from. The summing up of the evidence deposed, and the charge to
the jury have been made — but no word from the Black Woman.[10]

Cooper described "the Voice of the Black Woman" of the South as a
testifying voice, a voice that bears witness in the judicial process regarding
the rights of Black women and men in America. One is left with the image
of a Black woman or Black women singing *soprano obligato* in testimonial
of the experiences of Black women of the South. She shifted from musical
to justice metaphors to represent the voice of the Black woman as the voice
of a witness in a trial on the race problem:

It is because I believe the American people to be conscientiously
committed to a fair trial and ungarbled evidence, and because I feel
it essential to a perfect understanding and an equitable verdict that
truth from *each* standpoint be presented at the bar — that this little
Voice has been added to the already full chorus. The "other side"
has not been represented by one who "lives there." And not many
can more sensibly realize and more accurately tell the weight and the
fret of the "long dull pain" than the open-eyed but hitherto voiceless
Black Woman of America.[11]

Cooper described the Black woman as a witness. She portrayed her as
hitherto voiceless, but open-eyed. This woman, the personification of Black
women in America, had seen the evils of slavery, segregation, and discrimination, particularly in the South and could give testimony. Very few,
besides the Black woman, Cooper asserted, could more sensibly realize and
give a more accurate account of the pain of oppression in the South. Thus,
Cooper argued, this "little Voice" must be added to the chorus. That is,
the voice of the Black woman must also be brought to bear testimony and
to contribute to the analysis of a misapprehended problem. No one could
voice an analysis of America's race problem as Black women could, and no
one could reproduce that voice:

At any rate, as our Caucasian barristers are not to blame if they
cannot *quite* put themselves in the dark man's place, neither should
the dark man be wholly expected fully and adequately to reproduce
the exact Voice of the Black Woman.[12]

In referring to Black women collectively as "the black woman," Cooper
intended to speak both as a representative of Black women and in solidarity

with Black women. She particularly identified with Black women in the South, where she was born and raised.

Today, we might question Cooper's terminology of "the Voice of the Black Woman" as creating a false, monolithic portrayal of Black women as thinking the same thoughts, experiencing the same events. But, there was a sense of organization and unity among Black women who were beginning to organize to speak out on several issues: Jim Crow, segregation, lynching, rape, and the need for uplift. Black women were beginning to assert their ideas in the public sphere in heretofore unprecedented numbers on many agreed upon issues.

Moreover, the Black women's club movement was in full swing when Cooper wrote *A Voice from the South*. Cooper was part of an impressive network of eminent Black women leaders, all concerned with the development of Black womanhood and the uplift of the race. To the extent that they were in agreement that racism and sexism needed to be eradicated in America, Cooper was correct to describe the voices of Black women as one voice.

It is important to further observe that by referring to "the Black Woman," Cooper rendered Black womanhood, heretofore ignored and invisible to America's consciousness, visible. She rendered Black women larger than life. And, while on the one hand Cooper's description of the voice of the Black woman as "this little Voice" betrays the sense of isolation Cooper must have felt, it also belies her true feelings about that voice. Cooper's spelling of the word voice with a capital "V," reveals a spirit of defiance. To call her own voice or the voice of Black women "little" is a rhetorical gesture of nineteenth-century feminine politeness. It is also suggestive of the significance Cooper felt her intended audience, particularly white Americans and Black men, credited to Black women's voices.

Cooper's spelling of "voice" with a capital "V" is arresting. It stands in such sharp contrast to her description of Black women's voices as little, that it compels the reader to stop and question: Is the voice of Black women little, and to whose ears is the voice of Black women little? Not to Cooper, because she depicted that voice as large.

By techniques of spelling Cooper personified the voice of Black women as "the Voice of the Black Woman of the South." Such personification is often used in literature to designate divinities, goddesses, mythological figures, and the power of specific characteristics of human nature or the natural world. Through literary style, Cooper asserted the strength of the presence of Black women and of Black women's voices.

Cooper described the initial vocalization among Black women as being "with no language but a cry."[13] This initial cry was a primary sound of pain, outrage, and longing for freedom shared by Black women in America. It is more elemental than the specificity of articulations of precise methods for exacting social change. The feeling of outrage at America's social injustices regarding Black women and men was and is a shared feeling. Cooper's words suggest that Black women in post-Reconstruction America were essentially unified in their feelings of pain, suffering, and their cry for freedom and deliverance.

Cooper concluded her preface, "Our Raison D'Etre," by portraying the Black woman as a calorimeter, sensitive at every pore to America's social climate. One might look at feeling, sensitivity, and compassion in Cooper's thought as forms of moral reasoning. Because Black women were sensitive to the social climate, she argued, they were most qualified to testify on the problems of racism and sexism in America.

> Delicately sensitive at every pore to social atmospheric conditions, her calorimeter may well be studied in the interest of accuracy and fairness in diagnosing what is often conceded to be a "puzzling" case.[14]

Cooper described her own speech, surprisingly, as "broken utterances." Perhaps this description is, in part, rhetoric meant to foil the defenses of sexist and racist readers who would resist the idea of a Black woman educating them on the problems of sexism and racism. But this is also more than rhetoric. Cooper's words suggest that despite her own privileged educational background, her speech, too, has been crippled by the devastating effects of racism:

> If these broken utterances can in any way help to a clearer vision and a truer pulse-beat in studying our Nation's Problem, this Voice by a Black Woman of the South will not have been raised in vain.[15]

Cooper was aware of the singularity of her own voice as the author of *A Voice from the South.* She self-consciously created every aspect of the text, including its narrative voice. This voice was, in part, Cooper's literary construction of her own voice as narrator and, in part, her representation of the collective voices of the Black women for whom she saw herself as advocating.

Cooper indicated both her uniqueness in relation to other Black women and her solidarity with Black women in America by entitling her volume *"A" Voice from the South* rather than *"The" Voice from the South.* She was aware that she was limited in the extent to which she could speak for all Black women. But overall Cooper's language implicitly suggests that she saw her voice as a representative voice for the majority of Black women. Cooper was representative of the spheres in which she circulated, a group of mostly elite, educated Black women, although Harriet Tubman, uneducated, was also still an important voice among Black women lecturers. Cooper essayed to speak not only on the behalf of educated Black women, but on the behalf of uneducated Black women. Her primary concern was for their education and development.

Education was a means of developing eloquent speech that would belie stereotypes regarding the intellectual capacity for African Americans to analyze their own situation. Cooper was an example of what Black women could attain. She was living proof of her arguments for the education and development of Black women and the protection of their honor. The carefully crafted prose of *A Voice from the South* was evidence of the intellectual equality of Black women.

The Value and Significance of Woman's Voice

Why was the vocalization of woman's voice so important to Cooper? For some of the same reasons it is important to feminists and womanists today. The recognition of women's right to speak in traditionally male-dominated spheres was a problem in the nineteenth century, and in many respects, it is still a problem for women today. In nineteenth-century America, for women to speak on public platforms to mixed-sex audiences was considered "unladylike." Women who ventured to do so refused a model of subjugation and silence, or at most sweet, subtle whisperings to husband or father in the domestic sphere. They moved toward a model of bold vocalization.

In Cooper's view, it was subversive of every human interest that one-half of the human family be stifled. That is, to stifle women's perspective is counterproductive to the establishment of a good society. The world only half perceives truth. The presence of women's voices is necessary to complete the world's vision. Further, women's speech is of value and importance because women are linked with the world's wronged and suffering, for whom they must serve as interpreter and defender:

> It would be subversive of every human interest that the cry of one-half the human family be stifled. Woman, in stepping from the pedestal of statue-like inactivity in the domestic shrine, and daring to think and move and speak—to undertake to help shape, mold, and direct the thought of her age—is merely completing the circle of the world's vision. Hers is every interest that has lacked an interpreter and a defender. Her cause is linked with that of every agony that has been dumb—every wrong that needs a voice.[16]

Stifling women's voices, in Cooper's thought, incorrectly alters the world's vision. It undermines the best interests of everyone. Cooper described women as stepping down from the pedestal of statue-like inactivity in the domestic sphere to dare to think, move, and speak. To dare to think, move, and speak for Cooper was for women to shape, mold, and direct the thought of their age.

Cooper referred to a model of womanhood intended to represent white middle-class women, who were expected to remain in the domestic sphere. It is a model that Cooper herself, dependent on her employment as a teacher, could hardly have fully identified with. But she adopted it to make her argument for the need of women, of all races, to speak on political affairs.

For Cooper, because women were the most dominated group of human beings across cultures, women's issues were linked with every wrong that needed a voice. Cooper viewed women's oppression as affording the ability to interpret the interests of the weak generally. She presented women's power as the ability to interpret and defend the plight of the weak, the oppressed, from experiential understanding.

Women, Cooper's words suggest, have a distinctive and powerful ability to interpret every wrong and agony that has lacked a defender. Can women really interpret the interests of every oppressed group? Does this afford women too much power? Perhaps. The question arises: Which women will engage in shaping, molding, and directing the thought of their age? Educated white women and women of color? Where are the voices of the poor, the illiterate, of laboring women and men? Cooper's intention was not to establish a new imperialism. The value of her thought is that she recognized the interrelationship between various forms of oppression: sexism, racism, cultural imperialism. She purposed to raise women's consciousness, white and Black, to an awareness of the interrelated nature of the problem of oppression.

Cooper used language that was most accessible to highly educated persons. In order to effect social change, it was necessary to appeal to the sensibilities of those who had economic power to effect such change. Thus Cooper particularly addressed middle-class women and men. Mary Helen Washington notes that women in the racial uplift movement perceived that close identification with the issues and interests of poor and uneducated Black women entailed a great risk.[17] Perhaps for this reason, Cooper presumed to speak *for* them rather than *with* them or *beside* them. Today, womanists will want to speak in solidarity with Black women of all classes, rather than for them.

A Womanist Reflection on Cooper's Thought

What is the significance of Cooper's work for womanist theologians? Most basically, Alice Walker defines a womanist as a Black feminist or feminist of color. The term comes from the African-American folk tradition's use of the term "womanish," which means to act grown-up, responsible, and in charge.[18]

Jacquelyn Grant goes beyond Walker to describe womanism as "being and acting out who you are and interpreting the reality for yourself." She emphasizes the importance of Black women's autonomy and suggests that speech is an essential aspect of womanism. For Grant, an essential aspect of womanism is simply this: "Black women speak out for themselves."[19]

The self-possession of one's own voice, one might say, is an important aspect of womanism. Along with her contemporaries in the Black women's club movement, Cooper saw the need for Black women to speak out for themselves. Her work shares something in common with contemporary womanist interpretations of Black women's social-historical situation.

Moreover, Cooper was "womanist" in the sense that she was self-motivated and a leader. Also, the heights of Cooper's academic achievements demonstrate her search for knowledge, what Walker calls a desire to know "more" than is "good for one."[20] Further, as an educator, Cooper wanted her students to know more than was good for them; that is, she firmly held that they ought to have far higher educations than the dominant society thought Negro women and men ought to have. In the above respects Cooper embodied and expressed certain qualities that are currently attributed to womanism.

The context that Walker describes and Delores Williams identifies as important for womanist thought is the context of nonbourgeois Black folk culture.[21] Although Cooper did not fit that category, her slave birth gave her a sensitivity to anonymous Black women who were victims of the violent abuses of slavery. The legacy of the women affected her life's work. She recognized the anonymity of Black women's thoughts, feelings, and voices, and attempted, in the way that she best understood and knew how, to bring these voices out of anonymity. She did not speak with "the exact voice" of Black women in the sense of representing every particular viewpoint possible, but she did speak with the exact dignity of Black women for freedom and against social, economic, and educational injustice.

Moreover, Cooper in many respects shared an anonymity with other Black women. Cooper wrote and lectured fully aware that she might pass into anonymity.[22] Beneath the title, *A Voice from the South*, on the first title page of the text, she wrote: "With regret I forget if the song be living yet, yet remember, vaguely now, *it was honest, anyhow.*" As in the case of many Black women writers, African-American women and men have had to engage in a recovery of her writings.

Contemporary Black women can resonate with many of the problems, feelings, and solutions Cooper identified. To use her metaphor of music, *A Voice from the South* strikes a repetitive note in our ears. We have heard of the evils of domination she identifies. This repetitiveness ought to create a sense of discomfort. It ought to evoke an awareness of the discordancy in the world, an awareness that something is wrong. Part of the value of Cooper's writings is her identification of the gross discordancy in the human network of communities and relationships. This problem remains today.

Cooper's thought indicates very carefully and clearly that the problems of racism and sexism in America are not simply a Black problem or a woman problem; they are America's problem. And, more than that, the problem of the domination of the physically and militaristically weak by the strong — imperialism — is not simply an American problem, but a global problem.

Cooper, like contemporary feminist, womanist, and liberation theologians, analyzed particular forms of oppression and challenged specific structures of oppression. Unlike the liberation theologian, she presented no explicit definition of domination or oppression as "sin" or "evil." But Cooper viewed these problems as going against the principles of Christ as represented in the synoptic Gospels and other New Testament literature.[23] Womanist and liberationist theologians today recognize these problems as forms of institutional sin. That is, various forms of domination or oppression are deeply embedded within the structure of society and need to be eradicated.

Like Cooper, womanists today are aware of the subjugation of Black women's voices in American culture. And, looking to historical sources, the autobiographies of Black women evangelists like Jarena Lee, Amanda Berry Smith, Rebecca Cox Jackson, Zilpha Elaw, and Julia Foote, as well as political leaders from Maria Stewart to Ida B. Wells to Shirley Chisholm, echo the problem of men's efforts to silence the voices of Black women.

Cooper's passion for freedom from domination and her outrage at injustice gives her work both a timeless and a contemporary value and power. Cooper referred to the voice of the Black woman of the South, her own voice, as but a cry. In her movement from a cry of outrage, to broken utterances about suffering, to her bold vocalization of a gospel message of equality and freedom, Cooper's voice reaches from the past into the present to articulate a womanist analysis of oppression and freedom.

The Meaning and Power of Voice for Womanist Theologians

Perhaps it is in the passion for justice, freedom, and equality, along with outrage at the injustice of domination, that Cooper's voice can resonate with the voices of Black women, and women generally, today. There are many voices among Black women, as many voices as there are Black women. Theologians today must find ways of bringing these voices out of anonymity. It is necessary to find and employ ways of hearing the uniqueness and variedness of Black women's wisdom. One way of doing this is by turning to Black women's literature that mirrors the folk wisdom of Black women, as womanist theologian Delores Williams is doing, keeping in line with Alice Walker's understanding of womanism. Ethicist Katie Cannon similarly accesses Black women's folk wisdom through the works of Zora Neale Hurston and other Black women writers who follow in Hurston's Black anthropological tradition. In doing this, one need not exclude the voices of educationally privileged Black women like Mary Church Terrell, Ida B. Wells, Frances Ellen Watkins Harper, or Anna Julia Cooper. It is necessary to include a variety of voices in social, religious, and political discourse.

Each community, as well as each individual, has its own voice identifying the particularities of the problems of oppression. We need not expect the passion of each voice to have the same depth or tone. There are different levels of experience and awareness of the problem of oppression. One must recognize the value and integrity of the passion and outrage of a diversity of Black women's voices. Cooper was careful to point out that only Black women can speak with the exact voice of the Black woman. Today it is necessary to take this observation further. One must question the notion that there is such a thing as the "exact voice" of the Black woman. Further, like Cooper, it is important to practice what one preaches.

For Cooper, there was a *"Singing* Something" within human being that was part of the very being of God. This *"Singing* Something" is part of the "inborn human endowment," and "justifies the claim to equality by birthright."[24]

In 1945, in her published edition of her 1925 dissertation defense, "Equality of Races and the Democratic Movement," Cooper referred to human freedom as "a shadow mark of the Creator's image," a *"Singing* Something" that "distinguishes the first Man from the last ape, which in a subtle way tagged him with the picturesque Greek title *anthropos.*"[25] For Cooper, freedom and equality, universal birthrights, are something that sing within the human soul. This *"Singing* Something" is directly traceable to the Creator.[26] This *"Singing* Something" within human being, then, is part of the being of God.

For Cooper, humankind's creation in the likeness of God is more than merely imagistic. It is vocal. It is musical. It is auditory. She was interested in the sound, the words, the composition of God's voice. It is in song, in voice, that humankind is created in the image of God, or better, in the sound of God.

The entire body is engaged in voice: the lungs, the diaphragm, the voice box (the very breath of a human being, which is often symbolically equated with spirit). Also the head, the arms, the face, hands, legs, lips, tongue, and ears participate in the practice of vocal expression, whether in conversation, public speech, or song. Voice engages the whole person: the body, the mind, and feelings. Cooper's metaphor of a *"Singing* Something" points to the sacredness of human being as an energy and force that moves the body to action. Through voice one can assert the sacredness and beauty of Black women's bodies and lives.

Moreover, one can build on Cooper's use of metaphor to suggest that when Black women speak in the voice of equality and freedom, when Black women speak from a *"Singing* Something," Black women echo the sounds and lyrics of God's voice. Black women, in raising their voices, participate in an antiphony.

Antiphony has always been very popular in the Anglican tradition Cooper was a part of. Moreover, in traditional Black churches the practice of call-and-response between preacher and congregation during prayers, sermons, and singing is integral to the service. Black women raising their voices to call for freedom and equality are engaged in call-and-response with God, repeating God's words and ideals in the Black church tradition.

Cooper cited religion as the source for the power of voice in her essay "The Gain from a Belief," in which she described belief in religion as "a live coal from the altar which at once unseals the lips of the dumb."[27] The source of speech for Cooper was belief in religion. Although Cooper primarily cited Jesus and Christian principles as liberating, she cited religions around the world as holding this power.

For Cooper, with belief in the power of religion "all things are possible." Cooper explained that, "Jesus *believed* in the infinite possibilities of an individual soul." Faith that all things are possible, particularly social progress, empowers human beings to speak out. For Cooper, one might say, the voice of God is on the side of the oppressed. Humanity is found in setting forth the *"Singing* Something" within the human soul that responds to and resonates with a gospel message of freedom and equality for all.

The theme of coming to voice is essential to womanism. Voice calls attention to pain and suffering. Voice criticizes oppression. Voice offers and demands solutions to problems. Voice cries out in passion, anger, and outrage. Voice motivates others to follow. Voice shocks and touches people to respond. Voice challenges attitudes, social customs, and practice. Voice motivates reform. Voice calls people out for radical, revolutionary action. Voice resists systems of injustice.

If voice was not powerful, oppressors would not find it necessary to silence those they dominate. Cooper understood and practiced the power of voice. Moreover, she practiced what she voiced in her everyday life. She has left Black women in America a rich legacy of speech in action against the evils of sexism, racism, classism, and general domination of the weak by the strong. Black Women must continue this legacy of speech in action today.

NOTES

1. Undated autobiographical document by Anna Julia Cooper, Anna Julia Cooper Papers, Moorland-Spingarn Research Center, Howard University, reproduced in Louise Daniel Hutchinson, *Anna J. Cooper: A Voice from the South* (Washington, DC: Smithsonian Institution, 1981), 4.

2. Ibid., 19, 20.

3. Ibid., 61–67 ff. See also Mary Helen Washington, Introduction to *A Voice from the South,* by Anna J. Cooper, ed. Mary Helen Washington (Aldine Printing House, 1892; Reprint, New York and Oxford: Oxford University Press, 1988), xxxiii ff; and Sharon Harley, "Anna J. Cooper: A Voice for Black Women," *The Afro American Woman,* ed. Rosalyn Terborg Penn and Sharon Harley (Port Washington, NY: Kennikat Press, 1978), 92 ff.

4. The "M" Street School, Washington's Colored High School, moved into a new, larger building in 1916, and was renamed Dunbar High School.

5. Hutchinson, 147–152. Frelinghuysen was founded in 1906 to provide educational, social, and moral uplift programs for the children of former slaves. Its first president was Jesse Lawson, one of the school's major incorporators.

6. Cooper wrote a pageant, "From Servitude to Service," celebrating the lives of Black leaders in America. See Anna Julia Cooper Papers, Moorland-Spingarn Research Center, Howard University, Washington, DC.

7. Anna Julia Cooper, "Womanhood a Vital Element in the Regeneration and Progress of a Race," *A Voice from the South*, 9, 28. See also Barbara Andolsen's discussion of the ideal of true womanhood as used by Black and white feminists in *Daughters of Jefferson, Daughters of Bootblacks* (Macon, GA: Mercer University Press, 1986).

8. Anna Julia Cooper, *Equality of Races and the Democratic Movement* (pamphlet, privately printed, Washington, DC, 1945), 4–5. Cooper hypothesized that "progress in the democratic sense" was an "inborn human endowment," "a shadow mark of the Creator's image," an "urge cell," a *"Singing* Something" within human being.

9. Cooper, "Our Raison D'Etre," *A Voice from the South*, i.

10. Ibid., ii.

11. Ibid.

12. Ibid., iii.

13. Ibid.

14. Ibid.

15. Ibid.

16. Cooper, "Woman Versus the Indian," *A Voice from the South*, 121–122.

17. Washington, Introduction to *A Voice from the South*, xxx–xxxi.

18. Alice Walker, *In Search of Our Mothers' Gardens* (New York: Harcourt Brace Jovanovich, 1983), xi–xii.

19. Jacquelyn Grant, "Womanist Theology," in *African American Religious Studies*, ed. Gayraud S. Wilmore (Durham, NC: Duke University Press, 1989), 213.

20. Walker, *In Search*, xi, xii.

21. Ibid. See also Delores Williams, "Womanist Theology: Black Women's Voices," *Christianity and Crisis* (2 March 1987), 67.

22. Washington, Introduction to *A Voice from the South*, xxxix ff, for a discussion of this problem.

23. See Cooper, "Womanhood a Vital Element in the Regeneration and Progress of a Race," in *A Voice from the South*, 17, 18. See also Cooper's letter to Lyman Abott, Anna Julia Cooper Papers, Moorland Spingarn Research Center, Howard University, Washington, DC. Here Cooper writes of Christ as advocating the weak.

24. Cooper, *Equality of Races*, 5.

25. Ibid.

26. Ibid.

27. Cooper, "The Gain from a Belief," in *A Voice From the South*, 302.

PART IV

AS PURPLE
IS
TO LAVENDER

11

Women's Power—Women's Passion

And God Said, "That's Good"

Patricia L. Hunter

So God created humankind in God's image, . . . male and female God created them . . . God saw everything that God had made, and indeed, it was very good.
—Genesis 1:27, 31

"God said it, I believe it, and that settles it." No doubt you have seen this bumper sticker. What I find most intriguing about this maxim is, who gets to determine what God has said? There are many followers of the Christian faith who would say, "if it is in the Bible then God said it." Few Christians would dispute the belief that the Bible is the inspired Word of God. Indeed God has revealed God's self in history through scripture. Many oppressed communities have found strength and encouragement by reading Hebrew and Greek scriptures. God appears to be on the side of the oppressed—protecting, leading and admonishing those whom God calls God's own.

When Bibles are opened to the beginning of the Hebrew scriptures, readers encounter the Creation story. The reader is taken on a daily journey of how the world came into being. Sun, moon, stars, animals, and vegetation were all made intentionally. Finally, on the sixth day, the writer says that God created humankind. Both females and males were created in the image of God. At the end of the creation process, the author writes that God looked around on all that God had created and God said it was very good. That "very good" status was conveyed on heaven, earth, the firmament, animals, fish, plants and humanity. If *all* God created was very good, including humankind, then *all* women, regardless of ethnicity, class, varying abilities, or sexual orientation, are a part of God's very good creation. There have been tendencies to say certain aspects of our being are better than others. Philosophies and theologies have been based on a dualism or a dimensionalism where part of human nature is good and part is evil. However, it is my belief that all aspects of our being as women are good, including our emotions, our spiritual, physical, and sexual being.

It is not my intent to discuss scripture as being fallible or infallible. Neither will I discuss various methodologies of biblical criticism. What is critical for Christian women of color is to understand the contradiction of believing all of creation is good (including women of color) while treating ourselves as less than acceptable to God, and accepting despicable treatment from men and other women.

Perhaps the contradiction begins in our understanding of God. What does it mean to be female and to believe we are made in the image of God when God is known as Father, Lord, and Master? How can I be made in the image of God, when the words most often used to describe God are male and I am female? Not only are many words for God masculine, the words we most often use are words that connote power over another and fear of authority. The patriarchal titles of Lord and Master do not conjure loving or kind images for those whose history includes the enslavement of foreparents.

Patriarchy has evolved and come to be identified as a social structure where men dominate and oppress. Where patriarchy exists, one entity has power over, while another entity has less power or no power. The element of fear is not irrelevant to patriarchy, male domination or oppression. In order for people to stay in their place, with the oppressor in control, those with less power have to be terrified of the consequences if they upset the status quo.

Knowing God as father may be comforting to some. Those who had a supportive, loving father present in childhood may take comfort in knowing God as father. To only know or speak of God as father is limiting to those whose understanding of father is not positive. For those whose fathers were not present when needed, or who felt the pangs of hunger and poverty because of lacking financial support from their fathers, or who experienced physical and sexual abuse from their father, the image of God as father may be more painful than helpful.

It is naive to believe that creating God in the image of a male human being was and continues to be unintentional. Some may say the use of the word father for God is to refer to God as a parent. But if that were true, those same people would not have such a visceral reaction to the use of the words parent or mother in reference to God. To speak of God as father is intentional use of the masculine. Presenting God as male has legitimized male domination and power over women, children, and other living things. Having a male God means that only males are truly made in the image of God. Men have claimed, as their divine privilege, the right to order women's lives, control women's lives, and determine what activities are acceptable. Having a male God has led many to believe that women are something other than made in the image of God. If women are something other, then women are less than men who are truly made in God's image.

With the advent of womanist and feminist theology we now have ways to image God differently. God is no longer exclusively male. God is also female and God is also neither gender. God is no longer a God of power *over* God's creation, but a God who has power *with* God's creation. According to womanist theology, God no longer is created in the image of the dominate culture. Womanist theologians give God permission to be God all by God's self! It is no wonder that traditional systematic theologians find womanist theology threatening and therefore declare it a fad. Those who are accustomed to defining the Christian faith find it necessary to dismiss womanist theology as unimportant, lest they lose their control and power.

Reclaiming our womanhood and our ability to be womanish as a gift of God's grace is a painful and painstakingly slow process. Part of the pain lies in realizing a systemic conspiracy has been at work to prevent women of color from knowing their power and passion. Demonic "isms," such as racism, sexism, classism, heterosexism, imperialism, have worked in concert against women of color claiming their divine privilege to be who God has created them to be.

Each tool of oppression and prejudice must be confronted and dismantled. It is reasonable to turn to other women who have been isolated, marginalized, and oppressed to join us in demanding release from the "isms." The pain of oppression is compounded as we experience blatantly racist and other oppressive behaviors from well-intentioned European-American women. These women want to be known as our sisters, yet they participate in the conspiracy by denying the privilege that is theirs by virtue of the color of their skin. The pain continues when we meet women of color who are unaware that their power and passion have been taken from them. The pain deepens when we encounter those who are so pained by their powerlessness that they are determined to destroy any woman who has a sense of her own power or passion. We have lost, been denied, and given so much of ourselves away that we may not even know where to begin to find and reclaim ourselves.

If we start from a new premise that God is no longer male and *God is not made in the image of the dominate culture*, women of color can begin to reimage ourselves. Women of color can believe that we are also created in the image of God. If we, as women of color, are willing to reimage and redefine ourselves not as other but as Godlike, then innumerable ways of lifting self-esteem and claiming the right to live whole, healthy lives can emerge.

Perhaps one of the first ways to build our self-esteem is to name and claim our passion. Passion is more than lust and passion is not genitally focused. Passion consumes our total being—psychological, physical, spiritual, and sexual. Carter Heyward, in *Our Passion For Justice*, defines passion as

> a way of being in which anything less than spilling over with the Spirit of God is not enough; spilling over with desire to know and do the will of God in our daily work and play; with righteous and active indignation at injustice, with careful caring for others and self, with courage to stand up and be counted—when it counts; spilling over with integrity in relationship and with awareness of our oneness with all aspects and persons of creation.[1]

Passion is that unquenchable thirst for that which is not yet. Passion is that determined desire to know ourselves and others completely. Passion is our souls' desire for harmony born of justice. Audre Lorde, in *Sister Outsider*, speaks of the erotic power of women's lives. For Lorde, the erotic is not the pornographic exploitation that characterizes the sex for profit industry. Lorde speaks of the erotic as

> an assertion of the lifeforce of women; of that creative energy empowered, the knowledge and use of which we are now reclaiming in our language, our history, our dancing, our living, our work, our lives.[2]

To be in touch with our passion and to acknowledge our passion as a gift of God's "good" Creation is to give birth to a new way of being in the world. When we embrace our passion and acknowledge its power, we do not have to settle for the mediocre, the mundane, or that which causes harm to women. We can pursue that which affirms, gives life, and celebrates our presence. The power we experience by embracing our passion is not a power of military might or a power that leads to exploitation or destruction. The power we experience begins internally and then enables us to influence our surroundings. The power we have is a dynamic that gives us permission to claim our identity as we choose to be defined. Once we have embraced our identity, our power gives us the courage to accept others as they choose to define themselves. We do not have to fear someone just because they are different. Everyone need not be just like us in order to be acceptable.

The passion of African-American women has helped the entire African-American community survive. Our foremothers' passion enabled them to see a future where their children would have more options educationally, professionally, socially, and most assuredly economically. Our passion is born of our mothers. Our passion gives us courage to speak the unspeakable. Our passion compels us to speak the truth about our lives. Our passion is that life force that enables us to risk speaking the truth in the hope that our children will have even more options than we have today.

Those who are accustomed to defining women's lives find our passion and power threatening and dangerous, or at least disconcerting. One need not go any further than the church to see how the fear of women's passion and power is acted out. Why is it that even when our churches are 70 to 90 percent women, these congregations insist on having a male pastor? Why is it that in so many of our churches the decision-making body is all male or predominately male? Why is it that when an adolescent girl or young woman gives birth out of wedlock, she has to go before the congregation, ask for forgiveness and ask to be reinstated for membership while the father of the child, if he is in the church, does not? Why do we hear from so many pulpits that God does not call women to preach? Who is afraid of women preaching, God or men? Will the Christian message of love and salvation be compromised if women preach the gospel? The presence of women in prominent leadership positions and in significant numbers in the church is so threatening that the campaign of misogyny is waged and legitimized by prooftexted scripture. The campaign punishes those who claim their God-given power and passion as divine gifts of grace.

There exists a fallacy among Christians that we are not interested in power. If one appears interested in amassing power one could be chastised as being more interested in personal glory and acclaim than in sharing the gospel. No good Christian would want to be associated with James and John who wanted to be seated at Jesus' right and left hand when he came into his glory.[3] Yet those who create so-called "Christian moral standards" do so in a way that they maintain power over individual lives. They maintain power to name what is acceptable and what is not.

There seems to exist an underlying fear that if a woman is able to claim her own power and name her passion, she may define herself in a way that excludes those who have traditionally been in power as defined by patriarchy. One of the limitations of patriarchy, to which Christianity has succumbed, is to believe that some have power and some do not. It is outside the realm of traditional Christian thought to believe that everyone can have and does have power. To realize that one's position of privilege is obsolete and no longer needed or feared is a terrifying thought for those who have set themselves up as having power over human lives. So the campaign rewards and lifts up as examples those who give away their power and deny their passion.

If I had a dollar for every time I heard someone say, "It is not the men in my congregation that are against women preachers, it is the women," I could begin an early retirement. Statements of how women are unsupportive of each other point to the collusion of women to undermine one another, sometimes without even knowing it.

Our collusion to undermine women's power and authority keeps women bickering and men in charge. We do not come from the womb disliking or not trusting women. We are taught not to trust one another. We are taught that we are in competition with one another. We are taught that we have to watch out for other women, lest they take our men away from us. It is obvious who benefits from women not trusting women. Men benefit! More often than not the male pastor has coached, taught, and trained women in his congregation to be antagonistic to women preachers. For the male pastor, it is much safer for him to say, "It's the women in my congregation who are against women preachers," rather than admit he is afraid of losing his prestigious position if women are allowed to compete with him for pastoral positions and if women peel away the mystique of the pastorate.

There may be many reasons why some women in congregations are not supportive of women in ministry, but most of the reasons will fall under one of two basic premises—both of which involve the issue of power. The first reason is that women do not like or trust themselves as women. The second reason is that women do not feel women are good enough to have all the gifts God has given to humanity. We still believe some gifts are only given to or can be exercised only by men.

Most western women feel we are not sufficient just the way God created us. If we do not like ourselves—our physical features, our personalities, our emotional makeup, our spiritual dimension—we will not be attracted to these attributes when we find them in other women. If we spend enormous energy denying our passion, we will resent other women who dare to cultivate and thrive as a result of their passion.

One of the great paradoxes of women's lives is being taught not to trust one another (for the benefit of men), yet knowing those who will be there for us in our greatest hour of need and in times of celebration will be our sisters. This is not to say men are not present when the going gets tough. There are some men who are able to be present and helpful through difficult times. My experience leads me to believe these men are the exception rather than the rule. When we have to walk through the valley of the shadow of death, more often than not it is our sisters who will walk with us.

It is critically important for women of color to believe we are created in the image of God and that we are wonderfully made. We do not have to spend our energies trying to be something we are not or someone else. Women of African descent are beautiful with our larger sizes, intricately curly hair, adequate hips, broad noses, and other distinct features. To try and conform to a European image of beauty is to deny ourselves as being created in the image of God. To attempt to remake ourselves into someone else's image is a sin against God. God has not made a mistake in creating women of African descent!

The billion dollar makeup/make-over/weight-loss industry flourishes because most women, including myself, have received messages since we were little girls that something about our physical appearance is not adequate. The media and fashion industry reinforce those messages of inadequacy. The question to ask is, Who benefits from women of color thinking we are inadequate? It certainly is not women of color! We may try to straighten our hair, use makeup that was not created for women of color, surgically alter our facial features, and try diet program after diet program. After spending enormous amounts of money to re-create ourselves, we still feel we are not good enough and the feelings of inadequacy prevail. Since it seems that we cannot attain the perfect image, whatever that may be, we begin to feel like failures. Self-esteem plummets, hopelessness ensues, and the downward spiral to self-pity begins.

We can only imagine what our self-image would be like as adults if for the first twelve years of our lives we were told how beautiful we are. How empowering our lives would be if for the first twelve years of our lives we were taught that we are wonderfully made in the image of God. Our lives would be much different if we were told as little girls that it is truly a gift of God's grace to be born female. It is sobering to admit that the messages we receive as innocent little girls are far from these assurances. I am not saying that we are not to try and enhance who we are and what we have. There is a difference between trying to enhance ourselves and trying to recreate ourselves into someone else's image. We must take care of ourselves by living whole and healthy lives.

A life style that affirms women of color and helps maintain physical, sexual, emotional, and spiritual health is a must. Make time to eat nutritionally and exercise. Women have physical needs of touch and lovemaking. In the midst of all the demands on us, we have to be conscious of our need for intimacy, and find safe ways to fulfill our sexual desires. We must stop long enough to get in touch with our emotions.

In analyzing why women may not be supportive of other women in ministry, one cannot overlook how sexuality and ministry are interrelated. There is an erotic power in the pulpit. For generations men have benefited from the attention, flattery, and gifts given them by women in their congregations. For some women, the pastor becomes the husband or son they wished they had. Our society acknowledges, supports, and encourages this kind of behavior between men and women. But when the minister is female, women in congregations are very unsure of how to handle this different erotic power from the pulpit. When the minister is female, women in congregations are suddenly unsure whether the attention, flattery, and gifts they would have given male pastors are appropriate. If by chance a woman in the congregation becomes attracted to the woman pastor, a whole new can of worms is opened!

Finally, any discussion of power cannot minimize the influence of roles based on gender. Only in the past thirty years have women found greater acceptance in professional roles outside of nursing and education. The African-American community mirrors the general society when it comes to women in professional positions. It is perceived that women will do certain things and men other things. Men will be recognized for their divine gifts of leadership in the church and the community and women will be recognized for their gifts of leadership in the church, as long as it is not pulpit ministry. While general society is slowly accepting women in professional positions, the church community resists accepting women in professional ministry.

When congregations encounter women who preach and minister with divine power and grace, those women are considered exceptions. The belief that God does not call women to professional church leadership is psychologically and sociologically entrenched. It is very disconcerting to acknowledge that God calls women to be spiritual leaders when acknowledged or official history has not affirmed that reality. To realize God disregards our social norms regarding gender roles and does what God wants to do by calling women to pastoral leadership is to begin the process of questioning what other societal norms have been interpreted as divine will.

In order to embrace ourselves as women of color we must come to value our physical selves and understand our emotional makeup. Part of our power comes in knowing ourselves. We cannot know ourselves unless we are willing to be still and listen to the still, small voice within. When we stop to get in touch with our emotions, we must pay attention to all our feelings, even our rage. We cannot disregard our rage because it is too frightening to face.

As we analyze the state of the African-American community, it is no wonder that we as African-American women live in a constant state of rage. We are enraged with the economic injustices we must battle. We are enraged that Christianity has become frightened by that which can enhance our lives, namely our power and our passion. We are enraged that church doors of opportunity continue to close in our faces because of the color of our skin and our gender. We are enraged that some African-American men think we are their enemies and that we are only interested in male-bashing. We are enraged that standards of beauty seldom include characteristics of African ancestry. We are enraged that European-American women still claim not to know why we are angry. We are enraged when we are told to speak using less hostile words. We are enraged when we are told by well-meaning friends that our anger and our rage are inappropriate or unfounded. We are enraged when we are expected to instruct our oppressors on how to be justice-oriented.

We spend a significant amount of our emotional energy managing our rage. In fact, managing our rage is a survival skill we develop as little girls when we first begin to notice we are being treated differently than the boys or when we are treated differently than other ethnic children. Every day that goes by without destroying ourselves or those around us is a witness to God's grace and to our ability to cope with insanity and hatred.

The Holy Spirit's ability to give meaning and direction to our lives amid our rage is what sustains us. It is by God's amazing grace that we can turn our endless rage into a holy rage. With our holy rage we maintain our connections to the church, sometimes closely, other times tangentially. Our holy rage, in concert with our faith, enables us to believe in the power of the Holy Spirit to transform the church to be a place of justice and safety for women.

Why has the Black church been so obviously silent regarding the rights of African-American women? The Black church prides itself on speaking out on behalf of the "least of these" and the have-nots of its community. Throughout the turbulent history of African Americans, the Black church single-handedly kept the African-American community together. The Black church has been an advocate for civil rights, quality education, equal employment opportunities, and has spoken out against discrimination and apartheid in countries in Africa. Yet, when the women's movement began in the 1970s, pastors of our churches claimed women's liberation was a white woman's issue.

African-American male pastors had the audacity to say our women have always been liberated. Granted the women's movement of the 1970s was fraught with racism and most women's rights organizations continue to struggle with racism, but would African-American men accept the dominate culture defining for them the limits of their liberation?

African-American men expected African-American women to keep their mouths shut and let "our brothers" speak for them. The Black church has sinned in not caring, liberating, and empowering the very ones who support it, the women. Just as the Black church has criticized this country's policies and practices of discrimination, the Black church must be held accountable for the oppression it has leveled against its own women.

The question that is paramount for the survival of Christian women of color is whether Christianity as it has evolved, now embarking on the second millennium, is capable of doing women justice? Is Christianity as we know it today, entrenched in patriarchy and being male-defined, able to sustain and uplift women of color through the next millennium? No. The church must make a radical shift in its patriarchal, misogynistic theology if it wants to address the world's concerns in the twenty-first century.

The institutional church is teetering on becoming obsolete while the world moves forward. As we approach the twenty-first century, it seems that the church is stuck at the beginning of the twentieth century. When will the church catch up to the people it proposes to lead? The church cannot continue to oppress and ignore women in general and women of color specifically if it wants to have a prophetic place in the world and in women's lives.

If our historic Black churches are willing to leap into the twenty-first century, take advantage of current technology, and current political and social information, their chances of avoiding the current downturn in white mainline Protestantism may be avoided. God has not become obsolete and our need for a spiritually-based community is not obsolete. Only the ways of being the church of the early 1900s have become obsolete. Offering a critique of the Black church's strengths and weaknesses is risky business. Those who have benefited by the Black church's current systems and norms, be they oppressive or empowering, will rally vehemently to defend them. Those of us who have been marginalized because we refuse to support its oppression and bigotry may find ourselves even more marginalized. The church of the twenty-first century that speaks to the African-American community will be a church that believes all women are created in the image of God. The church will also believe that all God created is good. The church of the next century must be a church that is willing to address the interrelated issues of spirituality and sexuality. The church of the next century must be willing to confront patriarchy as a form of oppression for women of color. More than ever, our world is yearning for a community of faith to give witness to how being a follower of Jesus Christ can enhance the quality of life, facilitate healing, and bring peace with justice in this current day for all of God's creation.

NOTES

1. Carter Heyward, *Our Passion for Justice: Images of Power, Sexuality, and Liberation* (New York: Pilgrim Press, 1984), 21.
2. Audre Lorde, *Sister Outsider* (Trumansburg, NY: Crossing Press, 1984), 55.
3. Mark 10:35–40 NRSV (New Revised Standard Version).

12

The Sin of Servanthood

And the Deliverance of Discipleship

Jacquelyn Grant

A well-known theologian once warned us of answering questions that no one is asking. But Christian theology, he [Paul Tillich] argued, ought to correlate the questions emerging out of the human situation with the answers as they are found in the gospel message. I believe that a theologian's accountability ought to be to the community of believers that provide the new data for theological reflections. However, I equally believe that accountability does not imply uncritical acceptance of the oppressive controls placed on any particular human situation. That is, there must be a self-critical (evaluative) dimension to theology. In fact, theology must not only be reflection upon the lived realities of the faithful, but it must also be prophetic; that is, it must raise the critical and sometimes difficult questions that arise out of the various contradictions of life.

Many contradictions stared me in the face a few years ago when I was in midst of my dissertation process. The study, a comparative analysis of Black women's and white women's experiences of Jesus Christ, led me to exploring the lived realities of Black women and white women.[1] One theme that constantly emerged was that of "servanthood." Why is this the case? Could it be that women in general are believed to be, by nature, servants of men, and in the context of women's community, Black women are seen primarily as servants to all?

The theme "servanthood" was intriguing because of the contexts in which it was and is used. As critical components to Christianity, the notions of "service" and "servanthood," when seen against lordship, may be perceived as a necessary dialectical tension, but when viewed in light of human indignities perpetrated against those who have been the "real servants" of

199

the society, they represent contradictions. Indeed, we are all called to be "servants."

It is interesting, however, that these terms are customarily used to relegate certain victimized peoples — those on the underside of history — to the lower rung of society. Consequently, politically disenfranchised peoples have generally been perceived as the servant class for the politically powerful. Nonwhite peoples, it is believed by many white people, were created for the primary purpose of providing service for white people. Likewise, in patriarchal societies, the notions of service and servant were often used to describe the role that women played in relation to men and children.

As I examined the words and work of nineteenth-century feminists, I found that white women were challenging the fact that they were relegated to the level of "servants of men." They were incensed because they were being treated as second-class citizens in the larger society, and second-class Christians in the church. Certainly, any perusal of history in general, and women's history in particular, validates their claim.

Further, an examination of Black women's reality reveals that they are further removed from the topside of history. In fact, African-American women have been the "servants of the servants." It was clear that one of the best entrées for comparing the lives of white and Black women was through the study of slavery and of domestic service. This kind of comparison would allow us to answer partially the old theodicy question in relation to Black women — because service has been basically a life of suffering for those "relegated" to that state, the question to be raised is, why do Black women suffer so? Or even more pointedly, why does God permit the suffering of Black women? Does God condone the fact that Black women are systematically relegated to being "servants of servants?"

It is said that confession is good for the soul. Let me therefore confess my problem, at that time, with this line of research inquiry. Given the nature of Black women's servanthood/servitude, I found it difficult to settle for the use of such terminologies to describe their relationship with God. Servanthood in this country, in effect, has been servitude. It (service) has never been properly recognized. Servants have never been properly remunerated for their services. One could possibly argue that by definition, one does not engage in services for monetary gains, but for benevolent reasons instead. However, if this is so, one could ask, why is it that certain people are more often than others relegated to such positions? Further, why is it that these positions are more often than not relegated to the bottom (or at least the lower end) of the economic scale? Why is it that those so-called service positions that are higher or high on the economic scale are almost always held by those of an oppressor race, class, or gender? For example, public officials claim to be public servants; they are most often of the dominant culture, white and male. The hierarchy of the church claims to be servants of God and the people, yet they are likewise most often of the dominant culture — white and/or male. Generally and relatively speaking, they are economically well-off, or at least adequately provided for. This is not often true for service/servants on the lower rung of society. Why are the real servants overwhelmingly poor, Black, and Third World? Why is their service status always controlled by the upholders of the status quo?

These questions lead me to postulate that perhaps Christians, in the interest of fairness and justice, need to reconsider the servant language, for it has been this language that has undergirded much of the human structures causing pain and suffering for many oppressed peoples. The conditions created were nothing short of injustice and, in fact, sin.

Feminist Redemption of Servanthood

Feminists have attempted to redeem the notion of service, servant and servanthood. In explicating her position that Jesus is the representative for all, Letty Russell draws upon traditional phrases and words such as "Jesus is Lord" (*kyrios*) and "servant" (*diakonos*). Finding no problem with either of these terms, she emphasizes in her discussion that these functions are necessary. Recognizing the possible objection to the use of such metaphors as servant and Lord, Russell is quick to refer to the true meaning of servant, Lord, and lordship. Servant and Lord are defined not as the titles for the oppressed and oppressors, or inferior and superior persons, which they have come to mean in our unjust and oppressive church and society. But they are used to refer to "one divine *oikonomia*." In this sense, she does not only speak of the scandal of particularity, but also of the scandal involved in using the words servant and Lord together. At this point, the question is not how can the male be God, but how can the servant be Lord? The answer rests in Jesus' proclamation that he came not to be served but to serve *(diakonia)*. In the biblical sense, God is both Lord and servant; consequently, Jesus is characterized in lordship and servanthood:

> Neither Lord nor Servant can be removed from our description of God's self-presentation, . . . the key to understanding them is to allow them to remain together in the liberation paradox that witnesses to the story of God's *oikonomia*. The words cannot be separated if they are to be understood without leading to false dualism and false uses of power. The meaning of God's Lordship in Jesus Christ is clear only in relation to the purpose of that Lordship, which is service. The purpose of God's service and subordination in Jesus Christ is to establish the Lordship of God's love.[2]

Given the accounts of Jesus as recorded in the New Testament, it would appear that Jesus' reward for obedient servanthood was suffering rather than exaltation. What, therefore, is the relationship between servanthood and suffering? Is the servant always called to suffer?

In *Becoming Human*,[3] Russell discusses another scandal — that of suffering. How can he who is Lord also suffer? Additionally, if Jesus is Lord and Savior why do human beings suffer? There is suffering on the part of the divine as the divine has become human. It is through suffering that justice is established.

> God's power and glory are present in our human condition no matter what the dimension of our suffering, because in Christ's suffering God has chosen to stand with us. Yet when we look to see this power and glory in human life, it shines through most clearly in those whose lives are confronting the suffering by saying *no* [*italics mine*] to its dehumanizing power.[4]

Therefore, human beings are empowered to reject the dehumanizing aspects of suffering. Because of the act of caring, we know that human beings are destined not for suffering but for "partnership with God." Russell adds:

> When God's Spirit breaks into our lives . . . we suddenly discover that we are somebody, but not because of anything we have done. . . . We are somebody because we have accepted the presence in our lives of the One who calls us *partner*.
> It is in this and this only that we can glory, that our humanity is *more than* human because God has chosen to become a *nobody* and to share humanity with us.[5]

Christ connects God and humanity and is at the same time representative of the divine reality that is supreme. That reality is God. Additionally, Christ is the representative of the true/new humanity.

The old humanity/old creation in humanity is its fallen state. Human beings were overcome by their own weaknesses and limitations. This old humanity/old creation is the old order that is characterized by personal, political, and social sins, all of which have become translated into sociopolitical hierarchies for which the primary goal is domination of the strong over the weak. Consequently, old humanity/old creation is plagued with suffering, pain and unhappiness of the weak. The strong define humanity in a narrow way that protects their position as human beings, while the weak are considered nonhumans, nonpersons. The weak and helpless are bad, and the strong are good. In the old humanity, the concept of self as human is distorted on the part of both the weak and the strong. Thus, to overcome this fallen reality, Christ, the representative, must be affirmed.

Rosemary Ruether puts the primary critical question in its most simple, yet profound, way.[6] Given the realities of what maleness and femaleness mean in the church and in society, the question brings into focus elements of the very basic conflict in contemporary male-female relationship. Traditional understanding of the "nature of man" consisted of a dualism that kept men as "protectors" and women as the "protected." The perimeters of woman's sphere have been limited in order to maintain consistency with this social dualism. Women have begun to challenge the motives of such an arrangement—that is, they have questioned whether men have been protecting women or, in fact, protecting the "sacredness" of their privileged position. A male Christology, developed in the context of a Christian theology, which itself perpetuates sociotheological dualisms, is met with the same suspicion by feminists. If the male Christ has like investments in the sociotheological status quo, then he cannot be trusted to help women. Thus, Ruether asked, "Can a Male Savior Help Women?"

Later, in her book *To Change the World: Christology and Cultural Criticism*, the question becomes more pointedly theological and specifically soteriological: "Can a Male Savior Save Women?"[7] It appears that salvation in a patriarchal system is related to accepting one's designated place in the "order of Creation." This male Christ figure appears merely to put its stamp of approval upon the patriarchally defined place of women. It is here where Ruether prepares the way for her liberation approach to Christology when she poses the question, "Can Christology be liberated from its encapsulation in the structures of patriarchy and really become an expression of liberation of women?"[8] Ruether provides a positive response to the question. Two concepts are elevated, "service" and "conversion." Service must not be confused with servitude. In her view, "Service implies autonomy and power used in behalf of others."[9] We are called to service. Our conversion is to accept this call by abandoning previous, inaccurate notions of being called to hierarchical and oppressive leadership and power. The new Christology that is to be developed, then,

> does not exalt a new Lord that can be a role model for new roles of power and domination. Nor does it bring together male and female in sexist patterns of complementarity. Rather it is Christology of conversion and social transformation. Alienated power is overthrown. Those who presently have and represent power are called to lay this power down in service. The subjugated are lifted up. They will inherit the earth in the new liberated Kingdom of redemption. The despised of the present society lead the way into the Kingdom. Men leaders, even God, repent of domination; servants, women, the poor are liberated from servitude. This is a Christology of the process of conversion, the process of creating a new humanity of wholeness in mutuality.[10]

The way to this new humanity of wholeness is to be liberated from the various forms of oppression. Ruether states this explicitly in another place:

> Jesus as liberator calls for a renunciation and dissolution of the web of status relationships by which societies have defined privilege and

unprivilege. He speaks especially to outcast women, not as representatives of the "feminine," but because they are at the bottom of this network of oppression. His ability to be liberator does not reside in his maleness, but on the contrary, in the fact that he has renounced this system of domination and seeks to embody in his person the new humanity of service and mutual empowerment.[11]

It seems that Ruether is getting at the real issue at hand, "power." Here, service is connected with empowerment. The question that remains is, in what way(s) is there mutual empowerment? Does this mutuality extend to all of humanity?

Some Folk Are More Servants than Others

Both of these thinkers, Russell and Ruether, have provided reformulations that are helpful in making somewhat palatable a traditional Christian concept that is distasteful, to say the least, because of its history of misuse and abuse. They have articulated christologies of which service, suffering, empowerment and Lordship are integral parts.

As I examined my discomfort with this, I felt that perhaps my problem was with the ease with which Christians speak of such notions as service and servant. Perhaps my discomfort stemmed from the experiential knowledge of the Black community vis-à-vis service and particularly the Black women vis-à-vis domestic service. Black people's and Black women's lives demonstrate to us that some people are more servant than others. In what ways have they been substantially empowered? Has there been social, political, or economic empowerment? Is the empowerment simply an overspiritualization of an oppressed and depressed reality?

Studies in the area of Black women's work — domestic service — demonstrate the point that is being made here. It enables us to see not only that some people are more servant than other, but more specifically, that relationships among women of the dominant culture and minority women merely mirror the domination model of the larger society.

The abolition of slavery left intact the basic relationship between Black women and white women in particular and Black people and white people in general. For some, emancipation meant slavery without chains and for others it meant mere servanthood, and in fact, often servitude.

Post-slavery brought neither change in image nor significant change in the condition of Black people in the United States. The image was still that Blacks were inferior and that they were intended to service white America. Consequently, when Blacks, now free, sought work they were relegated to the service jobs and menial work of slavery days, which they did forcibly during slavery. For Black men this meant plantation/farm work, factory work (eventually), other service-oriented work and then no work.[12] For many Black women this meant sharing some of the work that Black men did as well as making up significant percentages of domestic servants in this country.

Studies of domestic servants show that Black women are more often in this category than any other group of people (perhaps with the exception of other third-world peoples today).[13] Between 1890 and 1920, while white female servants decreased, Black female servants increased, such that by 1920 forty percent of all domestic servants were Black women. Seventy-three percent of all laundresses were Black. Disproportionate numbers of Black women were (permanently) relegated to domestic work.[14] This was because Blacks and servants (especially in the South) were considered synonymous. David Katzman described the domestic service in the South as a caste system. Comparing the South with the North and West, he notes that servants were rarely found in lower middle-class or working-class families.

However, in the former slave states, Black servants were equally common in households headed by white-collar workers.[15] He further notes that the South has been called a "housewife's utopia."[16] This system in the South was a part of a larger racial caste structure in which, reminiscent of slavery, Blacks were servants and whites were masters and never the two should be changed. The domination/subordination relationship within the household mirrored the white/Black relationship in general and especially in the South.

Though legal slavery was abolished, much of the character of slavery remained for decades thereafter. This meant that basic relationships had not changed significantly, as we can see in two areas of Black life. (1) Though whites were not always able to use individual physical violence as measures of direct control and obedience, violence became incorporated as the basic program of the Ku Klux Klan and later in recognized law enforcement agencies under the guise of law or order.[17] As during slavery, tyranny was required to keep order. It was felt that violence was required to keep Blacks in their place. The result of the activities of the Ku Klux Klan and the law and order movements was that a disproportionate number of Blacks and particularly Black men were lynched and imprisoned.[18] (2) Specifically with regard to domestic servants, white women, as in slavery, superintended over household activities extending the close proximity between Black women and white women. White women were still in positions of authority over Black women and they demanded submission to their domination. In this context, generally, white women proved to be as oppressive as white men. Because domestic work was completely privatized, Black women suffered at the whims and wills of white women. As Katzman recognized, "Domestic servants then occupied a unique place in American society. They alone worked within the most private space within the female sphere; they alone entered the world designed to be insulated from the world of work; and they alone were thrust across the imaginary barrier into a family's private world."[19] Blacks were being lynched and imprisoned on the one hand, and privatized on the other. Essentially, they were still substantially controlled.

In the private family world we are able to note the continuation of many of the oppressive practices of slavery. Servants were often engaged for work with little or no guarantee that they would be paid. When they were paid it was often "slave wages"—that is, little pay for a great deal of work. Baker and Cooke in their 1935 study, "The Bronx Slave Market," uncovers the who, what, why, and when of northern servitude at its worst. "In the Bronx, a northern borough of New York City . . . exists a street corner market for domestic servants where Negro women are 'rented' at unbelievably low rates for house work."[20] Unlike the slave auction, buyers were primarily women and they negotiated directly with the workers, but like the slave auction, workers still got the "short end of the stick."

> Rain or shine, cold or hot, you will find them there—Negro women, old and young—sometimes bedraggled, sometimes neatly dressed— but with the invariable paper bundle, waiting expectantly for Bronx housewives to buy their strength and energy for an hour, two hours, or even for a day at the munificent rate of fifteen, twenty, twenty-five, or if luck be with them, thirty cents an hour.[21]

The relationship between white women and their Black women servants is depicted in two literary studies by two Black women, one of whom had personal experience as a domestic servant. Unable to find employment as an actress, Alice Childress, as many educated Black women have, found herself doing domestic work as a means of surviving. Based on her experience and research she wrote a book called *Like One of the Family* in which she employed wit to expose many lingering beliefs of white women about Black women. In spite of the fact that white women brought Black women into their homes to raise their children and clean their homes, they, white women, held that Black women were dirty, diseased, and dishonest. Consequently, Black women found themselves being asked for health cards to verify health status; and they also found monies laid in strange and unexpected places to test their honesty.[22]

Trudier Harris in *From Mammies to Militants* combines "folkloristic, sociological, historical, and psychological analyses with the literary ones." She proceeds to argue that "power relationships inherent in the concept of place, that blacks are always inferior to whites, provide the initial forces in which [to] view the interactions between black women and their adoptive white families."[23] Harris observed that the mammy turned militant when she migrated to the north; she became more assertive and independent.[24] Harris sums up the relationship between mistresses and maids, drawing a distinction between the South and the North by saying:

> The mistress does not expect the maid to be demanding, but the maid expects that of the mistress. The mistress expects the maid to accept

all hand-me-downs and service pans; the maid knows she is expected to accept these things and does so. The mistress thinks the maid will steal; the maid knows that and is therefore very careful to leave bills and coins precisely where she finds them. The mistress expects the maid to be a good mammy simply because, she believes, it's in her blood; the maid knows she is expected to give expert care to the mistress' children and neglects her own in order to be the ideal servant. ... The pattern was handed down from slavery and the majority of mistresses and maids are not inclined to alter it. But there have been a few iconoclasts, in art as in life. Between 1901 and 1977, some literary maids broke the mold shaped by southern attitudes and managed to bring new life to the worn portrayal of the domestic.[25]

Even in the North, however, the sociopolitical gap between Black women and white women differed so radically that the changed attitude on the part of Black women maids did not significantly change their status. White women were still dominant and Black women were still subordinate.

Though legally emancipated, servants were still essentially (treated as) property. The life of servants was almost as controlled as it was during slavery. Domestic service is personal service related so much to the personal property of slavery times that it too was unregulated by law. Still under the conditions of servitude, Black women, as Black people, were considered subordinate property and unequal in pursuit of life, liberty, and happiness. Katzman credits racial stereotype as the justification of the subordination of Black women in the South. According to popular views, Blacks "were childlike, lazy, irresponsible, and larcenous." They were worthless, dirty, dishonest, unreliable and incompetent.[26] In ruling over them, white women were only acting in the best "interest of all concerned."

As in slavery, the humanity of Black women was violated in domestic service. Again Black women were not human beings, but commodities for the convenience of white women (and men). White women, it was believed in the nineteenth century, were as different from Black women as night and day. Because of the strenuousness of housework and the delicateness of white women's physical make-up, white women needed protection from housework.

During the late nineteenth century, medical authorities cautioned women against demanding and enduring physical labor. According to medical guidebooks, adolescent middle-class girls should be excused from such hard physical labor as strenuous domestic chores. More mature women were advised against physical activity during menstruation, and it was widely thought that regular work schedules were injurious to a woman's health.[27]

Obviously the formulators of this belief did not consider Black women to be women. "That this advice was not applied to domestic servants simply underscored the differences between mistresses and servants."[28] Women had merely given further justification for servanthood as practiced in America. Because Black women were really not women, but property (or better still, animals), they could be used to further protect white women from the drudgeries of daily existence. Sutherland explains white women's *need* for servants:

> The dominant reason for employing servants during most of the nineteenth century was the exhausting, back breaking, unceasing nature of household labor. Housekeeping exacted dozens of daily, monotonous chores. Few housekeepers fluttered merely through their duties of dusting, mopping, scrubbing, and cooking. Even women who enjoyed housework found their multiple responsibilities a rather tough business, and some tasks, such as emptying chamberpots, changing infants, and cleaning up after pets and people with weak bladders and upset stomachs, were downright unpleasant. Servants were needed to spare American women the dirt, monotony, and drudgery of their own homes.[29]

The stereotype that Blacks are more suited for service work reflects the fact that even after slavery and to some extent even today, the term "chattels personal" can still be used to describe the way Blacks are treated, especially in the area of domestic service.

We could speak of many more stories of sexual exploitation where Black women have been violated; or political exploitation where their jobs were held hostage to force them to submit to "status quo politics"; or economic exploitation where they were systematically cheated. But suffice it to say that servanthood for Black women has led not only to the suffering of Black women, but also of the Black family.

These questions that Black women pose, then, coming out of women's experience, represent merely a microcosm of the larger society. What is the meaning of such conciliatory notions as "we are all called to be servants?" What is the significance of a distinction between service and servitude, when for Black women they have been one and the same? Service has not led to empowerment and liberation, but in fact has insured that they not happen. This leads to a theological dilemma.

Servanthood: A Theological Dilemma

The dilemma for me is a theological one that can be expressed in two questions. The first question emerges out of white women's claim that *women's experiences* is the source for feminist theology. In light of the data presented vis-à-vis the servant relationship between two groups of women in this country, my question is, which women's experience is the source of theology? Further, one could ask, how do these experiences impact the direction taken in one's theological perspective? Is it the experience of the daughters of slaveholders or the experience of the daughters of slaves? These two experiences are irreconcilable as they stand. Certainly, servanthood is not the only dimension of women's experiences. But still, before we can realistically talk about reconciling the women of both groups, we must find that which is required for eradicating the pain and suffering inflicted by the one group upon the other. We must ask, how is the gulf bridged between two groups of people who, though they have lived in close proximity, have radically different lives?

Womanist theology acknowledges these experiences. They cannot be covered up or swept under the rug, so to speak; they must be confronted with intentionality. To speak of sisterhood prematurely is to camouflage the reality. We must begin to eliminate the obstacles of sisterhood—the hate, the distrust, the suspicion, the inferiority/superiority complex. The same can be said about humanity in general. Racism, classism, and other forms of oppression are still deeply embedded in the church and society. Until the relational issues are adequately addressed, it is premature (or at least not very meaningful) to speak of such things as reconciliation and community. In other words, we must seek salvation, for we've been living in a world of sin. That is, we've been perpetuating the sins of racism, sexism, classism and so forth.

Second, I am led to ask, how does one justify teaching a people that they are called to a life of service when they have been imprisoned by the most exploitative forms of service? Service and oppression of Blacks went hand in hand. Therefore, to speak of service as empowerment, without concrete means or plans for economic, social, and political revolution that in fact leads to empowerment, is simply another form of "overspiritualization." It does not eliminate real pain and suffering, it merely spiritualizes the reality itself. It's one thing to say that people spiritualize in order to "make it through the days, weeks, and months" of agony. But it is another to give the people a "pie in the sky" theology, so that they would concern themselves with the next world in order to undergird the status quo. The one can be seen as liberating while the other is oppressive.

The one begs respect; the other begs the question: how do you propose that we are called to service to Jesus, the one who has been sent by God to redeem us, when both God and Jesus have been principle weapons in the oppressors' arsenal to keep Blacks and Black women in their appropriate place? Both God and Jesus were portrayed as white and male and interested primarily in preserving the white patriarchal and racist status quo. In light of that then, do we simply answer Bill Jones' question—yes, God is a white racist[30]—not only that, but God is also a male chauvinistic pig—an irredeemable sexist? Is God actually responsible for the systemic pain and suffering of Blacks and women? Does God condone the servanthood relationships between Blacks and women? If we are unwilling or unable to accept the proposition implied in an affirmative response to these questions, then how are the redeemers liberated from the oppressive structures of the oppressor? How do we liberate God? Bill Jones answers this inquiry by proposing that reality must be viewed from a humanocentric perspective. In other words, the conditions that existed have resulted from human beings' will for evil and not from God's will. Effectively, Jones has liberated the redeemers from the structure of oppression by locating them strictly in the human world. When applied to the notion of servanthood, one can squarely locate the problems with oppressive human beings. The sin of servanthood is the sin of humanity that results from the sociopolitical interests of proponents of the status quo and their attempts to undergird their intended goal through psychological conditioning that comes partially with the institutionalization of oppressive language, even theological language.

Theological Language and Liberation

The language that we use to talk about God more often than not says more about the speaker than about God. Understanding the context of the speakers, then, is critical for interpreting the language about God. In his discussions of theological language, William Hordern[31] argues for the necessity of identifying correctly the particular game being played as a prerequisite for the language to be used for asking questions as well as providing answers. Specifically, he addressed the inappropriateness of using theological language to answer questions of the sciences. A scientist, who is a Christian, may answer questions consistent with Christian belief, but the rules and regulations that govern scientific language are not appropriate for theological language.

It would seen to me, however, that further explorations into theological language need to be done. What is appropriate or adequate theological language? Language, including theological language, arises out of the context of the community, or the experiences of the people. The recent debate about inclusive versus exclusive language demonstrates not only how language emerges out of community situations, but also how powerful language really is. Those who are in control of the dominant culture are in control of the language and consequently, men have produced language that is advantageous to men and disadvantageous to women. Language functions the same in oppressive idealogy and theology. For example, in racist idealogy and theology, in color symbolism, Black is invariably evil and white is good.

Much of Hordern's argument referred to above is designed to respond to the charges of analytical philosophers that theological language is nonsense. When we explore the relationship between theological language and, for example, political language vis-à-vis uses of servanthood language, we are able to see the political implications of theological language. Oppressors, for example, always have the advantage of determining whom the real "servants" are. Even with institutional hierarchies that claim to be servants (be they church or government related), it is often difficult to determine which is more important, being served or serving.

What happens when political and social language and interests are used to give content to theological language? Certainly, during most of American history, there has been an infusion of theological teachings with unjust political and social agenda of oppressors. For example, Black people were taught that service to oppressors was mandated by God. Indoctrination came through the various instruments given Blacks, such as the catechism where it was clearly taught that God and the white man were the same.[32] Given the continued use of the notion of servanthood, especially throughout the South, after slavery and even until recent times, the attitudes have survived "emancipation." The idea referred to above by Katzman, that being servant and Black in the South were synonymous, still exists. Further, the reality is that though it is not always explicitly said, this attitude goes beyond the South.

A Black woman Ph.D. candidate in religious studies recently told of her experience in a northern seminary of constantly being presumed to be the maid by both professors and students. Serving is reserved for victims, while being served is the special privilege of victimizers, or at least representatives of the status quo. These privileged servants are often served by servants who are in fact often treated as slaves. The process of euphemizing is often used to camouflage the real meaning of the language.

Clarice Martin, in her article "Womanist Interpretations of the New Testament," provides insights into the dangers of euphemizing and cautions us against it. To the tendency of some to interpret the Greek *doulos* as *servant,* Martin argues that the correct interpretation is *slave,* and to interpret it otherwise would be to camouflage the real injustice in relationships of biblical times and of today. She challenges,

> A womanist critical biblical hermeneutics, then, must not only critique the tendencies of the biblical writers and traditioning processes themselves, but must also analyze contemporary scholarly and popular interpretations and appropriations of those traditions, and the underlying theoretical models. A womanist biblical hermeneutic must clarify whether the "*doulos*" text, potential "texts of terror" for black people, can in any way portend new possibilities for our understanding of what actually constitutes the radicality of the Good News of the Gospel.[33]

A language needs to be adopted or emphasized that challenges the servant mentality of oppressed peoples and the oppressive mentality of oppressors.

From Double Consciousness to Deliverance

African-American thinker W. E. B. DuBois is helpful, perhaps not in resolving the dilemma identified in this essay, but certainly in helping us to see more clearly the African-American reality. In articulating the spiritual struggle of Black people, DuBois speaks of a double consciousness.

> After the Egyptian and Indian, the Greek and Roman, the Teuton and Mongolian, the Negro is a sort of seventh son, born with a veil, and gifted with second-sight in this American world—a world which yields him no true self-consciousness, but only lets him see himself through the revelation of the other world. It is a peculiar sensation, this double-consciousness, this sense of always looking at one's self through the eyes of others, of measuring one's soul by the tape of the world that looks on in amused contempt and pity. One ever feels his twoness—an American, a Negro; two souls, two thoughts, two unreconciled strivings; two warring ideals in one dark body, whose dogged strength alone keeps it from being torn asunder.[34]

When I consider the "twoness" or "double" nature of the Black consciousness (and in fact the triple nature of Black women's consciousness), I am able to reconsider my thesis that this servanthood theme in Christianity needs to be eliminated from Christian theology for it has outlived its usefulness.

What we find instead is the capacity of Blacks to live in two or more worlds at the same time. They understood what their relationship with the other world—the white world—was to be. Even when they did not accept it, they understood it nonetheless. Survival made this a necessity.

For Black people the double-consciousness meant that Blacks, to some degree, functioned in the white world on terms defined by that world. In the white world, Blacks were referred to as "uncle," "joe," "tom," "aunty," and "mammy." It is also the case that Black people functioned in their own world based on their own self-understanding. Black people in their churches knew themselves to be "deacon," "trusty," "mrs.," "sister," and "brother." This point was perhaps not adequately expressed by DuBois, for Blacks indeed did not always see themselves through the eyes of white people.

With this in mind it is possible to understand the birth of the Black church. It was a public declaration that our self-understanding took precedence over the definition of the other world or the external world. In this context we can be truly servants of the living Christ. This brings me back to my original problem regarding Black women and servanthood. What sense does it make to rejoice in the service of a man (Jesus), who has been used not to save but to exploit?

The triple consciousness of Black women makes it possible to see how they were able to liberate redemption as they overtly and covertly challenged the assumption of the racist and sexist status quo. That triple consciousness gave them the possibility of experiencing a liberating Jesus even as they were given a racist and sexist one. It enabled me to better understand how Black women relegated to domestic service could go to church on Tuesday, Wednesday nights and Sunday morning and testify of being a better servant of the Lord and Savior Jesus. What they were saying was perhaps what the early church was saying to the Roman Empire when they professed Jesus Christ as Lord. Or what Karl Barth and the confessing church of Germany were saying when they gave their allegiances to Jesus rather than to Hitler, or what the Southern African writers of *The Kairos Document* meant as they proclaimed a living and just God.

Perhaps what these Black women were saying is that what "I am forced to do on Monday through Saturday is redemptive only in the sense that it facilitates survival." In this sense, then, Martin Luther King, Jr., was right, suffering is redemptive.[35] True redemption takes place when one experiences the redeemer even as it is in the context of oppression. Their speaking of such titles as Lord and Master with regard to Jesus and God meant that the lords and masters of the white world were illegitimate.

The church and/or religious experience for African Americans allowed them the opportunity to express their spirituality freely—at least to a certain degree. For African-American women the third level of consciousness is accented as we consider the limitations placed upon women even within the church/religious sphere. This third consciousness level caused some women to challenge the church internally and in other instances it resulted in women leaving the church still in the pursuit of liberating themselves and Jesus.

When Jesus was liberated from the oppressive theology of the white church and the white consciousness, Black women were able to see themselves as "servants" of the Christ and not of the oppressive world. It was Jesus who befriended Sojourner Truth when no one else could or would; it was Jesus that made Jarena Lee preach anyhow. In more recent times, it was Jesus that provided guidance for Mary McLeod Bethune and Jesus that motivated activist Fannie Lou Hamer. Black women/African-American women were constantly liberating Jesus as Jesus was liberating them.

Where then is the dilemma? If I listen to Black women's communities I would say that the dilemma is at the point of having to live in two and sometimes three different worlds, their world and the world of oppressors (the white world and the male world). Womanist theology is committed to bringing wholism to Black women. Being a servant of the redeemer means joining in the struggle of the redeemer against oppression, wherever it is found. If the source is white women, that is, being consumed in the universal definition of women's experiences, then Black women must continue to challenge the oppressive notions. This may mean challenging traditional notions of servanthood and embracing a more liberating understanding of the self.

An Invitation to Christian Discipleship

DuBois's notion of double consciousness is helpful in understanding how oppressed peoples are able to live in a world designed to keep them in an appointed place, and yet move beyond that world. Martin Luther King, Jr.'s notion of "suffering servant" explains how Black people and Black women were able to make sense out of, and possibly bring hope out of, apparently hopeless life situations.[36] Whereas both of these interpretations are helpful as a part of the survival strategies of Black people, they are unable to provide adequate substance for liberation. For liberation to happen the psychological, political, and social conditions must be created to nurture the processes. Servant language does not do this. What is the best way to create these conditions?

Susan Nelson Dunfee has suggested that we must move beyond servanthood, for traditional notions of service (and altruism) do not provide an adequate way of interpreting the Christian experience of liberation. The category that is most helpful for her is that of "friendship." Jesus, she argues, calls us to be friends, for "the freedom and authority grounded in the friendship of Jesus would empower women to our liberation."[37]

Though the category of "friendship" is helpful in undercutting the "domination/submission" model inherent in the servanthood model, I would suggest that the model of discipleship implies more of an empowerment model, particularly for a group of people, women, who have not been considered to be disciples. As a part of most church programs/services, there is usually an opportunity to "join church," as some would say, or to become Christian. It is often referred to as the "call to Christian discipleship." The truth of the matter, however, is that when women "join the church," they are not allowed to become full members, with all of the rights and privileges invested therein; rather, they are only permitted to become servants. Contrary to popular beliefs, women are not full members because they are not given opportunities for full participation at all levels of the church, particularly at the decision-making levels. Women must be invited into the power houses of the church and society to participate on all levels.

Given the overwhelming racial and gender politics that relegate Blacks, other third-world peoples and women to the level of mere servant, there stands a great need for a language of empowerment. Servanthood language has, in effect, been one of subordination. Perhaps, we need to explore the language of discipleship as a more meaningful way of speaking about the life-work of Christians. We are all called to be disciples. True, the "disciples' club" has been given to us as an "old boys' club." I'm not suggesting that the goal of women and minority men ought simply be to join the "old boys' club." What I am suggesting instead is that the club may need to be shattered, and the real discipling network must be restored.

Womanist theology seeks to foster a more inclusive discipleship. The kind of wholism sought in womanist theology requires that justice be an integral part of our quest for unity and community. I would suggest that the discussion above indicates that, minimally, three areas of concern must be addressed in theological reformulations.

First, we must resist the tendency of using language to camouflage oppressive reality, rather than eliminating the oppressive reality itself. My distaste for the use of such terms as "service" and "servant" is paralleled by similar suspicion in using such terms as "reconciliation," "covenant relationship," "unity" or "community." How can we realistically talk about these things when we are not yet seriously grappling with racism, sexism, classism, and other oppressive structures that plague our reality? It is tantamount to the concern for peace, without equal love for justice and liberation. The fact of the matter is that these terms — service, reconciliation, community, etc. — are apparently nonthreatening. Who can be against them? But just as service and servanthood have historically slipped into servitude, these concepts run the similar danger, if the conciliatory language is not given substance with actions of justice. All too often, notions of reconciliation, convenantal relationship, unity, and community mirror those in the system of domestic service relationships. The needs of one group (partner) are universalized in such a fashion that those on the topside of history are the beneficiaries of the system; and those on the underside of history are mere victims of the relationship. Topsided people often presume knowledge of the answers; consequently, they invalidate even the questions of those who live on the underside of history. Transformations of traditional oppressive relationships enable us to reject the presumptions of dominant-culture people.

For example, real concern for liberation may mean relinquishing our preoccupation with reconciliation and peace. Instead, our energies must be refocussed upon liberation and justice — after all, true liberation and justice include reconciliation and peace anyway. In the same way, this means that being a true "servant" may mean relinquishing the dubious honor of servanthood.

Second, we must resist the tendency of relegating some to the lower rung of society. Certainly, the data I have articulated above strongly indicates that some people are more servant than others. Any Christian relationship must eliminate the injustices of such relationships. In fact the kind of relationships that have existed between women (and men) of the dominant culture and third-world women (and men) must be destroyed. A few years ago, the argument of some feminists on the question of sin was that women needed to reexamine the question of sin as it has been interpreted traditionally within the context of patriarchal Christian community. When we examine women's experiences, we may discover, they argue, that perhaps pride — one of those old patriarchal sins — is not the sin of women, but instead, too much pride is sin. In the same vein, I would argue that perhaps, for women of color, the sin is not the lack of humility, but the sin is too much humility. Further, for women of color, the sin is not the lack of service, but too much service. The liberation of servants means that women will no longer shoulder the responsibility of service. Oppressed people, women of color, men of color will no longer be relegated to the place of servanthood and servitude. But, there will be justice in living the Christian life. Justice means that some will give up, and some will gain; but all will become disciples; that is, simultaneously, oppressors must give up or lose oppressive power, as oppressed people are empowered for discipleship.

Third, we must resist the tendency of devaluing the lives of people by virtue of who they are. The data strongly demonstrates that some people are victimized even to the extent of having their very humanity denied. How can justice be a reality when servants are considered less than human? The affirmation of humanity must move far beyond mere words to deeds of justice. This justice must be more than mere equality. Certainly, minimally it must include equality. Fannie Lou Hamer challenged us at this point when she challenged us to move beyond equality. The affirmation of humanity causes us to move beyond the mere acceptance and acknowledgment of societal and church structures—political, social, and theological. These oppressive structures that render and keep "some people more ser-vant than others" must be eliminated. The church does not need servants, as oppressively conceived of and experienced by many; the church needs followers of Christ—disciples.

Women have been invited to become disciples. In the historical records, women were left out of the inner circle of the disciples. Therefore, women must be empowered to become disciples. The language of discipleship for women provides the possibility of breaking down traditional stereotypical, exclusivistic understandings of discipleship. Overcoming the sin of servant-hood can prepare us for the deliverance that comes through discipleship.

NOTES

1. Jacquelyn Grant, *White Women's Christ and Black Women's Jesus* (Atlanta: Scholars Press, 1989).

2. Letty M. Russell, *The Future of Partnership* (Philadelphia: Westminster Press, 1979), 67.

3. Russell, *Becoming Human* (Philadelphia: Westminster Press, 1982).

4. Ibid., 57.

5. Ibid., 58-59.

6. Rosemary Ruether, "Christology and Feminism: Can a Male Savior Help Women," *An Occasional Paper* of The Board of Higher Education and Ministry of the United Methodist Church, I (25 December 1976).

7. Ruether, *To Change the World: Christology and Cultural Criticism* (New York: Crossroad, 1981).

8. Ibid., 47.

9. Ruether, "Christology and Feminism," 5.

10. Ibid.

11. Ruether, *To Change the World*, 56.

12. See statistics as summarized in the U.S. Department of Commerce, Bureau of the Census, "The Social and Economic Status of the Black Population in the U.S.: American Historical View, 1790–1978" (Current Population Reports Special Studies Series #80). To see the consistent high unemployment rates of Blacks

relative to whites (and Black men relative to white men), see reports from the U.S. Department of Labor, Bureau of Labor Statistics.

13. Some major studies on domestic servants are: David Katzman, *Seven Days a Week: Women and Domestic Service in Industrializing America* (New York: Oxford University Press, 1978); Sutherland, *Americans and Their Servants* (Baton Rouge: Louisiana State University Press, 1981); Faye E. Dudden, *Serving Women: Household Service in Nineteenth-Century America* (Middletown, CT: Wesleyan University Press, 1983). For particular Black emphasis see: Elizabeth Ross Hayner, *Negroes in Domestic Service in the United States* (Washington, DC: The Association for the Study of Negro Life and History, Inc., 1923; reprint, *The Journal of Negro History* 8, no. 4, [October 1923]). W. E. B. DuBois included in the *Philadelphia Negro* a study of domestic servants conducted by Isabel Eaten, "Special Report of Negro Domestic Service in the Seventh Ward" (Millwood, NY: Kraus-Thomas Organization Ltd., 1973). Literary studies include Alice Childress, *Like One of the Family . . . Conversations from a Domestic Life* (Brooklyn, NY: Independence Publishers, 1956) and Trudier Harris, *From Mammy to Militant Domestics in Black American Literature* (Philadelphia: Temple University Press, 1982).

14. White females (especially immigrants) used domestic service as a stepping stone to other more decent women's occupations — office clerks, stenographers, typists, bookkeepers, cashiers, accountants, store clerks and saleswomen, and telephone operators. As white women in this field declined significantly, Black women increased to 40 percent. In 1920 they were 73 percent of all laundresses. In 1910 and 1920 Black women were 0.5 percent and 1.3 percent in nonagricultural occupations. By 1920 only 7 percent native born and 20 percent immigrant women were servants. Katzman, *Seven Days a Week*, 72-73.

15. Katzman, 185.

16. Ibid.

17. For a history of the Ku Klux Klan see Marion Monteval, pseud., *The Klan Inside Out* (Westport, CT: Negro Universities Press, 1970); William J. Simmons, *The Klan Unmasked* (Atlanta, GA: William E. Thompson Publishing Co., 1923); and Charles Tyler, *The K.K.K.* (New York: Abbey Press, 1902).

18. Ida B. Wells, *Crusade for Justice: The Autobiography of Ida B. Wells,* ed. Alfreda Duster (Chicago: University of Chicago Press, 1970), especially pp. xxi and xxii and Chapter 6. In 1895 Wells published *A Red Record: Tabulated Statistics in the United States 1892–1893–1894* (Chicago: Donohue and Henneberry).

19. Katzman, 148.

20. Ella Baker and Marvel Cooke, "The Bronx Slave Market," *The Crisis* 42 (November 1935), 330.

21. Ibid.

22. Alice Childress, *Like One of the Family . . . Conversations from a Domestic Life* (Brooklyn, NY: Independence Publishers, 1956).

23. Harris, xii.

24. Though Harris gives precise examples of her argument in several literary works, there is evidence to suggest that maids in the North were generally or significantly no more "powerful" or independent than maids in the South. See the study by Baker and Cooke as an example.

25. Harris, 20-21.

26. Katzman, 186 and 188. The irony of these beliefs is that these were the people that whites had to care for their children and their homes.

27. Ibid., 149.

28. Ibid.

29. Sutherland, 10-11.

30. William Jones, *Is God a White Racist?* (New York: Anchor/Doubleday, 1973).

31. William Hordern, *Speaking of God, The Nature and Purpose of Theological Language* (New York: Macmillan Company, 1964).

32. Albert Raboteau, *Slave Religion* (New York: Oxford University Press, 1978), 162-163.

33. Clarice Martin, "Womanist Interpretations of the New Testament: The Quest for Holistic and Inclusive Translation and Interpretation," *Journal of Feminist Studies in Religion* 6, no. 2 (Fall 1990): 41-61.

34. William E. B. DuBois, *The Souls of Black Folks* (New York: A Signet Classic, New American Library, 1969), 49.

35. Martin Luther King, Jr., "Suffering and Faith" in *A Testament of Hope*, ed. James Washington (New York: Harper & Row, 1986), 41.

36. Ibid.

37. Susan Nelson Dunfee, *Beyond Servanthood: Christianity and the Liberation of Women* (New York: University Press of America, 1989), 159.

13

"The Wounds of Jesus"

Justification of Goodness
in the Face of Manifold Evil

Katie Geneva Cannon

Twenty years ago, a minister friend of mine, Dr. G. Murray Branch, posed the question that captures the essence of the problem of evil as it has resounded down through the ages from the African-American pulpit, "Can God create a rock that God can't pick up?" Without doubt the African-American sermon is the earliest form of spoken religious art wherein the Black church community wrestles with how evil can occur in a world created by a benevolent God.[1]

Put another way, this inquiry, "Can God create a rock that God can't pick up?" is the fundamental query that deals with the traditional theological problem concerning transgressions that proceed directly from human sin — structures of domination, subordination, and constraints that reinforce and reproduce hierarchies based on race, sex, class, and sexual orientation. These sermons sometimes address those ills suffered because of physical and natural calamities and the immense human suffering that follows in their wake — disease, tempest, fire, famine, flood, tidal wave, earthquake, drought. African-American preachers in my church community have been particularly interested in framing and arguing the question of moral evil due to our suffering and the identification and solidarity that creates two-thirds of the human family who are hungry, have no homes, have no schools or medicine for their children, no pure water to drink, and no work.

African-American sermonic texts have been the most vital factors in explaining moral evils such as chattel slavery, economic impoverishment, wars and the atrocities they involve.[2] The sacred rhetoric produced by African-American preachers validates and makes coherent the yearnings of Black Christians to explain moral evil inflicted by human agency.[3] Yet, many of these texts have been passed over, basically unnoticed. The substantial omission of African-American sacred rhetoric from theological discourse on the nature, explanation and remedy of evil flows quite naturally from scholars using analytical frameworks that take the European-American religious experience as the norm.

In broad outline, the dominant tradition poses the problem of evil like this: If God is omnipotent, omniscient, and omnipresent, then God would prevent evil if God wanted to. And if God is a perfectly good God, then of course God would want to prevent evil if God could. Thus, if God is all-powerful, all-knowing and ever-present and is also perfectly good, then God *could* prevent evil if God *wanted to*, and God would *want to* prevent evil if God *could*.

My primary goal in this essay is threefold: (1) to examine theodicy as it is presented in the ecclesiastical texts embedded as distinctive rhetorical units in Zora Neale Hurston's canon; (2) to critique Hurston's sermon, "The Wounds of Jesus,"[4] as a sketch of the problem of evil in AfroChristian sacred rhetoric; and (3) to construct, even in the barest outline, my own composite womanist matrix as to the corpus of sermons in the African-American women's literary tradition.

Numerous African-American novelists have included sermons in their work.[5] I do not want to suggest that the AfroChristian teachings espoused in this essay constitute the whole of the preaching tradition in African-American literature. "The Wounds of Jesus" in *Jonah's Gourd Vine* by Hurston deserves special attention, however, because it reproduces certain AfroChristian ethical conventions and cultural patterns concerning theodicy. By placing this sermon in a context where its worth and value can be reassessed and redefined, I am naming some of the preferred meanings, values, and interpretations of evil—those favored and transmitted through AfroChristian religious rhetoric. Thus, it is the many issues connected with a womanist interpretation of the African-American church community's justification of divine goodness in the face of manifold human experience of evil that this essay addresses.

Hurston's Ecclesiastical Texts

I first became interested in examining the problem of evil as it is embedded in the ecclesiastical rhetoric in African-American women's novels while completing research for my dissertation on "Resources for a Constructive Ethic for Black Women with Special Attention to the Life and Work of Zora Neale Hurston."[6] The personal joy of studying Hurston's canon is the sheer fact of being able to read about the familiar world in which the African-American church community that I know most intimately is made visible. Hurston included explicit theological materials in her work, ranging from full-length sermons, prayers, and proverbs to the passing acknowledgment of religious persons, places, and things. In her work, my Afro-Christian culture is mirrored and writ large.

Even though Hurston was not, at least in the traditional sense, a religious novelist, contestable ethical issues and religious imagery pervade her work. Hurston's writing preserves, like forms embedded in prehistoric ore, traces of her Baptist upbringing. Her characterization of the Reverend John Buddy Pearson and his sermon, "The Wounds of Jesus" in *Jonah's Gourd Vine*, draws heavily upon her own experiences. As the daughter of a southern Black Baptist preacher and therefore a direct heir to the worshiping Christian community, Hurston expressed the creative spiritual force around which the Black church is organized and from which the Black community draws its prophetic nourishment.

For Hurston, preaching in the Black idiom is an essential creative aspect of African-American culture. Black preaching is not theoretical, factual reporting of AfroChristian theological doctrines and dogmas that vindicate God in the face of evil.[7] Instead, these sermonic texts are pastorally engaged writings that reflect the teachings of the Black church community concerning God's redeeming love.

As an outstanding novelist, cultural anthropologist, folklorist and critic, Hurston's extreme closeness to the sensibilities of her unlettered characters, along with her meticulous collection of folklore, legends, superstitions, music, and dance of the common people, enable her work to serve as a rich repository of resources helpful in delineating the moral counsel cultivated by African Americans. Working both as a collector and a systematizer, Hurston collated and classified AfroChristian expressions and various theological themes that help us understand the religious vernacular that dominated African-American Christian culture during the first half of the twentieth century.[8]

For instance, all four of Hurston's novels are packed full of exemplifications of independent actions of the Black community expressing our loves and frustrations in the context of our faith or lack thereof. *Jonah's Gourd Vine* (1934) is a literary allusion (Jonah 4:6–10) to various ways that the protagonist has great and sudden growth and after an act of malice, withers and experiences a tragic end.[9] *Their Eyes Were Watching God* (1937), her second novel, is a drama based on the values of the community and the tension that arises when there is a conflict between what the community advises Black women to do and what, in fact, is done, especially when the mirror in the Black woman's soul (her eyes) is focused on God. According to Hurston's biographer, Robert Hemenway, the novel, *Moses, Man of the Mountain* (1939), is nothing less than Hurston's attempt to kidnap Moses from the Jewish-Christian tradition, claiming that Moses' true birthright is African and that his true constituency is African American. *Seraph on the Suwanee* (1948), Hurston's last novel, has a title that suggests winged celestial beings, possibly angels or flying serpents of uncertain identity. The plot is filled with ironies and ambiguities of self-improvement and self-extension, not with a world of earthly victims whose survival and transformation depend upon a change of heart by their antagonists.

Three of Hurston's short stories, "The Fire and Cloud," "The Seventh Veil" and "The Woman in Gaul" include biblical imagery allowing Hurston's stories to produce a particular representation of AfroChristian theological understanding of God's gift of freedom to act rightly or wrongly. These fictional narratives do not obscure or deny the existence of the ugly dimensions of human nature, circumstances and conduct, but rather through the full, sharp, and inescapable awareness of them, they show the meaningfulness of Black existence. By confronting and contending with the internal absurdities and ever-impending frustrations in the reality of African Americans, Hurston sets before us the problem of evil and the possibilities of endurance.

Between 1926 and 1944 Hurston wrote, alone or in collaboration, eight plays.[10] *The First One* (1927), a one-act mythic drama of the legend of Ham, won the 1927 *Opportunity Magazine* award. In *Mule Bone* (1930), a folk-comedy in three acts,[11] Hurston dramatized the religiosity that existed outside the traditional ecclesial boundaries of mainline Protestantism so as to disclose the interior faction of a town divided between Black Baptists and Black Methodists. *The Fiery Chariot*, a one-act comedy, focuses on a slave's nightly prayer for deliverance from bondage; but the God of Western Christianity is indicted as an ineffective liberator. The characters in these plays draw on the wisdom of their personal strength and determination to protect themselves from the brutality of dehumanizing situations. These texts function as indices and theoethical messages for African Americans, in terms of using the symbols of the curse of Ham's son, Canaan, a mule bone, a fiery chariot, and the conflicts between light-skinned and dark-skinned people to provide some means of balance, an equilibrium that makes suffering bearable. By ironic juxtaposition and emblematic situations, the protagonists counter existing myths so as to present African Americans as complex human beings who have survived and prevailed in racist/sexist/capitalist constellations.

In all of these writings, Hurston presented sacred rhetoric that represents the diverse ways that African-American people of the working poor social strata bring our folkways to the experience of the Christian gospel. Hurston described the various ways that Black Christians, particularly of my social location, use biblical symbols and images to neutralize the brutality of oppressive and exploitative systems in our struggle to maintain our humanity, our integrity and our sanity. Hurston portrayed Black protagonists lifting up aspects of the biblical legend in order to validate the deep religious bent manifested as a major sustaining power in the church community. Such AfroChristian religious symbolism is integral to the unique character of Hurston's texts.

In essence, Hurston's portrayal of the Black preacher is one of the most colorful and dynamic figures illuminated in American literature. She recognized, with W. E. B. DuBois (the eminent sociologist who wrote about the survival of Black religious culture at the turn of this century), that the Black preacher was "the most unique personality developed on American soil."[12]

"The Wounds of Jesus"

Hurston's most famous religious narrative is the sermon I have singled out earlier, "The Wounds of Jesus," wherein Hurston recognized the sermon as a critical cultural phenomenon of African-American culture. Hurston's sermon on the crucifixion of Jesus is a pivotal text in African-American letters. With notable skills and sensibilities, she captures in writing the distinctive style of Black oratory so as to give evidence of previously spoken-only understanding of certain religious truths. Hurston's sermonic eloquence can be judged as equal, if not superior, to the very best masters of the oratory art in any age.

Hurston's sermon was disclaimed by the *New York Times* as "too good, too brilliantly splashed with poetic imagery to be the product of any Negro preacher." On May 8, 1934, Zora Hurston wrote to James Weldon Johnson expressing her disappointment with the white critic's ignorance of the place and power of the sermon in AfroChristian culture. And, this is what Hurston said:

> He means well, I guess, but I never saw such a lack of information about us. It just seems that he is unwilling to believe that a Negro preacher could have so much poetry in him. When you and I (who seem to be the only ones even among Negroes who recognize the barbaric poetry in their sermons) know that there are hundreds of preachers who are equalling that sermon weekly. He does not know that merely being a good man is not enough to hold a Negro preacher in an important charge. He must also be an artist. He must be both a poet and an actor of a very high order, and then he must have the voice and figure. He does not realize or is unwilling to admit that the light that shone from *God's Trombone* [sic] was handed to you, as was the sermon to me in *Jonah's Gourd Vine*.[13]

Hurston was very upset with the review from the *New York Times* because she knew that her sermon, "The Wounds of Jesus," was an exemplary text.

Like the genre of Black preaching it reflects, "The Wounds of Jesus" must be understood within a particular AfroChristian cultural context of a particular time. As a sermon set in the first quarter of this century, it is wedded to the prophetic traditions of Amos, Hosea, Isaiah, and Micah, and is divorced from the brand of homiletics that shaped preaching as linear, bland, and formally speculative as in the European-American tradition.[14] "The Wounds of Jesus" is a recital of God's dealings with people in times past, as well as a proclamation of the relevance of God's message in relation to the particular pain and anguish of contemporary church folks. The sermon is saturated with Bible verses. Thus, a knowledge of scripture comprises the foremost requisite for the Black preacher's proposition that God could create a universe containing evil.

In other words, this sacred rhetoric, originating in the book of Zechariah, chapter 13, verse 6, and Isaiah, chapter 53, verse 5, serves both as reflections of the liberative reality about which AfroChristians speak and as clues and allusions to the oppressive reality under which we live. The problems and issues explored in this sermon show us how African-American people understood every believer in Christ as a friend of Jesus and how every sin committed in the house of friends is a wound to Christ. What is indisputable in this sermonic text is the existence of a strong religious imagination that formed and substantiated belief in the goodness of God, who vouchsafes a liberating redeemer whose potency eases the burden of Black people's afflictions.

The preacher of Hurston's sermon, the Reverend John Buddy Pearson, is well acquainted with biblical texts that explain why a perfectly good God permits human sin to occur. He says that when God said, "Let us make human beings in our image, after our likeness," the elders who were members of the heavenly court adamantly cried out, "No. No. No.," arguing that if God decides to make human beings, they will sin. Rev. Pearson then asserts that it was at this point in the creation of the world that God promised to send a redeemer. For Pearson, the incarnation of Jesus Christ was God's forethought, God's remedy for human sinfulness, a part of God's original intention. To make this theological point another way is to say that evil is not sidestepped or explained away as the absence of good but instead it is exposed as an essential element in the completion of human history, a presupposition for the fulfillment of the divine purpose in creation.

Pearson is not bothered by the chronological distance between the biblical era and the present. Operating on a sense of sacred time, he extends time backwards so that the congregation can experience an immediate intimacy with biblical characters as faith relatives. The trials and triumphs of Zechariah's wounds in the house of his friends, Isaiah's measure of the sea in the hollow of his hand, Mark's worms that never die, Ezekiel's fire that never quenches, Matthew's secrets kept from the foundation of the world, John's bread of life, and the psalmist's mountains that skip like lambs are all interwoven throughout this sermon as the preacher interprets the crucifixion of Jesus against a wider narrative of atonement and redemption. In other words, Hurston aligns Reverend Pearson with earlier Black preachers whose sermons rehearse the gospel stories in the language and culture of the people. Pearson's sermon is full of analogies and parables that compare and juxtapose contemporary problems of evil with and alongside ancient dilemmas in the biblical text.

Second, this sermon utilizes the medium of metaphorical adornment in order to make the sacred discursive narrative visible to the listeners. As a storyteller and a mythmaker, the Black preacher combines a disciplined imagination with realistic reflection, converting the sermon into a genuine art form. This sermon reiterates the macro-signs of suffering and evil in a white supremist, patriarchal society by signifying African-American Christians' understanding of how God is greater than all instances of evil. This ethical value operates in the church community and promotes a life sustaining faith praxis. Such rhetoric functions to restore self-confidence, giving Black believers back our nerve, especially when we are confronted by the morally repugnant white supremacy.

Articulating in rhythmic fashion, the Black preacher presents a word-picture of problems created by morally offensive actions that human beings perform. Images are not merely hinted at in Black preaching but symbols and metaphors become alive to the listener, taking on fixed character in the tradition of their origin and past adventures.

Again, using "The Wounds of Jesus" and Hurston's character, Rev. Pearson, we are presented with a concretized dramatization of how Jesus loved us before the creation of the world. Dispersed throughout the sermonic text is Jesus' declaration that if and when we do evil, Jesus will pay our bond before God's mighty throne. Rev. Pearson says that Jesus left heaven with all of its grandeur, disrobing himself of his matchless honor, yielding up the scepter of revolving worlds, clothing himself in the garment of humanity in order to rescue his friends from the clutches of evil and damnation. Thus, like his preaching forebears, Rev. Pearson's sermonic text moves from an ardent apprehension of a theological image, figuratively expressed, to more and more precise comprehension, until the hearers are able to make the connections between the metaphorical statements and their real lived situations.

The third and final theme at the core of this text is dominant Christocentrism. Black preaching is concerned with the revelation of God in Jesus Christ. The person and the work of Jesus Christ is the basis for all theological propositions that claim that God created a universe containing evil. This sermon exposes the dialectical tension of those who have suffered not only the pain of evil perpetrated by so-called Christian friends, but also alludes to the structural differences that exist in political rights and economic realities for African-American people. The text of "The Wounds of Jesus" provides a framework that gives substance and reality to Afro-Christianity's ethical understanding of reconciling evil with the active morality of Christians. This sermon brings together theological assent wherein the existence of Jesus as Redeemer is embraced prior to any rational consideration of the status of evil in the world.

Pearson preached that the damnation train pulled out from the Garden of Eden loaded with cargo going to hell, running at breakneck speed all the way through the law, the prophetic age, the reigns of kings and judges, plowing through the Jordan on her way to Calvary. Jesus stood out on the train track like a rough-backed mountain and shed his blood in order to derail the train of damnation. "He died for our sins, wounded in the house of His friends." This fundamental religious lore embodying African-American people's understanding of evil and suffering implies that human sins commited against humanity are in flagrant opposition to Divine Goodness. The evil that we do unto one another inflicts wounds not only on Jesus but on all of creation. The mountains fall to their rocky knees and tremble like a beast. The veins of the earth bleed. The geological strata falls loose and the chamber of hell explodes. In "The Wounds of Jesus" the redemption story begins with creation and ends with consummation at Calvary.

Womanist Queries for the Black Preaching Tradition

Since completing my dissertation on Hurston, I have continued to research the sacred rhetoric in African-American women's writings. I have found that sermons, prayers, and proverbs as religious events continue to make their way from the substratum of church life and religious activities into literary form in the work of Black novelists such as Nella Larsen, Jessie Fauset, Margaret Walker, Alice Childress, Sarah Wright, Toni Morrison, Alice Walker, Paule Marshall, and Gloria Naylor. These women do not write as exponents of the African-American religious tradition, but they convey religious sensibility central to the Black community throughout their work. As creators of literature, these women are not formally historians, sociologists, or theologians, yet the patterns and themes of their writings are reflective of historical reality. They are sociologically accurate and describe the religious convictions that undergird the ethical practice of my church community.

In other words, Black women novelists give me a way to look at AfroChristian thought outside of the institutional and traditionally articulated expressions of faith. As participant-interpreters of the African-American experience, Black women novelists coalesce their sociocultural perspectives with their intimate knowledge of AfroChristians' words and colorful ways of speaking. By presenting widely used cultural forms of sermons, prayers, and proverbs of *what is*, these writers enable me to do ethical analysis beyond the limits of the parochial situation of my denomination as well as propositional identities such as creeds, theologies, and books of order concerning *what should be*.

For example, Nella Larsen's Reverend Mr. Pleasant Green in *Quicksand* (1928), Margaret Walker's Brother Ezekiel in *Jubilee* (1966), Alice Childress' Reverend Mills in *A Short Walk* (1979), Paule Marshall's Reverend Morrissey in *Praisesong for the Widow* (1983), and Gloria Naylor's the Right Reverend Michael T. Hollis in *Linden Hills* (1985) all use the poetic style and fixed forms of speech that are endemic to the Black preaching experience. In order to illuminate the charismatic and ecstatic forms of expression as well as the rational medium of Black preaching, these novelists blend the sophistication and savvy of the urban church with the earthiness and mother wit of the rural tradition. Their sermons are consistent with the framework, the structure and organizing principles that have emerged from within the Black church and conform to the general rules of preaching in the Black idiom. The sermons in these novels are not just fictional tools but cultural truths, which, in turn, allow me to investigate whether or not these texts are normatively appropriate to mobilize a nonpatriarchal Black theology for today.

Thus, I contend that Black women writers add an important voice to the discussion of the sermon as genre and preaching as process. For more than two and a half centuries Black religious thoughts have been expressed in a variety of forms, mainly nonliterary. However, the sermons of the preliterary oral tradition are explicit in these novels. The Black women's literary tradition allows me to get behind the verbal compositions of the Afro-Christian experience so as to decode, question, and challenge the givens of patriarchal consensus reality contained therein. Thus, I maintain that if one wants to turn to a body of writings that incorporates the seminal experiences of evil, suffering, and God's goodness in Black lives, it is to African-American women's novels that one turns.

It is not possible to discuss and analyze the texts of male ministers without recognizing the gender dimension: that the majority of the faithful who heard and who continue to hear these sermons are women. Since women outnumber men in church congregations, our experiences need to be interfaced with how the sacred rhetoric reflects and mirrors the social, cultural, and religious realities of Black church patriarchy so that we can evaluate these sermons historically in their own time and assess them ethically in terms of a womanist scale of value.

For instance, when we turn to the experience of Black churchwomen to establish criteria for interpreting and determining the worth of sermonic texts we need to ask, What difference does it make that African-American women hear sermons like the ones embedded in this literary tradition wherein the feminine pronoun is used to refer to the sun, the moon, lightning and long-legged faith, who has no eyes? The linguistic sexism of Rev. Pearson results in nouns with feminine pronouns all having form without substance. Using gratuitous expressions, the preacher paints a picture of creation with the sun gathering up her fiery garments and wheeling around the throne of heaven while the moon grabbed up the tides of the ocean, dragging a thousand seas, as the lightning zig-zagged across the sky licking out her fiery tongue. And yet at the most crucial moment in history when Jesus is crucified, an angel who stands at the gate with a flaming sword pierces the moon and she runs down in blood while the sun bats her fiery eyes, puts on her judgment robe, lays down in the cradle of eternity, and rocks herself into sleep and slumber.

What do we do with sexist paradigms and negative female imagery included and promoted in such sermons as "The Wounds of Jesus" wherein the female damnation train that is carrying people to hell at breakneck speed throws her cow-catcher and murders Jesus? As womanist theologians, what are we doing to counter negative real-world consequences of sexist wording that reinforces sexist cultural realities? How disruptive is such gendered-biased language and androcentric sermons for social relations within the African-American family?

As Christian scholars committed to the well-being of the African-American community how are we refuting gender stereotypes that are dehumanizing, debilitating, and prejudicial to African-American women? Can we change male supremist attitudes by prescribing alternatives to discriminatory word usage in Black preaching? What are the essential liberating strategies that African-American clergywomen use in our own sacred rhetoric that encourages an ethic of resistance to evil? What are we doing that will allow a womanist ethic to emerge, an ethic that shows how Black women, underneath patriarchal teachings and relations of domination, are complex life-affirming moral agents?

This theoretical frame of questions is at once a comparative and an ideal construct, in terms of employing a critical and interpretative apparatus of selection and evaluation in order to gain knowledge about the judgment and criticism of women in relation to systemic evil and inevitable suffering. A womanist ethical critique helps us delegitimize the patriarchal teachings of the Black church. By disentangling the textual marginalization of women, we can find clues to Black churchwomen's moral agency and restore, as much as possible, the rich traditions of women's contributions to African-American theological thought. This matrix serves as a model for understanding the silences, limitations and possibilities of cultural patterns and forms that are unique and peculiar to the Black church community. It also enables women to see the constraints and limitations of male-defined and male-dominated religious ideas that have been fed to AfroChristian women for hundred of years in the name of natural order. By using womanist ethical questions to measure the worth of sermonic texts, we become aware of the ways in which widely accepted patriarchal beliefs and cultural practices dictate Black theology.

My womanist queries for the Black preaching tradition ask new questions of these ecclesiastical texts in order to unmask both linguistic and material reality. By combing Black sermons for womanist meaning, I want to show how this genre functions as an essential AfroChristian theological resource with ethical impact that can be calculated politically. Sermons are conduits for many of the theological and intellectual preferences within Afro-Christianity, in terms of keeping certain theological ideas and social habits alive in the Black community's mind.

Therefore, I contend that a womanist liberation matrix breaks the silence of Black sermons, wherein African-American women's history and pastoral praxis are placed in dialogue with the androcentric interests and perspectives that function as inclusive concepts in AfroChristian patriarchal culture. By looking at when and how the feminine is mentioned in these texts, I am analyzing the AfroChristian sacred canon for the ethical "stuff" that can give the contemporary Black churchwoman a greater sense of being, that can validate, make coherent, and give meaning to the dailiness of life as it relates to risk-and-security, weakness-and-strength, death-and-life. Furthermore, a womanist methodology critically analyzes sociocultural conditions and contexts in order to burst asunder the dominant understandings of theodicy and produces new archetypes that release the AfroChristian mind and spirit from the manacles of patriarchy, in order for Black women to emerge and to discern just what kind of moral agents we really want to be.

Conclusion

Womanist liberation ethics and the Black women's literary tradition have much to contribute to one another. The fruitful interaction between these two fields of inquiry enables me as an ethicist to examine the patriarchal apparatus of African-American Christian sacred rhetoric so as to assess whether or not these cultural treasures reinforce dehumanizing images or produce liberating paradigms for churchwomen. By critiquing the modes of religious expression and theoethical systems of representation that emerge, my intent is to unmask the Black church community's uncritical connections to the dominant traditional theological "worries." The point of much African-American women's spirituality as expressed in the literature is that it does not begin with questions about the omnipotence, omniscience, and omnipresence of God and then move to justify God's goodness given evil. Rather, womanist protagonists contend that God's sustaining presence is known in the resistance to evil.

My hope is that this essay serves as one of the vehicles for weaving and shaping the liberating sacred rhetoric of the Black church community. In order to judge and assess the ongoing value of AfroChristian sermons, Black liberation ethicists must continue creating modes of critical inquiry that allow African-American women, and others who cast their lot with us, to evaluate sermonic texts from a womanist perspective. When we exegete the established canon of intellectual AfroChristianity,[15] we stretch sermons to their raw state of exteriority, so as to break with specifiable social, structural, and cultural constructs that mock, demean, and exclude Black women. Those who form and maintain the patriarchal apparatus of AfroChristianity must realize that the Black church is in crisis and that the African-American church community has to respond to womanist theological interests and concerns if it wants to survive. Thus, our task as liberationists is to continue debunking, unmasking, and disentangling the messages in African-American sacred rhetoric, so that together we can expose the various ways that their representations embrace the well-being of us all.

NOTES

1. The importance of sermons in biblical discourse is discussed in David T. Shannon's essay "An Ante-bellum Sermon: A Resource for an African American Hermeneutic" in *Stony the Road We Trod: African American Biblical Interpretation*, ed. Cain Hope Felder (Minneapolis, MN: Fortress Press, 1991), 98–123.

2. Zilpha Elaw, *Memoirs of the Life, Religious Experience, Ministerial Travels and Labours, of Mrs. Zilpha Elaw, An American Female of Colour* (London: T. Dudley and B. Taylor, 1846); James Walker Hood, *The Negro in the Christian Pulpit; or, The Two Characters and Two Destinies Delineated in Twenty-one Practical Sermons* (Raleigh, NC: Edward Broughton, 1884); Bishop Lucius Henry Holsey, *Autobiography, Sermons, Addresses and Essays* (Atlanta: Franklin Printing and Publishing Co., 1898); William E. Hatcher, *John Jasper: The Unmatched Negro Philosopher and Preacher* (New York: Revell, 1908); William Henry Furness, *The Ministry of Women* (N.p., 1842); and Amanda Berry Smith, *An Autobiography: The Story of the Lord's Dealings with Mrs. Amanda Berry Smith, the Colored Evangelist* (Chicago: Meyer, 1893).

3. William Lloyd Imes, *The Black Pastures—An American Pilgrimage in Two Centuries: Essays and Sermons* (Nashville: Hemphill Press, 1957); Charles A. Tindley, *Book of Sermons* (Philadelphia: Charles A. Tindley, 1932); James H. Robinson, *Adventurous Preaching* (Great Neck, NY: Channel Press, 1956); Samuel Gandy, ed. *Human Possibilities: A Vernon John Reader* (Washington, DC: Hoffman Press, 1977).

4. This sermon was given by C. C. Lovelace and heard by Zora Neale Hurston at Eau Gallie in Florida, 3 May 1929, and originally published in *Negro: An Anthology*, ed. Nancy Cunard (London: Wishart, 1934), 35–39.

5. For other instances of sermons in the African-American literary tradition see the following: Paul Lawrence Dunbar, *The Uncalled* (1898; reprint New York: Negro Universities Press, 1969), *Joggin' Erlong* (New York: Dodd, Mead & Co., 1906) and *Lyrics of Lowly Life* (New York: Dodd, Mead & Company, 1901); James Weldon Johnson, *God's Trombones: Seven Negro Sermons in Verse* (New York: Viking Press, 1927); Walter White, *The Fire in the Flint* (1924; reprint New York: New American Library, 1969); Jean Toomer, *Cane* (New York: Boniand Liveright, 1923); James Baldwin, *Go Tell It On the Mountain* (New York: Grosset & Dunlap, 1953), *Notes of a Native Son* (New York: Dial Press, 1955), *The Fire Next Time* (New York: Dial Press, 1963), and *Just Above My Head* (New York: Dial Press, 1979).

6. Published as *Black Womanist Ethics* (Atlanta: Scholars Press, 1988).

7. Henry H. Mitchell, *Black Preaching* (Philadelphia: Lippincott, 1970); Ella P. Mitchell, ed., *Those Preaching Women* (Valley Forge, PA: Judson Press, 1985); Robert T. Newbold, Jr., ed., *Black Preaching: Selected Sermons in the Presbyterian Tradition* (Philadelphia: Geneva Press, 1977); Mervyn A. Warren, *Black Preaching: Truth and Soul* (Washington, DC: University Press of America, 1977); Joseph A. Johnson, Jr., *The Soul of the Black Preacher* (Memphis: C.M.E. Publishing House, 1970).

8. Also, examine Hurston's nonfiction, *Mules and Men* (Philadelphia: Lippincott, 1935); *Tell My Horse* (1938; reprint Berkeley, CA: Turtle Island, 1981); and *The Sanctified Church* (Berkeley, CA: Turtle Island, 1983).

9. Zora Neale Hurston to Carl Van Vechten, 28 February 1934, James Weldon Johnson Memorial Collection of American Literature, Beinecke Rare Book and Manuscript Library, Yale University.

10. The four plays not discussed in this paper are "Spears," now lost, which won honorable mention in the 1925 *Opportunity Magazine* contest; "Color Struck," published in *Fire!* in 1926; "Fast and Furious" (1932) and "The Great Day" (1932), musical revues.

11. Ruthe T. Sheffey, "Zora Hurston and Langston Hughes's 'Mule Bone'; An Authentic Folk Comedy and the Compromised Tradition," *The Zora Neale Hurston Forum* 2, no. 1 (Fall 1987): 49–60. Reverend Long points out that by the law of the Bible in Judges 15:16, Samson slew a thousand Philistines with the jaw-bone of an ass . . . a mule is more dangerous the further to the rear one goes, a mule's hock bone must be much more dangerous than the jaw-bone of an ass.

12. W. E. B. DuBois, *The Gifts of Black Folk: The Negroes in the Making of America* (New York: Washington Square Press, 1970).

13. Zora Neale Hurston to James Weldon Johnson, 8 May 1934, James Weldon Johnson Memorial Collection of American Literature, Beinecke Rare Book and Manuscript Library, Yale University. The review was by John Chamberlain, *New York Times*, 3 May 1934, 7.

14. See Yngve Briolioth, *A Brief History of Preaching* (Philadelphia: Fortress Press, 1945); C. C. Morrison, *The American Pulpit* (Chicago: Christian Century Press, 1925); Robert T. Handy, *A Christian America: Protestant Hopes and Historical Realities*, 2d. ed. (New York: Oxford University Press, 1984).

15. bell hooks and Cornel West, *Breaking Bread: Insurgent Black Intellectual Life* (Boston: South End Press, 1991), 131–146.

14

The "Loves" and "Troubles" of African-American Women's Bodies

The Womanist Challenge to Cultural Humiliation and Community Ambivalence[1]

Cheryl Townsend Gilkes

As part of the racial oppression that African-American people experience, cultural humiliation based on beauty norms [2] has serious implications for the self-esteem of African-American women and men. Such a concern may seem trivial in the face of drugs, violence, poverty, and social isolation, but many current social problems are often tied to low self-esteem or self-hatred. Self-hatred or damage and brokenness to our inner visions make it impossible for us to make and share effective "liberating visions" for our community and our world.[3] Self-hatred may be one of the deepest sources of conflict and turmoil *within* the African-American community. This may be especially true concerning women and their bodies. Damage and fractures to our inner visions surrounding women and their bodies show themselves when we are confronted with public events such as the Mike Tyson/ Desiree Washington case or the Vanessa Williams/Miss America scandal. By focusing on that dimension of Alice Walker's womanist idea/ideal that emphasizes love of self, others, and the life-affirming aspects of community life, I hope to show the importance of confronting this cultural humiliation and its consequences within ourselves.

Cultural humiliation assaults Black women by undermining their capacities for self-love. A womanist approach to life and living underscores the importance of self-love for celebrating and resisting in a hostile society. The loves and troubles of Black women's bodies represent a very narrow dimension of experience that has accumulated a weighty cultural burden.

In attempting to grasp this weighty cultural burden, I first try to show that a major component of racial oppression — cultural humiliation — is highlighted by the paradoxes and conflicted inner visions surrounding embodied experience, the loves, and the troubles. I then explore the roots of the "loves" and "troubles" in terms of the importance and power of experience. I attempt to juxtapose these experiences with the power of society to insinuate itself at the roots of our trouble. I conclude by focusing on the truly revolutionary nature of the challenge Alice Walker presents through her womanist idea. The ethical challenge to live out the mandates of love in a hateful and hate-filled world is a constant struggle and demands an attitude of resistance that must be embraced through what bell hooks calls "a process of critical remembering."[4] It is such a process, most often seen in the testifying of religious experience, that transforms individual victories over stumbling blocks and the destructive fury of society into prophetic resources for the larger community. Such resources, I hope to show, are essential for the kind of ministries necessary to empower and equip African-American women for full resistance to dehumanization and for full participation in the project of a truly humane society and world.

Cultural Humiliation and Conflicted Inner Visions

Complexity and diversity are the foundations of any truths to be told about African-American women in the United States. Both Alice Walker[5] and Mary Church Terrell have observed that African-American women collectively come from a "flower garden" full of "universalist" potential with families of people ranging through "brown, pink, and yellow, and our cousins are white, beige, and black." Black people generally and Black women most specifically are arrayed across the entire spectrum of female difference. The experience of these differences enables women to offer insights on life that never take so-called female privileges for granted. African-American women are also able to assess the underside of the cultural privileges associated with physical appearance and body size in a way that women of other ethnic groups, particularly white women, are not challenged to do. While sometimes the physical differences among African-American women have been a source of conflict and tension, my own experience, my observations of politically active African-American women, and my intense study of recent public events persuade me that conflict with one another is not the most critical problem African-American women face.[6] The paradoxes of being African American and female, of crossing an entire spectrum of embodied experience, and of being able to compare the experiences of different body types, sometimes within one's own family, may have contributed more to women's solidarity and critical empathy than to their division.

The historically conditioned responses of white people to the differences among African-American women and their bodies have been more of a problem and reflect more accurately the sexist and racist pathologies of American culture. If the responses of white people were the only problems, things would be easy. The racialized sexism and the sexualized racism of the larger society have elicited a wide range of responses among Black people themselves as they have constructed strategies for survival and politics of resistance and liberation. As a result, there is within the African-American community a history of ambivalence about issues of physical appearance.

This ambivalence may be the source of the most critical "troubles" that are stumbling blocks on the pathway toward a healthy self-love. The stumbling blocks of ambivalence are found everywhere. Women across the full spectrum of African-American experience, from the lightest to the darkest and from the largest to the smallest, contribute to a fund of knowledge that highlights the paradoxes, the loves, and the troubles, of existing in a Black and female body in America. In spite of the high premium placed on culturally exalted images of white female beauty and the comedic exploitation that surrounds the large Black woman, many African-American women know that the most respected physical image of Black women, within and outside of the community, is that of the large woman. Although it is respected, it is a culturally deviant image that is not necessarily loved. It is an image of power in a community where women need to be fortified and empowered. Yet some of the most powerless women in the community struggle with overweight and its unhealthy consequences. It is an asexual image[7] that sometimes permits escape from the constant harassment and sexual aggression, accurately called "hitting on," that disproportionately pervade the lives of those Black women who most approximate white cultural ideals.[8] In the era of "fitness and health," that same image is officially labeled "obese" and makes every large Black woman an immediately suspected case of bulimia.[9]

This essay borrows its title from a collection of Alice Walker's short stories entitled *In Love and In Trouble: Stories of Black Women*. A friend, taking a final examination in an English class, was asked to discuss the loves and the troubles present in Walker's stories. That question made me realize that the characters of Walker's stories exhibit self-destructive stumbling blocks right alongside self-constructed inner resources as they seek to live an ethic of love and resistance and to sustain life and hope. Walker's characters reflect the larger African-American experience as they play out the consequences of conflicted inner visions, inner visions that are the personal sources of cultural ambivalence and a barrier to self-love.

In one story, "The Welcome Table," we see the way inner visions can be tangled in contradiction. An elderly Black woman who precipitates an apoplectic and apocalyptic crisis in a segregated church one Sunday morning is strengthened by Jesus, whom she images as white, who meets her at the point of violent rejection, and walks with her and talks with her as she travels to glory. One observes the woman with wonder, strengthened and joyous in her meeting with Jesus, at the same time one wonders about the image fixed in her mind, an image from a picture stolen from her white lady's Bible.[10] Such conflicted inner visions are at the heart of the embodied experiences of African-American women.

Conflicted inner visions come from mixed messages and the world is full of mixed messages about being Black and female. Where our bodies and our appearance are concerned, because of the many mixed messages from within and outside of African-American culture, we are loved and troubled almost constantly. If we deviate from the dominant culture norms by being too dark or too light, we suffer a myriad of assaults on our self-esteem at the same time that we may discover that our bodies are a peculiar refuge from some forms of destructions and humiliations. If we are light and European-looking, we may find it easier to become campus queens, wives, and girlfriends, but we may have trouble being taken seriously as leaders in our churches, organizations, and communities unless we are attached to a man. Our so-called European "good looks" also mean that our behavior is excessively scrutinized for flaws in our commitment to and solidarity with "the Folk" at the same time we hear echoes of envy and longing when someone mutters, "All that yellow wasted." If we are dark and full-featured we are often made to feel unloved and unlovable, and if we are light and fine-featured we find ourselves asking, like Alice Walker's Squeak/Mary Alice, "do you really love me, or just my color?"[11] If we are dark and full-featured, particularly if we are large, members of our community presume that we are ready to take charge of our church organizations and our little brothers and sisters before our childhoods are over. If we are women clergy who are dark and large, we are attacked for embodying a mammy stereotype; however, if we are light and thin we are told that we are "too pretty to preach."

Because we are African-American, the assaults on our lives and bodies are historically molded and take on a more ominous character and meaning. We find that our history of racial oppression has always been sexualized. And that all sexism is racialized and often by homogenizing it we miss the peculiar ways sexism is able to reinforce racial privilege for some and sharpen the consequences of racial oppression for others. Racialized sexism, particularly in the form of the specialized sexism that assaults African-American women, compounds our own community's ambivalence about the meaning of being Black and female in America. This ambivalence is a source of the "multiple jeopardy" that characterizes our experience of oppression.[12]

Sociologist Deborah King, in her analysis of "multiple jeopardy" as a context for consciousness and feminist potential, points out that African-American women are a highly diverse group of women. Part of that diversity is tied to the various resources and disadvantages associated with our varying class, educational, and other status positions. From a sociological perspective, status can include dimensions of physical appearance, for instance, color, size, and conformity to appropriate gender images combined with the limits and options for roles and rewards that society assigns to physical appearance. Because of the high premium placed on physical appearance in our society, the vulnerabilities associated with race, class, and gender are greatly affected by the options, barriers, and limits created by physical appearance.

More than anything else, the diversity of experience related to physical appearance alone exposes the limitations of terms such as *double whammy* or *double jeopardy*. In spite of their rhetorical convenience and their contributions to rendering African-American women more visible, King points out that terms like double and triple jeopardy often obscure "the dynamics of multiple forms of discrimination." She argues:

> Unfortunately, most applications of the concepts of double and triple jeopardy have been overly simplistic in assuming that the relationships among the various discriminations are merely additive. These relationships are interpreted as equivalent to the mathematical equation, racism plus sexism plus classism equals triple jeopardy. . . . Such assertions ignore the fact that racism, sexism, and classism constitute three interdependent control systems. An interactive model, which I have termed multiple jeopardy, better captures those processes.[13]

As part of this multiple jeopardy, these simultaneous and interacting oppressions have a multiplier effect. The dynamism in King's model is intensified by the wide range of experiences that are possible in individual African-American women's lives, making possible a very broad context for Black women's resistance. The ability to resist, however, is dependent on how widely perspectives on issues of struggle are shared. Damaged and conflicted inner visions limit that ability to build upon the multiple potentials for resistance implied in the multiple dimensions of oppression.

The contradictions surrounding African-American women's experiences shape both personal and communal perspectives on culture and social change. African-American women have opportunities throughout their lives to develop insights on Black, white, male, and female experiences. These insights inform not only their strategies for survival in a hostile society but also the ideas and actions they use to challenge an oppressive society through social movements and through individual acts of resistance. Patricia Hill Collins describes African-American women as the "outsiders within,"[14] occupying statuses that differed mightily from those presumed appropriate for white women. Calling these statuses "contradictory locations," Collins identifies them as the source of "a peculiar marginality that stimulated a special African-American women's perspective." She explains that:

> Black women's position in the political economy, particularly ghettoization in domestic work, comprised . . . [a] contradictory location

where economic and political subordination created the conditions for Black women's resistance. Domestic work allowed African-American women to see white elites, both actual and aspiring, from perspectives largely obscured from Black men and from these groups themselves.[15]

While on the one hand such women experienced, according to Collins, a "sense of self-affirmation" by "seeing white power demystified," they also experienced at a very basic level the fact that they could "never belong. . . ."[16] Not only is such knowledge, from Collins's perspective, a source of profound frustration, it is also a source of creativity. This self-understanding, often shared in the communal spaces of women's life – their churches, their clubs, and their beauty parlors – evolves into a standpoint from which African-American women's ideas about life and society develop into what she calls "a recurring humanist vision."[17] This vision is deeply implicated in a legacy of organized activism and personal resistance. Both King and Collins point to the diverse ways in which African-American women have participated in actions and movements that have challenged racial oppression and have opened the doors for other groups to launch similar challenges. However, it is the poetic vision of Alice Walker that has provided the most succinct and probative perspective on the critical power embedded within Black women's history and experience and the need for certain stances to be taken within one's personal experience in order for that power to be realized.

The Womanist Idea and Ideal

Walker's term *womanist* and the complex definition that accompanies it underscore the powerful critique of oppression and potential for human liberation that can emerge from reflection on being Black and female in America. She takes a position. I think we do Walker a disservice when we use her term *womanist* as simply a label for Black women feminists and their intellectual efforts in order to distinguish them from white women feminists and their efforts. Walker's idea of Black feminism lays out very clear positions that Black women ought to adopt based upon the best traditions ingrained in their legacy of struggle, survival, and the construction of African-American women's culture. It is an ethical evaluation of African-American women's history that extracts a set of principles that women may choose as their orientation to the world.

Clearly, by Walker's standards, not all Black women are womanists, but the womanist potential is embedded in all Black women's experiences. Her word is part of a dictionary-style definition that she wrote, according to Karen Baker-Fletcher, in response to her editors' queries regarding the existence and meaning of a term she had used in her essays and the title of her book. Her term touched a deep spiritual nerve among African-

American women in a way that no other African-American artist or critic had been able to do.[18] Because of the term's spiritual implications, Walker has probably reached more ordinary women in the Black community than any other Black feminist thinker and writer. My own encounter with the term sparked a period of introspection and "critical remembering." Walker's perspective helped me to re-member the voices that had helped to shape my own inner vision. Through re-membering these voices, the personal emerged more forcefully as a didactic resource. Walker extracted the heroic consequences of difference and the process by which these consequences became elements of a *critical* consciousness.

For African-American women, the pain of simply being embodied — coping with others' responses to our hair, skin, and size — can overshadow the strengths and options. The pathetic dimension too often obscures the heroic possibilities. William H. Grier and Price M. Cobb early recognized the extremely negative implications of Black women's experience.[19] Other observers, when attempting to make sense of Black life and culture in a racist society, also dwell primarily on the deprivations. Walker insisted that the experience of suffering and oppression can be a resource for liberating vision and spiritual growth. Walker asserted through Celie that the voice of "poor colored women" can make a difference. When Celie shocked her friend Shug with her comments about God, Celie shouted, "Let 'im hear me, I say. If [God] ever listened to poor colored women the world would be a different place, I can tell you."[20] Celie, like Sojourner Truth and Harriet Tubman, discovers that her voice and her testimony of experience has the power to "turn the world right side up" and "to shake a nation." Walker makes the heroic and critical side of being Black, female, poor, and oppressed most explicit in her definition of womanist. Where the tension between the pathetic and the heroic fosters ambivalence, Walker pushes us toward clarity.

Walker's idea contains a vision in which the ambivalences of African-American culture toward women, their roles and their images, are resolved. Her perspective is historically and traditionally grounded. The appropriate heroic models for her are women like Harriet Tubman, Mary Church Terrell, and Josephine St. Pierre Ruffin. Without ever mentioning their names, she taps into the legacies of struggle and collective work each has left behind. She calls us to emulate the boldness and daring of Harriet Tubman, a woman who just could not leave her community behind as a runaway from slavery. She asks us to think like Mary Church Terrell who thought that African Americans should call themselves "colored" because the diversity of African Americans was so broad. Although "colored" achieved only limited success, Terrell's vision was one that included the most privileged and the most deprived and sought to affirm and embrace the full range of images from the darkest to the lightest. Walker sees important models in the assertive and premature adulthood of women such as Ida B. Wells-Barnett, who lied about her age in order to secure a teaching job as a teenager, and Nannie Helen Burroughs, who was serving the National Baptist Convention in an executive capacity by the age of eighteen. In the tradition of Josephine St. Pierre Ruffin, Walker clearly reasserts the validity of the definition of a "woman's movement" as a movement led by women for "the survival and wholeness of the entire people, male and female."

Not only does Walker point to the dimensions of difference among African-American women as a source of "universalist" humanism, but she centers love as the orientation women should have to the world around them. In her articulation of the "loves" that a good woman should express, and of course a womanist is a good woman, Walker emphasizes those things that make possible what has come to be called "the beloved community." As one reflects upon these loves, it becomes clear that these loves oppose directly the central hatreds of this age. We live in a society that hates poor people and yet Walker calls us to love "the Folk." We live in a society that hates challenges to rigid order and hierarchical authority in its religious life and yet Walker insists that we love "the Spirit." In a society that in its hatred of poor people and fat people has allowed the ethic that "a woman can be neither too rich or too thin" to rain down life-threatening terrors on women, Walker exalts "food and roundness." And most importantly, in a society that pulls its various cultural hatreds together in such a way as to destroy and victimize Black women, Walker passionately emphasizes the importance of self-love. "Loves herself. *Regardless*."

These loves are on a collision course with the troubles that comprise the cultural humiliation of African-American women. In this context of dehumanization, Walker's challenge to love creates a context of *re*humanization. These loves must be seen as ethical positions associated with a good womanist. Walker emphasizes those dimensions of African-American culture that have helped African Americans maintain their sanity and humanity under impossible circumstances, spirituality and those things most associated with its expression—music, dance, and the Spirit. These loves are interwoven with ideals that should be part of the fabric of a humane spirituality, love of "the Folk," love of "struggle," and the love of oneself, "regardless."

On Loving Food, Roundness, and the Self

Linked within this list of loves, almost like the germinal center of a beautiful flower, is the deceptively revolutionary insistence, "Loves love and food and roundness." These loves of love and roundness and food seem almost ethereal and apolitical until they are placed in the context of contemporary culture. In my personal encounter with Walker's *womanist,* I stopped there. As a large, full-featured, dark brown African-American woman, I recognized a revolution in her call to love. Walker's emphasis remembered for me my own struggles with community and culture. My own experience and my understanding of the history of cultural humiliation embedded in American racism made it abundantly clear that these loves are not only a source of celebration and bonding in a human community, but also a protest against a culture that systematically assaults the self-esteem of African-American women.

Edwin Schur has pointed to the importance of "gender norms" in defining the position of women in our society. These norms include narrow European standards of beauty, a model of marriage and motherhood that enforces economic dependence, and social and intellectual subordination. Violation of these norms brings about the exclusion and punishment of women in a variety of ways. African-American women, by choice and by circumstance, violate nearly every dimension of American gender norms. Failure to meet society's beauty norms is, in Schur's terms, "visual deviance." Visual conformity in the United States, of course, is tied to an idolatry of whiteness. African-American women, in terms of their color alone, stand in opposition to the culture's idolatry of whiteness. For this opposition, they are assaulted from outside their communities, but African-American women who are too dark face an outrageous complex of attitudes and behaviors from within their own communities. Often the behavior of men and their stated preferences for lighter-colored women reflect the men's own self-hatred, but in spite of changes brought about by the Black Power Movement, Alice Walker is still able to lament, "If the present looks like the past, what does the future look like?"[21]

Physical, psychological, and emotional assaults against women are endemic. However, the culture's approach to African-American women, their images, and their life styles has been a central thrust in the continued humiliation of the entire African-American community. The assault on Black women has been so effective that in recent times, the African-American community has turned against its women as the source of its problems rather than as heroic resources in the constant struggle against racial oppression. As a result, African-American women have waged more struggle on behalf of men as part of their commitment to the entire community than I think Black men have waged on behalf of women. Some would argue that women have done more for the men than women have done for themselves. They have also been forced to justify themselves within and to their communities — a distracting process that deflects energy from the real struggle.

Straight talk about the loves and troubles of our bodies is almost impossible because there is so much pain. Paradoxes become apparent in very strange ways. Recently, when speaking at a conference, I pointed out the ways in which we needed to engage in ministry that addressed the ways in which the culture responded differentially to little girls who were considered "pretty" and those who were considered "ugly." This "pretty"/"ugly" dichotomy is so taken for granted within Black culture that it is almost never discussed. Girls not considered beautiful by white American standards, if they are part of families and communities who take education and achievement seriously, are groomed to be good students and to be leaders. The others may also be groomed that way, but unless they grow up in middle-class settings where certain protections are in place, they walk a very treacherous pathway to adulthood that may leave them educationally and professionally underdeveloped and very vulnerable targets for all sorts of sexual aggression and exploitation. The failures of African Americans to address this problem is evident in the sad and sorry history of Black women in beauty pageants.

When I pointed to the problem of young African-American girls and their self-esteem, one man got up and expressed amazement that when he would stop little girls in the grocery store and ask them if they were going to grow up to be Miss America, the little girls would scowl at him. His point was that at a young age they already seemed to know they were rejected. I responded that although he meant well, he was not only being cruel to them by simply asking the question but failing to reckon with the problems embedded in these pageants that Black people, because of their history in the United States, should intuitively recognize.

Until the early 1960s Black women were not permitted to enter the Miss America Pageant.[22] Although many Black fraternal organizations and most Black colleges had contests, the college competitions and most fraternal pageants never involved any kind of swimsuit competitions and still do not. As one observer pointed out, the swimsuit competition has one purpose: to answer the question, "How does she look without any clothes?" Because of the withering feminist critique the Miss America Pageant has elicited, one need only watch annually to see the pageant's incremental response. Since the 1960s, scholarship, education, and ideologies of professionalism have gained greater prominence. In 1991 and 1992, program segments featured interviews with former contestants from various states and former Miss Americas describing the careers and family lives the scholarship aid had made possible. Because the swimsuit competition is particularly indefensible, it has been recast as a display of "fitness and health." One year the pageant organizers went so far as to eliminate the wearing of high heels with swimsuits. Although the contestants were in their bare feet, every one of the women walked across the stage on her toes. Two years after Vanessa Williams entered, won, and embarrassed the pageant, the scoring system was changed to make it possible to win without winning in the swimsuit competition.

African-American women winners at the state level and the four who have served as Miss Americas have had a powerful impact on the pageant's attempt to maintain its relevance. The Miss America Pageant, however, is a genteel upper-middle-class institution that masks and mystifies a more sinister culture of female sexual exploitation, abuse, and violence. The display, exploitation, and abuse of African-American women is probably at the genetic core of this institutionalized misuse of women.

African-American women were probably the first women in the United

States to be displayed publicly without clothing. Slave auctions often drew crowds of observers because, in their display of women to be sold as slaves, they pandered to white prurient interests. Black women's bodies were the objects of intense public curiosity.[23] The sexual exploitation endemic to slavery was made possible by the violence and abuse. Women were flogged and tortured just like men. Angela Davis points out that women who participated in revolts or engaged in violence were sometimes killed more brutally than the men.[24] Where men were hanged, women were burned at stakes. It is almost as if the American cultural rituals of immolating Black men during lynchings after slavery had their antecedents in attempts to control Black women during slavery. The sexual abuse and violence went hand in hand and sometimes choices about survival were made by weighing the option of nonviolent submission against near-suicidal attempts at resistance. Often survival was possible at a high personal cost. There were historical and cultural costs as well.

The abuse and degradation of slavery was the first step in a devaluation or labeling process that shaped attitudes and actions toward Black women. These attitudes and actions are so specialized and so deep that they even carry over into pornographic depictions.[25] African-American women's status as degraded sexual objects during slavery was carried forward to argue for the necessity of segregation after slavery. Beliefs about the sexuality of African-American women fueled ideologies that supported the lynching of their men. Those sexual images helped to carry forward the Jezebel image that had become a fixed stereotype associated with slavery. Additionally the images associated with women's roles as workers also carried forward the deviant image of Mammy—the loyal faithful worker who was also large, loving, and asexual. The oppositional dichotomy between the light-skinned, sexy, and European-looking Black woman and the large, loving one became a fixed feature of American culture. Within African-American culture itself, such images became lovingly lionized as the dichotomy between women "built for comfort" and those "built for speed." Indeed Black popular culture became far more affirming of big women than white popular culture.[26]

All human experience is embodied experience and the consequences of cultural humiliation are most dramatically shown with reference to the body. Not only is experience embodied, but stereotypes, pernicious cultural representations of people, are also embodied images. All racial stereotypes are usually named images attached to an image of a body, and all of those named images are gendered. Distorted Black images come in male and female form, so for the male Sambo image, there is the female mammy image. For the image of "Zip Coon" there is Jezebel. Hollywood depictions often ally Mammy with Sambo and Jezebel with Zip Coon. Implied also are presumptions about sexuality and danger. The safe, emasculated, Black male is paired with the large, highly respected, and loving Mammy. Her industriousness is often contrasted with his laziness. Their lack of apparent sexuality is tied to her enterprise and his economic ineffectiveness and laziness.

If stereotypes are any guides to actual social roles, it is a paradox that the most symbolically privileged image of white women, the fragile-blond-beauty queen, is diametrically opposed to the most exploited image of Black women, the large physically powerful "mammy." Barbara Andolsen, in her powerful exploration of the ethical implications of racism, particularly in the form of racial and cultural privilege, for American feminism, points to the victimization of African-American women by cultural definitions of beauty. She points out that while both men and women have been victimized, men's popular images have changed more radically and become more varied than have women's images. Indeed Andolsen argues that the differential impact of white beauty standards serves to maintain divisions among women, even Black and white women who are both feminists.[27]

My own experience as a dark, plump, African-American woman informs my reading and hearing of Walker's call to love food and roundness. Her call also challenged me to examine the scripts of my childhood and see the sources of my own conflicted inner visions. I am not a woman who became plump as the years have passed, but I have been so my entire life. My childhood doctor, a very loving Armenian woman named Agnes Grace Israelian, vehemently warned me during one of the many times I tried to lose weight that I was never to attempt to drop below one hundred forty pounds. By insurance company standards that is still overweight for my height. My parents' marriage was the union between a family of little women and big men. My mother weighed only eighty-seven pounds on the day she married my ex-football-player father. My father's genes are clearly dominant; I look like and am built like my dad. However since my mother had rickets as a child, her size may also be a function of some deprivations in early childhood.

My mother's lack of experience with fatness forced me to navigate the treacherous waters of American body culture without the compasses and maps that often make "becoming a woman" a taken-for-granted process, regardless of how painful and destructive. I was actually forced to think about myself and my size and where I fit in the community and the family as my friends at school thought up newer and more creative names for my size and as my mother and her relatives agonized over strategies to make me slimmer. My family's quest to keep me at the same size as my many smaller friends is a rich catalogue of tragicomical failures. I drank 1950s skim milk. I was given special candy as an appetite suppressant. I was enrolled in dance classes at a very early age and encouraged to practice at home. I was divested of my Easter baskets and relieved of my jelly beans by Easter Monday. No desserts were served with dinners until after my brothers were born, eight and nine years after me. My brothers of course were encouraged to grow "big!" like the men of my father's family. I can now laugh about the strategies they tried. As a result, I am a big woman who does not have a ravenous sweet tooth and can let chocolate candy sit in the refrigerator for months and years at a time. My mother would also control my ability to snack through careful rationing of money. When I did develop a taste for Dorothy Muriel sugar cookies, I had to choose between the cookie and my carfare home. Every stolen cookie required a two-mile walk to get home. A fairly healthy consequence is that I love to dance and to take long walks in urban areas.

As the cultural critiques embedded in feminist and womanist ideas have pointed out, becoming women in contemporary culture often means being shaped by painful experiences shaped lovingly and caringly by other women. The ideals embedded in Walker's idea highlight the ennobling and empowering dimensions of mother-daughter dialogues. These are meant to counter the demeaning and destructive exchanges that often shape our feelings about our bodies and our life styles. Because these dialogues continue throughout life, our experience as Black women often entails overhearing and assimilating a wide range of conversations among our mothers and "othermothers," all of which serve to build and shape our inner vision.

My mother wanted me to be a "normal" size and I am sure that the times I came home and cried about my friends' name-calling only spurred her on to greater efforts. However, her zeal to slim me down led to statements while eating such as "You're digging your grave with your fork!" I was repeatedly warned that "children have heart attacks too." Fortunately growing up in most Black families provides many voices for our inner visions and our many mothers have "no clips on their lips." My great-aunt and grandmothers saw things differently, and said so. They thought my mother was too thin and told her so in front of me. They delivered a set of counter messages along with a dazzling array of delectably cooked dishes for their very special niece and grandchild. I may not have a sweet tooth, but no spare rib, chicken leg, or green vegetable is safe in my presence. My propensity to eat fried chicken with a knife and a fork was carefully cultivated with rewards of peach ice cream by my Savannah, Georgia-born grandmother.

My size, and my size alone, exposed me to a diverse set of voices during the formation of my cultural world. The smaller and shorter friends at school were quick to taunt me with a range of names. Their favorite was "Baby Huey." It was probably the most accurate since I was always so much taller. Since being large meant that I was also full-featured, there were occasional words about this as well. Ironically many of these same children liked to come home with me after school. We would play "school" and they would elect me teacher since I looked the oldest, *because of my size*. I was also allowed to preside and preach at pet funerals, probably for this same reason. The negative messages about size were also countered with positive messages from men and women at church who said I was simply a "big" girl. They worked hard to make me feel comfortable. At the same time my peers and my mother impressed me with my visual deviance, my peers, my family, and my church encouraged me to occupy leadership roles and to excel in other ways. The negative voices about my size often came from the same chorus as the positive voices about other aspects of myself. Fortunately I was in a structural position and an institutional setting where the positive voices had a greater opportunity to be heard.

Walker is insisting that African-American women must not hate themselves. In spite of the overwhelming storm of cultural humiliations we are faced with everyday, especially regarding our bodies and our psyches, part of our struggle is to live the loves. In the context of a misogynist world that lies to women about not being too rich or too thin, Walker's insistence that a womanist "loves love and food and roundness" takes on the character of a revolutionary manifesto. For women like me, encountering the womanist idea involved hearing a persistent and prophetic call to sift through the oppositional tensions among the voices of our inner vision and choose the heroic over the pathetic. "Regardless," of all else that may claim our energies and challenge our being, we are challenged to encourage the manifestation of self-love.

Living the Loves in a Hateful World

African Americans' existential ambivalence about their bodies may be the most personally painful legacy of slavery and racial oppression in the United States. The consequences of that ambivalence for women may be the most dangerous and debilitating. Black men also have injured self-images but they are able to defend themselves from certain kinds of assaults and have almost nothing to fear in terms of assaults and sexual harassment from women. There are also lucrative outlets for Black men to use their bodies while maintaining tremendous illusions of power and in some cases real power. Most women are as defenseless now as they were during slavery and in some ways they may be more so. Given the problems of poor urban neighborhoods, the large slave community may have been more effective at defending its members. Slave communities may also have been more unified. The womanist idea is a call to the kind of unity that creates a community climate that is nurturing and empowering. When all of its implications are examined, the womanist idea as defined by Walker is a call to healing, spiritual wholeness, celebration, and struggle. Taken with Walker's other writings, it is an unambivalent and unconflicted call for the affirmation of life and all that sustains a healthy life. Walker is insisting that we must repair our inner visions in order to live the loves in a hateful and troubling world. She believes, and I agree with her, that if we are able to live this ideal it will benefit our world, not just our community.

It is no accident that many white women feminists, from Sarah Evans to Hillary Rodham Clinton, point to specific Black women as role models who freed them from the guilded prison of silence, physical fragility, and intellectual subordination. For many women in the civil rights movement, women such as Fannie Lou Hamer, Ella Baker, and Ruby Doris Robinson were voices and images that empowered. Marian Wright Edelman, her prominence enhanced by her mentoring role to Hillary Rodham Clinton, was also one of the women of the civil rights movement whose actions and choices provided models of strength and self-actualization. These women reflect the adjectives that emerge from Walker's description of a womanist as someone who is serious, responsible, courageous, and mature. African-American women's history is full of revered women whose critiques and contributions placed them in direct conflict with the prevailing norms and conventions of womanhood in the United States. Walker has called us to maintain our connection with that history by adopting this revolutionary standpoint of womanism.

Walker's call and its application to the lives of African-American women are also challenges to a society whose evil is fractionated and diffuse. African-American women are not the only women who suffer from cultural definitions of beauty and body image. However they are the only group that must sustain itself independently of these ideals because of the ontological impossibilities surrounding the vast majority. It is ironic that the parents of the two darkest Miss Americas, Marjorie Vincent and Debbie Turner, actively discouraged their daughters in order to protect them. These two women, in my opinion, expanded the value of professional aspirations as competitive currency in the Miss America Pageant. The contestants in their cohort were older and more heavily representative of graduate and professional students. Vanessa Williams, ironically, had not entertained a thought of winning the pageant and basically competed because it was a summer job opportunity for a dance and theater major. Yet even in her downfall she contributed to changes that served to devalue the swimsuit competition. The only parent who actively encouraged her daughter was Mrs. de Gaetano, Suzette Charles's mother, who herself had wanted to compete in the Miss America pageant but was prohibited by its "white only" rules.[28] All four Black women who served as Miss Americas were in some way or another part of the world of ontological impossibility and because of their peculiar marginality, they changed dimensions of the pageant.

The sordid history of African-American women and the exploitation of our bodies is not over. We are developing a contemporary roll call, names like Anita Hill, Vanessa Williams, and Desiree Washington, to remind us. Both the Vanessa Williams scandal and the Mike Tyson case point to the fact that Black women are still peculiarly victimized by the cult of beauty and the culture of sexual exploitation, abuse, and violence it masks. *And* they are vulnerable *within* the community as well as in the society at large. Karen Baker-Fletcher notes that the National Baptist Convention's support of Mike Tyson, while remaining silent about (and actually tacitly supporting) Desiree Washington's victimization and vilification, disrespects the history of struggle waged by Black women on behalf of the entire community and sidesteps the problem of sexual violence and abuse in our own communities.[29] This situation is a stark reminder that we are all victimized and therefore we must each be someone who, in Walker's words, "loves struggle." If, through loving ourselves "regardless" and repairing our inner visions, we save our own lives, we have taken the first step toward our "response-ability" to save our brothers and sisters. Self-love then is probably the most critical task we complete in establishing our commitment "to survival and wholeness of entire people, male and female."

NOTES

1. The author gratefully acknowledges the support of the W. E. B. DuBois Institute for African American Research and Colby College in the writing and production of this paper.

2. For an expanded discussion of beauty as conformity or deviance from social norms, see Edwin Schur, *Labeling Women Deviant: Gender, Stigma, and Social Control* (New York: Random House, 1984). I depend heavily on Schur's perspective in my own analysis of African-American women's deviance in terms of their labor history. See Cheryl Townsend Gilkes, " 'Liberated to Work Like Dogs!': Labeling Black Women and Their Work" in *The Experience and Meaning of Work in Women's Lives*, ed. Hildreth Y. Grossman and Nia Lane Chester (Hillsdale, NJ: Lawrence Erlbaum Associates, 1989).

3. For the different kind of "liberating visions" that emerge from our various life histories, see Robert Michael Franklin, *Liberating Visions: Human Fulfillment and Social Justice in African American Thought* (Minneapolis, MN: Augsburg Fortress Press, 1990).

4. bell hooks [Gloria Watkins], "Loving Blackness as Political Resistance," in *Black Looks: Race and Representation* (Boston: South End Press, 1992), 19.

5. Alice Walker, "Womanist," in *In Search of Our Mothers' Gardens: Womanist Prose* (San Diego: Harcourt Brace Jovanovich, 1983), xi-xii.

6. Some Black feminist critics see African-American women's anger at one another as one of Black women's biggest problems. While it is sometimes a problem, it is not *the* problem. For some more pessimistic discussions see bell hooks, *Black Looks* and Audre Lorde, *Sister Outsider* (Trumansberg, NY: Crossing Press, 1984), especially her essay "Eye to Eye: Black Women, Hatred, and Anger."

7. On the asexuality of the "Mammy" image associated with the large Black woman, see Barbara Christian, *Black Feminist Criticism: Perspectives on Black Women Writers* (New York: Pergamon, 1985), and Deborah Gray White, *Ar'n't I A Woman: Female Slaves in the Plantation South* (New York: W. W. Norton and Co., 1985).

8. Michelle Wallace tried to talk about this disparity in her book *Black Macho and the Myth of the Superwoman* (New York: Dial Press, 1978). She had difficulty making herself understood, however, because she uncritically used the term "prettiest" to talk about the problems of teenagers in the ghetto whose appearance most conformed to white norms.

9. This is not to ignore the very real risks that African-American women face. In her introduction to Georgianna Arnold's essay "Coming Home: One Black Woman's Journey to Health and Fitness," Evelyn C. White, editor of *The Black Women's Health Book: Speaking for Ourselves* (Seattle, WA: Seal Press, 1990), points out that

as "American women have gotten increasingly heavier" the problem has "been even greater for black women." Not only do we have increased risks of heart disease, diabetes, and high blood pressure, but we also may be more victimized by our social circumstances. According to White, "Researchers believe that social factors including self-image, career and marital expectations, education, images in the media and role models can influence weight gain."

10. Walker, *In Love and In Trouble: Stories of Black Women* (New York: Harcourt Brace Jovanovich, 1973).

11. Walker, *The Color Purple* (New York: Harcourt Brace Jovanovich, 1992, Tenth Anniversary Edition), 92.

12. Deborah K. King, "Multiple Jeopardy, Multiple Consciousness: The Context of a Black Feminist Ideology," in *Black Women in America: Social Science Perspectives,* ed. Micheline R. Malson, Elisabeth Mudimbe-Boyi, Jean F. O'Barr, and Mary Wyer (Chicago: University of Chicago Press, 1988), 265-295.

13. Ibid., 270.

14. Patricia Hill Collins, "Learning from the Outsider Within: The Sociological Significance of Black Feminist Thought," *Social Problems* 33, no. 6 (1986): 14-32. See also Collins, "The Social Construction of Black Feminist Thought" *Signs: Journal of Women in Culture and Society* 14, no. 4 (1989) and *Black Feminist Thought: Knowledge, Consciousness, and the Politics of Empowerment* (Cambridge, MA: Unwin Hyman, Inc., 1990).

15. Collins, *Black Feminist Thought,* 11.

16. Ibid.

17. Ibid., 37-38.

18. Karen Baker-Fletcher, "Womanism: It's More Than Blush." *Que Pasa? Information by Racial/Ethnic Clergywomen* (Louisville, KY: Women's Ministry Unit, Presbyterian Church [U.S.A.], February 1993), 1.

19. William H. Grier and Price M. Cobb, "Achieving Womanhood," in *Black Rage* (New York: Bantam Books, 1968), 32-45.

20. Walker, *The Color Purple,* 187.

21. See Walker's essay by this same title in *In Search of Our Mothers' Gardens,* 290.

22. Lois W. Banner points out that the Miss America Pageant, beginning in 1921, "made a national ritual of the . . . powerful notion that the pursuit of beauty ought to be a woman's primary goal." For a general history of beauty that includes the Miss America Pageant as a pivotal social institution, see Banner's book *American Beauty: A Social History through Two Centuries of the American Idea, Ideal, and Image of the Beautiful Woman* (New York: Random House, 1983). My general observations on the Vanessa Williams affair are drawn from my own extensive and uncatalogued clippings collection on the subject of African-American women and beauty pageants.

23. Some of the more egregious examples of this can be found in Sander L. Gilman, "Black Bodies, White Bodies: Toward an Iconography of Female Sexuality in Late Nineteenth-Century Art, Medicine, and Literature," in *"Race," Writing, and Difference,* Henry Louis Gates, Jr. (Chicago: University of Chicago Press, 1986), 223-261.

24. Angela T. Davis, *Women, Race, and Class* (New York: Random House, 1981).

25. Alice Walker offers a forceful analysis of this in her essay "Coming Apart,"

in *You Can't Keep a Good Woman Down* (New York: Harcourt Brace Jovanovich, 1981), 41-53.

26. I am grateful to Deborah King who provided examples from her popular culture collection, particularly references to songs such as "Big Leg Woman with a Short Mini Skirt" (Israel Tolbert on Warren Records, Stax Records Distributor, 1970).

27. Barbara Andolsen, *"Daughters of Jefferson, Daughters of Bootblacks": Racism and American Feminism* (Macon, GA: Mercer University Press, 1986).

28. Ironically "Charles" is Suzette de Gaetano's stage name. Her father, who is white, understood the culture of sexual exploitation and abuse well enough to insist that his daughter never be photographed out of his presence. The Rev. Samuel D. Proctor, in a sermon before the National Convention of Gospel Choirs and Choruses in 1984, pointed out that the history of white America's response to our "little light girls with funny eyes" should have prompted more surveillance of Vanessa Williams's employers on the part of her father. Vanessa Williams herself later pointed out that other well-known actresses had shared stories of their own exploitation by photographers.

29. Karen Baker-Fletcher, "Tyson's Defenders and the Church of Silence," *New York Times* (29 March 1992, Opinion section), 17.

Contributors

Karen Baker-Fletcher is assistant professor of theology and culture at Claremont School of Theology, Claremont, California.

Katie Geneva Cannon is associate professor of religion at Temple University, Philadelphia, Pennsylvania. She is the author of *Black Womanist Ethics*.

M. Shawn Copeland is assistant professor of theology and Black studies at the Divinity School, Yale University, New Haven, Connecticut.

Cheryl Townsend Gilkes is the John D. and Catherine T. MacArthur associate professor of sociology and African-American studies at Colby College, Waterville, Maine.

Jacquelyn Grant is associate professor of systematic theology at Interdenominational Theological Center, Atlanta, Georgia. She is the author of *White Women's Christ, Black Women's Jesus*.

Patricia L. Hunter is an ordained minister and the representative for the Pacific Northwest, The Ministers and Missionaries Benefit Board of the American Baptist Church.

Cheryl A. Kirk-Duggan is an ordained minister and a doctoral student at the Baylor University School of Religion. She holds a B.A. and M.M. in music and a M.Div.

Clarice J. Martin is associate professor of New Testament at Colgate Rochester Divinity School/Bexley Hall/Crozer Theological Seminary, Rochester, New York.

Rosita deAnn Mathews is an ordained American Baptist minister and the first African-American woman to be chief of Chaplain Service in the Veterans Administration Medical System. She works in Northampton, Massachusetts.

Jamie T. Phelps, O.P., is assistant professor of doctrinal theology at the Catholic Theological Union, Chicago, Illinois.

Marcia Y. Riggs is associate professor of Christian ethics at Columbia Theological Seminary, Decatur, Georgia.

Emilie M. Townes is assistant professor of Christian social ethics at Saint Paul School of Theology, Kansas City, Missouri. She is author of *Womanist Justice, Womanist Hope*.

Delores S. Williams is associate professor of theology and culture at Union Theological Seminary, New York, New York. She is the author of *Sisters in the Wilderness: The Challenge of Womanist God-Talk*.

Frances E. Wood is the former program director for the Center for Domestic and Sexual Violence, Seattle, Washington.

Index

Abraham, 84
Adam, 133
Aggie, 120
Allen collection of slave songs, 132, 136-37, 147n7, 152
Americans and Their Servants (Daniel E. Sutherland), 208
Amos, 223
Amott, Teresa L., 51
Andolsen, Barbara, 243
Andrews, William, 20
Angelou, Maya, 16
Antihistemi, 92
Augustine, St., 16, 18
Authority, 86-87; as domination and as partnership, 86
Autobiography, 16, 21, 28; African-American, four elements, 17-18; women's, 18-20
Autobiography of Malcolm X (Malcolm X), 16
Baker, Ella, 206, 246
Baker-Fletcher, Karen, 6, 172, 237, 246
Baldwin, James, 2
Barth, Karl, 137, 213
Beauty as conformity, 247n2
Becoming Human (Letty Russell), 201
Berger, Peter, 14
Berry, Polly, 121
Bethune, Mary McLeod, 213
Bible, 21, 122
Black Theology of Liberation (James Cone), 131, 138-40
Book of Margery Kempe (Margery Kempe), 19
Branch, G. Murray, 219
Brand Plucked From the Fire: An Autobiographical Sketch by Mrs. Julia A. F. Foote (Julia Foote), 131

Braxton, Joanne M., 29, 121
Brent, Linda. *See* Harriet Jacobs
Brothers and Sisters to Us (U.S. Catholic Bishops), 54
Brown, Elsa Barkley, 130
Bulimia, 234
Bunyan, John, 16
Burroughs, Nanny Helen, 239
Butterfield, Stephen, 17
Canaan, 222
Cannon, Katie Geneva, 37, 182, 219
Carby, Hazel, 110
Caruthers, Richard, 135
Catholicism and slavery, 53
Charles, Suzette. *See* Suzette de Gaetano
Childress, Alice, 206, 226
Chisholm, Shirley, 182
Christianity favoring slavery, 52
Christology, 203
Church, Black, 170n52, 212; institutional, 41-43
Classism, 52, 54, 56, 57, 173, 191, 236
Clifford, Carrie W., 73
Clinton, Hillary Rodham, 245-46
Club movement, Black women's, 70-72, 177; a religious movement, 72-74
Cobb, Price M., 238
Collins, Patricia Hill, 236-37
Comedy, 157
Common Destiny: Blacks and American Society (Gerald Jaynes and Alfred Moss, Jr.), 52
Cone, James H., 38, 131, 138-40, 145-46
Confessions (St. Augustine), 16, 18
Constitution, U.S., 26, 35n80
Context, 16, 18, 152-54
Cooke, Marvel, 206
Cooper, Anna Julia Haywood, 6, 172-84